Basics of California Law
for LMFTs, LPCCs, and LCSWs
Fifth edition

Benjamin E. Caldwell, PsyD

Basics of California Law for LMFTs, LPCCs, and LCSWs
Fifth edition

ISBN 978-0-9989285-2-4

Cover image: Shutterstock. Used under license.

Ben Caldwell Labs
6222 Wilshire Blvd, Suite 200
Los Angeles CA 90048

www.bencaldwelllabs.com
ben@bencaldwelllabs.com

Ordering Information:

Special discounts are available on bulk purchases by educators, corporations, associations, and others. For details, contact the publisher at the above listed address.

U.S. trade bookstores and wholesalers: Please contact Ben Caldwell Labs at support@bencaldwelllabs.com.

To those therapists
past, present, and future
working to make the rules work better

▶ Acknowledgments

Since the first edition of this book was released in 2013, I have been often honored and humbled by those who have chosen to use it and who have come to me with compliments, questions, and feedback. My most sincere thanks go to all of those who have assisted with this ongoing project in ways big and small.

I am indebted to my current and former colleagues at California State University Northridge, The Wright Institute, Alliant International University, Caldwell-Clark, AAMFT, AAMFT-California Division, Noteware Government Relations, the California Board of Behavioral Sciences, and many others for their suggestions, support, and guidance as I have learned about the laws of California and the process of changing them.

My team at Ben Caldwell Labs, including Jeffrey Liebert and Emma Jaegle, has been consistently tremendous in providing background research, edits, and production support.

Sara Acharya provided valuable legal review and feedback that has made this fifth edition even stronger. My deep thanks as well to Aimee Clark, Diane Gehart, Olivia Loewy, Sean Davis, and Scott Woolley – friends and brilliant therapists all – for their support with this and prior editions.

My Dad, Chris Caldwell, edited an earlier edition of this book to make it, in a word, readable. Every edition that has followed has been better because of it. Thanks, Dad.

I am particularly indebted to my wife, Angela. Her guidance on this and every previous edition has been kind and wonderful. It is the depth of her support, and her belief in the importance of this project, that are truly exceptional, though. It is not overstating things to say that this book would not be possible without her.

My thanks to the many students, faculty, clinicians, and supervisors who have used and offered comments on earlier editions of this book. Those suggestions have real impact, and I hope you see your input reflected here.

I am sure I missed naming some important people here, and for that I can only offer my apologies. I am profoundly grateful to each of you.

▶ About this guide / Disclaimers

This guide is focused on state law and professional ethical codes in place as of January 2018 unless otherwise noted. Laws and ethical codes change quickly, and it is the responsibility of the therapist to stay current. In addition, **this guide is a summary; it is not meant to cover every situation a therapist may encounter related to the topics discussed here. The author assumes no liability for errors, omissions, or changes in legal or ethical standards. Additional state and federal laws and professional guidelines beyond those mentioned here may govern your work based on your clientele and work setting.**

This guide is for informational purposes only, and reflects a clinician's plain-language reading of the law. No part of it may be construed as legal advice. This text is NOT a substitute for consultation with a qualified attorney. I am an educator and a practicing Marriage and Family Therapist, and not an attorney. If you are in need of legal advice, I strongly encourage you to make use of the legal resources available to you through your professional association and your professional liability insurance carrier.

Links to online resources are presented here for reference purposes only. Any link to an outside resource should not be viewed as an endorsement of that resource (or as the resource endorsing this book). While every effort has been made to ensure that the links here were functional and accurate as of the time of publication, information on the Internet changes frequently. It cannot be guaranteed that the links here are current or accurate. The author assumes no responsibility for the accuracy, currency, or completeness of information on linked web sites, or for the functionality of those sites.

▶ Copyright notice

Contents

Detailed Contents

1. Licensing..25

2. Supervision 69

3. Unprofessional Conduct...............99

4. Confidentiality 131

5. Documentation.......................................153

6. Families and Children......................181

7. Abuse reporting 199

8. Business and Marketing 221

9. Technology 255

10. Advocacy 277

Appendix 309

Introduction

There is great responsibility that comes with being a mental health professional. You are entrusted with the ability to diagnose a person as mentally ill, and then to work with that person in a private, confidential setting as they tell you about their deepest thoughts and fears. Every time a client comes to a family therapist, a clinical counselor, or a clinical social worker, they place a great deal of trust in that professional to act responsibly in their professional role.

Overwhelmingly, mental health professionals *do* act responsibly in that role. When we discuss Unprofessional Conduct (Chapter 3), we'll review just how rare it is for a lawsuit or disciplinary action to succeed. But even understanding that most therapists, counselors, and social workers are ethical, responsible professionals, the vulnerability our clients bring to us means that those few professionals who don't follow the rules can do a great deal of harm.

This is perhaps the first and most important point to understand about the rules of our professions: **They don't exist for our benefit.** They *do* benefit us, by clarifying standards such that frivolous complaints and lawsuits can be easily disposed of, by creating clear standards and expectations for our work, and by demonstrating to the public that we hold ourselves to those lofty standards. But fundamentally, the legal and ethical rules for mental health care exist to protect the public *from* us. Or at least, from the worst of us.

There are three sets of rules that govern mental health work: **Laws**, **ethics**, and the **standard of care**. Laws trump everything else; if there is a direct conflict between your professional code of ethics and the law, the law generally wins (although you should follow the law with the strongest possible adherence to the ethics code).[1] If one simply sets a higher standard than another, then following that higher standard should mean you are behaving in both a legal and ethical manner.

Laws are developed by legislators and regulators. The laws that govern a profession typically define what you *must* or *must not* do within your professional role. They provide legal recourse for a client who is severely mistreated, as that person can file a civil lawsuit, or a complaint against a professional's license. For either of those to be successful, it must be demonstrated that the professional violated the law.

Codes of ethics are developed by professional associations to help define their work. The public is protected because they can trust that a mental health professional is following a set of agreed-upon rules for their care. The professionals also benefit, by virtue of less government regulation (lawmakers are much more reluctant to add regulations to a profession when the profession seems to be adequately governing itself). Sound ethics codes help shield professionals against malpractice lawsuits, since professionals can use them to demonstrate they have followed standard rules of the profession.

Codes of ethics vary in their design, with some written more narrowly to make enforcement easier, and others written with more aspirational language to help guide professionals in what ideal behavior looks like. In the mental health professions, ethical codes often seek to achieve both enforceability and guidance for more ideal behavior. When the American Association for Marriage and Family Therapy (AAMFT) updated its Code of Ethics for 2015,[2] they added aspirational elements for the first time. The National Association of Social Workers (NASW) Code of Ethics[3] is a good example of a code

---

[1] AAMFT Code of Ethics preamble; ACA Code of Ethics subprinciple I.1.c; NASW Code of Ethics preamble
[2] AAMFT Code of Ethics
[3] NASW Code of Ethics

that includes significant guidance not just on what social workers are *required* to do or not do, but also on the kinds of behavior they strive for.

Regardless of an ethics code's design, there will invariably be times when elements of the code fail to offer clear guidance to a therapist wondering how to handle a particular situation, and times when different parts of the code appear to conflict. One recent and controversial example has been the problem of religious therapists refusing to treat gay and lesbian clients. While such refusals would appear to violate the anti-discrimination clauses of each profession's code of ethics, the therapists involved would argue that if they were forced to provide treatment to a population their religious beliefs preclude them from supporting, they would be violating the ethics clauses demanding competent treatment.

In situations where there is no clear legal or ethical guidance, therapists are expected to follow the *standard of care* for their field. Essentially, the standard of care is whatever practices most other people in the profession are following in a particular situation. This is why it is so important, and so helpful, to consult with colleagues and supervisors when you are unsure how to best handle a situation. Gathering ideas from those you trust in the field can help you to know whether a standard of care exists for your specific situation, and if so, how to best follow it.

Your best sources of information when seeking a specific, applicable standard of care for your situation are writings in the field, and your supervisors and colleagues. As should be obvious, the best sources of information when it comes to ethical guidelines are the codes of ethics themselves (their web addresses appear in the appendices at the end of this book). There are also a number of great texts offering general discussion of legal and ethical issues in the mental health professions, geared toward anyone in the country. But the mental health professions are regulated at the *state* level. Where can you go to learn about the *California* laws that govern Licensed Marriage and Family Therapists (LMFTs), Licensed Professional Clinical Counselors (LPCCs), and Licensed Clinical Social Workers (LCSWs)?

I wrote this book to be the answer to that question.

For the actual language of the law, you can download the free compilation put together every year by the Board of Behavioral Sciences (BBS), our licensing board.[4] However, there is nothing to translate that legal language to plain English, and it can often be difficult to find the specific information you are looking for.

This book aims to make that easier. While it is, by design, a summary – state law offers many more specific rules than could be covered here – it seeks to address key elements you need to know as a practitioner.

How to use this book

Depending on where you are in your career, you may have purchased this text as a class requirement, as part of preparing for a BBS exam on the way to licensure, or as a general reference. I hope that it works well as any of those. I have tried to make each chapter as independent as possible, so that if what you really need is information about abuse reporting, as one example, you can simply jump ahead to that chapter.

You will notice more than 500 footnotes in this text, most of which include specific references to sections of law or other relevant information. Please make use of them! Doing so will help you to learn about the language and structure of the law itself. They also can help clarify any elements of this text you are having struggles with.

It is worth repeating here the disclaimer that appears before the Table of Contents. **While I hope this book is a valuable reference, it is NOT a substitute for legal advice from a qualified attorney**. This book does not cover every situation you will encounter, nor does it include every state law impacting mental health work. Laws and regulations can change quickly, so I can't be held responsible for errors or omissions here. I am a practicing LMFT who teaches law and ethics at the graduate level, and I am **not** an attorney. If you are in need of legal advice, you can likely get it at no charge from your professional association or your professional liability insurance carrier.

---

[4] Board of Behavioral Sciences (2018). *Statutes and Regulations Relating to the Practice of Professional Clinical Counseling, Marriage and Family Therapy, Educational Psychology, and Clinical Social Work*. Sacramento, CA: BBS.

Links

Internet addresses referenced in this text are to official sources whenever possible. Of course, information online changes quickly, so I cannot assume any responsibility for the accuracy or functioning of any of the sites linked here. But I hope you will find the links to be useful when you want more in-depth knowledge or direct legal language on the issues covered here. Links provided here of course do not represent endorsement of the linked sites, nor their endorsement of this book.

Some notes on terminology

Throughout this guide, I use the following acronyms:

BBS - The California Board of Behavioral Sciences, which is the state licensing board for Professional Clinical Counselors, Clinical Social Workers, and Marriage and Family Therapists. The BBS also licenses Educational Psychologists (LEPs), however, LEPs are not a focus of this text.

LCSW – Licensed Clinical Social Worker.

LMFT – Licensed Marriage and Family Therapist.

LPCC – Licensed Professional Clinical Counselor.

I also use the following terms to refer to stages of the licensing ladder. These terms apply to all three professions (marriage and family therapy, clinical social work, and professional clinical counseling):

Licensee – Those who are fully and actively licensed by the Board of Behavioral Sciences (LMFTs, LCSWs, and LPCCs). If you are not yet fully licensed, you are not a licensee.

Registrant – MFT, PCC, and CSW associates. Such individuals have completed their master's degrees and are registered with the BBS but are not licensed.

Trainee – Those who are completing required experience as part of their graduate degree program. These individuals are not licensed or registered with the BBS, but their work is still governed by California law and regulation.

What's new in the fifth edition

This edition marks the largest change in this text since the first edition was released in 2013. Of course the book is updated to 2018 law and professional ethics codes, including the new NASW Code of Ethics that took effect January 1, 2018. But that's only the beginning.

Several chapters have been rewritten or reorganized to make them more useful and specific. Chapter 2 on Supervision, for example, is almost entirely new, save for the requirements for supervisors that had been included in prior editions. It includes information on Employment Law that has not been covered here before. Chapter 5 has changed from a chapter on informed consent to a more complete chapter on Documentation. Chapter 6 includes significant discussion of Family Law for the first time, filling a gap that instructors had rightly been asking me to fix for years. Chapter 7 is now specific to Abuse Reporting. Chapter 9 on Technology has new information on telehealth platforms. And Chapter 10 on Advocacy includes new information on the importance of courage when making a difference that extends far beyond the walls of your therapy practice.

In the fourth edition, we introduced "Room for Debate" discussions at the end of several chapters. We've added more of those here, highlighting additional elements of law that are presently unclear, controversial, or (in my admittedly biased view) problematic. These sidebars will demonstrate how the *application* of the law is often much more complicated than simply understanding the *letter* of the law. My thanks to Emma Jaegle and Jeffrey Liebert for writing arguments on some of these sections. Hopefully the discussion there will be thought-provoking.

Of course, we've also fixed typos, updated references, and made some stylistic changes, all in the interest of keeping the book fresh and engaging. We plan to continue making updates, so if you see anything here that needs fixing or that you think should be added, please don't hesitate to reach out. (More on that below.)

Updates and corrections

I've done my best to make sure that everything in this book is accurate, to the best of my knowledge, at the time of publication. Laws and ethical standards can change quickly, and sometimes I make mistakes just like anyone else. If I become aware of any significant errors in this book, corrections will be posted at bencaldwelllabs.com.

Trademarks and web site links

Product and web site names used throughout this book are trademarks of their respective owners. The use of those names is for informational purposes only, and is not intended to imply endorsement of those products or sites.

Feedback

Your feedback can help make future editions of this book even better! I would love to hear your comments and suggestions. You can send them to me by email at ben@bencaldwelllabs.com. As I said, I'm not a lawyer, so please do not send any questions requesting legal advice; those are better directed to an attorney. But feedback on what you found helpful in the book, and what could be changed for the future, is always welcomed.

Let's get started!

1

Licensing

Becoming a licensed mental health professional is no small task. It is a difficult, expensive, years-long journey. For many, reaching licensure is the achievement of a dream, or at least a major life goal.

The physical license is a piece of paper. But what it represents is much larger: It is the state's way of informing the public that you met all of the criteria to be considered safe to practice mental health care independently. The more you think about it, the more important that stamp of approval becomes. You are entrusted by the community around you to work with people in their most vulnerable emotional states, alone and behind closed doors. You are entrusted with the ability to diagnose someone as having a mental illness. You are held up as one of society's experts in emotional health and behavior change.

In return for this social recognition and trust, you agree to be held to higher standards than the general public. Our codes of ethics, our unprofessional conduct statutes, and our standards of care all represent obligations that you willingly take on through the process of becoming a licensed mental health professional.

When you consider all of the hard-earned rights and responsibilities that come with licensure, it is easy to see why many counselors and therapists are bothered by unlicensed professionals, with little or no training, claiming to offer treatments for mental or emotional problems. Later in this chapter, we'll talk about life coaches, consultants, and other unlicensed professionals.

▶ Differences between professions

I frequently hear the argument that there are no meaningful differences among the mental health professions. After all, each of the master's-level mental health professions can assess, diagnose, and treat the full range of mental and emotional disorders in the *Diagnostic and Statistical Manual* through the use of psychotherapy. So why do we even have different licenses?

It is interesting to me that when I hear this argument, it is almost always from someone who practices in California. Therapists and counselors in other states generally seem to have a clearer sense of professional identity.

One reason for this might be that California therapists are often trained and supervised primarily by members of other professions. To be sure, one can get licensed as an LMFT or LPCC without ever having been supervised by someone in the same profession. (Clinical Social Workers *do* have to have some of their pre-license experience supervised specifically by LCSWs.) However, I would argue that being supervised outside of one's own profession is not ideal preparation for one to really become a member of that profession. LMFTs typically do not know how social workers are trained, what texts they read, and how they are brought into the social work field. The same could be said for any other cross-disciplinary understanding. **While the master's-level mental health professions often perform similar work functions, they do so from very different underlying philosophies.**

The act of spelling out those differences is hardly a distant memory. LMFTs and LPCCs each had states where their professions were not licensed until 2009, when Montana (LMFTs) and California (LPCCs) passed laws that completed 50 states of licensure for each profession. In the years before, as LPCCs and LMFTs went around the country arguing for distinct licensure in each state, both professions regularly made the argument that the two operate from distinct histories, distinct skill sets, and distinct bodies of knowledge. They had to make those arguments to gain licensure; if you can't convince a state government that what your professional group does is meaningfully different from what other, already-licensed groups do, that state government will not see a need to create a new license type.

To understand the differences between professions succinctly, let's start from a problem. Let's say that Diego is a 38-year-old Latino man who is married and works in a bookstore. He comes to therapy with severe anxiety. The different mental health professions will likely start from very different places as they seek to answer the question, "Why is Diego struggling with anxiety?"

Psychology

Although this text does not focus on Psychologists, understanding their perspective can be helpful. **A traditional Psychologist would examine Diego's inner world to find the root of his dysfunction.** Whether looking to his childhood (as a Freudian would) or looking to his present (as a behaviorist would), the focus will be on Diego as an individual. Furthermore, traditional psychology would focus on pathology – rooting out what is wrong with Diego individually.[5]

Professional Clinical Counseling

The professional clinical counseling field emerged from school and career counseling. While they focus today on mental health, **LPCCs are likely to see Diego's struggle as an individual, developmental issue.** They will examine his psychological and social development and his current functioning, and treatment will focus on helping Diego improve overall development and wellness (including treatment of mental illness).

Clinical Social Work

Clinical social workers place their focus on connecting people with the resources they need to function well. Those resources may be internal (such as personal skills and strengths, some of which Diego may not be utilizing to their potential) or external (such as community

---

[5] Yes, this is an oversimplification, and today's field of Psychology is much more expansive. We'll get there. Stay with me.

resources and support groups). Traditionally speaking, **LCSWs are likely to see Diego's struggle as a resource issue,** and will work with Diego to gather the internal and external resources needed for him to control and ultimately overcome his anxiety.

Marriage and Family Therapy

LMFTs look at behavior in its social and relational context. Perhaps Diego's anxiety has emerged as a result of tension in his work or in his relationships. Perhaps his anxiety is even adaptive when considered in its context – for example, if he receives more support from his boss or from his partner when showing outward signs of anxiety. Ultimately, LMFTs believe that no behavior exists in a social vacuum, and will work with Diego – as well as other family members and other important people in Diego's life, if appropriate – in an effort to make the anxiety no longer necessary.

Areas of overlap

As you can see, **none of these philosophies is any better or worse than the others. They're just different.** That matters a great deal as new professionals are being trained and socialized into their respective professions. Of course, the perspectives above are purist ones, and even looking at things from that purist perspective, there is significant overlap between these philosophies for dealing with many problems. When handling adjustment issues with children, for example, LMFTs and LPCCs may work very similarly.

Each of these fields has also been influenced by the others. Using Psychologists as an example, there are now Community Psychologists (who share a great deal in common with LCSWs in their approach), Family Psychologists (who share a great deal in common with LMFTs), and Counseling Psychologists (who share a great deal in common with LPCCs). The professions all benefit from this cross-pollination, which helps us communicate effectively with one another and assess clients more thoroughly. But each profession has a skill set that can be broken down into three categories:[6]

1. Tasks that all mental health professionals should be able to do, and that all would do about the same way (for example, suicide assessment).
2. Tasks that all mental health professionals should be able to do, but that each profession would do from a different conceptual framework.
3. Tasks that the specific profession should be able to do that other mental health professionals would *not* necessarily be expected to do.

That last category is important. LPCCs are expected to be able to not just intervene when clients are experiencing problems, but to know how to promote resilience and optimal functioning throughout the lifespan.[7] LCSWs are expected to use their work not just to provide immediate support to their clients, but to advance human rights and social and economic justice.[8] LMFTs are expected to be familiar with a wide variety of couple- and family-level interventions and to be able to understand and assess the functioning of complex family systems. In each case, members of the other professions *could* have been trained in these tasks, but they probably were not. And that would not be a weakness in their training, but rather an example of how each profession is different.

We all do many of the same things in assessing, diagnosing, and treating mental illness. But it is quite a disservice to the professions to suggest we are all the same. Ideally, we benefit from the differences in perspective we may have with our colleagues.

---

[6] The AAMFT Core Competencies illustrate this idea well. American Association for Marriage and Family Therapy (2004). *Marriage and family therapy core competencies.* Alexandria, VA: AAMFT.
[7] Council for Accreditation of Counseling and Related Educational Programs (2016). *CACREP Accreditation Standards, Section 2: Professional Counseling Identity.* Alexandria, VA: CACREP.
[8] Council on Social Work Education (2015). *Educational Policy and Accreditation Standards.* Alexandria, VA: CSWE.

▶ Defining "scope of practice"

A profession's scope of practice outlines the activities one can legally do as part of that profession. It helps define the boundaries of a profession, and the differences between one profession and another. An LCSW is allowed to practice therapy, but not brain surgery, because of the different scopes of practice between LCSWs and physicians.

All of the master's-level mental health professions discussed here are able to perform psychotherapy within their scope of practice. (Using the terms "psychotherapy" and "psychotherapist" in advertising does come with specific additional requirements. See Chapter 8.)

Scope of practice vs. scope of competence

Of course, you will never be an expert in *everything* that can be done under your license. In order to engage in any activity as a professional, in addition to that activity being within your profession's legal scope of practice, that activity also must belong to your personal scope of competence. Your scope of competence consists of those activities that you have appropriate education, training, and experience to do on your own.

For you visual learners, here's the difference in table form:

Table 1.1: Scope of practice vs. scope of competence

	Scope of Practice	Scope of Competence
Applies to:	**Everyone in your profession equally**	**You specifically**
Defined by:	**State law**	**Your education, training, and experience**
Can you expand yours?	**No** (unless you get additional licenses)	**Yes,** through additional education, training, and experience

▶ Marriage and family therapy scope of practice

Normally in this text, I present a clinician's understanding of state law, and offer references to the actual letter of the law. When dealing with scope of practice, I find it helpful to review the actual letter of the law, so I've copied it below – with some notes to help you understand its meaning.

MFT Scope of Practice in California law[9]

For the purposes of this chapter, the practice of marriage and family therapy shall mean that service performed with individuals, couples, or groups wherein interpersonal relationships are examined for the purpose of achieving more adequate, satisfying, and productive marriage and family adjustments. This practice includes relationship and pre-marriage counseling.

(Continued on the next page)

A clinician's translation

LMFTs do not just work with couples and families; they work with individuals and groups as well.

This nicely lays out the relational philosophy of LMFTs: They examine people in their relational context, and work to make that relational context more satisfying.

[9] California Business and Professions Code section 4980.02

MFT Scope of Practice in California law[10]

(continued)

The application of marriage and family therapy principles and methods includes, but is not limited to, the use of applied psychotherapeutic techniques, to enable individuals to mature and grow within marriage and the family, the provision of explanations and interpretations of the psychosexual and psychosocial aspects of relationships, and the use, application, and integration of the coursework and training required by Sections 4980.36, 4980.37, and 4980.41.

A clinician's translation

This phrase establishes MFTs as psychotherapists, and was key to the determination that MFTs can legally use psychological tests. Testing is an "applied psychotherapeutic technique."

While the words "assess," "diagnose," and "treat" are not anywhere in the MFT scope of practice language, they are required to be trained in these skills. This passage in the MFT scope of practice means they are allowed to use those skills to assess, diagnose, and treat in practice.

[10] California Business and Professions Code section 4980.02

Restriction on psychological testing

Contrary to a common misunderstanding among mental health professionals, LMFTs in California <u>are</u> allowed to do psychological testing. They simply must meet two conditions:

- The LMFT must have appropriate training in the instrument used.
- Testing must be case-specific and within a therapeutic context. That is, LMFTs can do psychological testing only in the context of an ongoing therapy relationship.[11]

These conditions are specified in a 1984 California Attorney General's opinion. It emerged after a long and contentious debate between Psychologists and LMFTs about whether such testing was within the LMFT scope. To this day, I frequently hear from MFT students whose graduate courses in assessment included incorrect information that discouraged students from using instruments that they would be legally allowed to use in practice.

While the Attorney General's opinion specifically referred to *licensed* MFTs, there is nothing there to suggest that the conditions would be any different for prelicensed MFTs, so long as they are working under appropriate supervision.

---

[11] Van de Kamp, J. K. (1984). *Do marriage, family and child counselors have the statutory authority to construct, administer, and interpret psychological tests?* California Attorney General opinion no. 83-810, June 28, 1984.

▶ Professional clinical counseling scope of practice

Professional clinical counselors are the newest mental health professionals in California. The PCC scope of practice was carefully developed through negotiations with the BBS and the other mental health professions in California. It is more detailed than the scopes of the other professions.

PCC Scope of Practice in California law[12]

(1) "Professional clinical counseling" means the application of counseling interventions and psychotherapeutic techniques to identify and remediate cognitive, mental, and emotional issues, including personal growth, adjustment to disability, crisis intervention, and psychosocial and environmental problems, and the use, application, and integration of the coursework and training required by Sections 4999.32 and 4999.33.

(Continued on the next page)

A clinician's translation

This establishes PCCs as psychotherapists.

As is the case for MFTs, the PCC scope does not directly use the words "assess," "diagnose," or "treat" in relation to mental illness. But this language makes clear that these tasks are within the PCC scope. PCCs' scope includes the assessment, diagnosis, and treatment of mental disorders.

_____

[12] California Business and Professions Code section 4999.20(a)

PCC Scope of Practice in California law[13]	A clinician's translation
(continued)	
(2) "Professional clinical counseling" includes conducting assessments for the purpose of establishing counseling goals and objectives to empower individuals to deal adequately with life situations, reduce stress, experience growth, change behavior, and make well-informed rational decisions.	This allows PCCs to use psychological tests, but there are important limitations on this. See the next page.
(3) "Professional clinical counseling" is focused exclusively on the application of counseling interventions and psychotherapeutic techniques for the purposes of improving mental health, and is not intended to capture other, nonclinical forms of counseling for the purposes of licensure. For the purposes of this paragraph, "nonclinical" means nonmental health.	This language clarifies that career and other non-mental-health counselors do not need a PCC license.

[13] California Business and Professions Code section 4999.20(a)

Restriction on working with couples and families

Because they are not required to have any training or supervised experience working with couples and families prior to licensure, **LPCCs are prohibited from assessing or treating couples and families unless they have completed all of the following:**

- **6 semester units or 9 quarter units of coursework** in couple and family therapy, **or a named specialization in couple and family therapy** on their degree
- **500 hours supervised experience** with couples, families, and children
- **6 hours of continuing education (CE) on couple and family work** in each renewal cycle[14]

Of course, PCC associates and trainees (and, for that matter, licensees) who are under supervision and working toward the completion of these requirements are able to see couples and families. Indeed, many of those who complete these requirements (excepting CE, which is after licensure) do so within their regular degree program and supervised experience.

Because working with children necessarily involves working with their families (see Chapter 6, Families and Children), LPCCs wishing to work with children would be wise to complete these additional requirements. LPCCs who have not completed the above requirements, but who are working individually with minors, can still meet with parents for the purpose of informing them about their child's treatment progress and doing aftercare planning.[15] They simply cannot *intervene* on a family level.

---

[14] California Business & Professions Code section 4999.20(a)(3)
[15] California Code of Regulations section 1820.5(d)

Restriction on psychological testing

Professional clinical counselors are able to use psychological tests and measures. However, **LPCCs are explicitly prohibited from using any of the following testing procedures**:[16]

- Projective tests of personality (such as the Rorschach)
- Individually administered intelligence tests
- Neuropsychological testing
- Utilization of a battery of three or more tests to assess psychosis, dementia, amnesia, cognitive impairment, or criminal behavior

"Assessment" as it relates to tests and measures for LPCCs is also specifically defined as an activity done "as part of the counseling process."[17] This would appear to mean that, similar to LMFTs, LPCCs cannot engage in psychological testing with people who are not engaged in an ongoing counseling process with the LPCC.

Additional definitions

The LPCC scope language includes two other important definitions. First, it clarifies that "professional counseling does not include the provision of clinical social work services."[18] That is simply a recognition (one of several in the LPCC licensing act) that LPCCs and LCSWs practice distinct professions.

Second, the bill includes a definition of "counseling interventions and psychotherapeutic techniques" that reinforces the philosophical distinctiveness of the LPCC profession. It notes that while LPCCs work in a variety of ways, using many different theories and approaches, all LPCCs' interventions "include principles of development, wellness, and maladjustment."[19]

---

[16] California Business & Professions Code section 4999.20(c)
[17] California Business & Professions Code section 4999.20(c)
[18] California Business & Professions Code section 4999.20(a)(4)
[19] California Business & Professions Code section 4999.20(b)

▶ Clinical social work scope of practice

The clinical social work scope of practice skillfully integrates CSWs' roles as psychotherapists with the values traditionally underlying social work in all its forms. Notice the inclusion of terms like "resources," "human capabilities," and "potential."

CSW Scope of Practice in California law[20]	A clinician's translation
The practice of clinical social work is defined as a service in which a special knowledge of social resources, human capabilities, and the part that unconscious motivation plays in determining behavior, is directed at helping people to achieve more adequate, satisfying, and productive social adjustments. The application of social work principles and methods includes, but is not restricted to, counseling and using applied psychotherapy of a nonmedical nature with individuals, families, or groups; providing information and referral services;	This is a reference to how social workers are trained. The term "special knowledge" makes clear that this training is distinct from that given to other professionals.
	This establishes CSWs as psychotherapists. Psychotherapy, for the purposes of the CSW scope, is defined in the next paragraph (see next page).

(Continued on the next page)

---

[20] California Business and Professions Code section 4996.9

CSW Scope of Practice in California law[21]

A clinician's translation

(continued)

providing or arranging for the provision of social services; explaining or interpreting the psychosocial aspects in the situations of individuals, families, or groups; helping communities to organize, to provide, or to improve social or health services; doing research related to social work; and the use, application, and integration of the coursework and experience required by sections 4996.2 and 4996.23.

Psychotherapy, within the meaning of this chapter, is the use of psychosocial methods within a professional relationship, to assist the person or persons to achieve a better psychosocial adaptation, to acquire greater human realization of psychosocial potential and adaptation, to modify internal and external conditions which affect individuals, groups, or communities in respect to behavior, emotions, and thinking, in respect to their intrapersonal and interpersonal processes.

This makes clear that CSWs are not limited to working with individuals. They also can work with couples, families, and groups.

This language, a parallel to the MFT and PCC scopes, was added in 2014. It clarifies, as one example, that CSWs can do substance abuse treatment, as this is required in their training under section 4996.2.

This is the closest the CSW language gets to saying that CSWs assess, diagnose, and treat the full range of mental and emotional disorders. As is the case for the other professions, the integration of required training (see above) makes clear that CSWs can perform those tasks.

---

[21] California Business and Professions Code section 4996.9

▶ Licensure status

When you begin your work experience during your degree program you are an unlicensed and unregistered **Trainee** in the eyes of the state. Trainees must be engaging in their work as part of a recognized degree program,[22] and must be under supervision. Some CSW programs refer to their students who are completing required work experience as "interns," which gets confusing because "intern" was also the prior title for post-degree, pre-license MFTs and PCCs. Throughout this book, I simply refer to pre-degree therapists as trainees and post-degree, pre-licensed therapists as associates.

Once you complete your degree, you register as an **Associate**.[23] Associates are working on their supervised hours of experience for licensure. (Individuals and agencies with marketing materials that included the previous MFT and PCC title "intern" can continue to use those through the end of 2018.[24])

Associates and trainees within a mental health profession have essentially the same scope of practice as those who are licensed. While there are some activities trainees cannot take part in (like supervision via videoconferencing), the acceptable clinical activities of licensees and prelicensees are largely the same. However, associates and trainees typically must have their work supervised by a qualified supervisor. In addition, there are a number of non-clinical restrictions on what associates and trainees can do. They cannot be paid directly by clients, and they cannot rent their own office space, as two examples.[25] And there are a number of external limits on the roles of prelicensed therapists. For example, some insurance plans will not reimburse for services provided by an associate or trainee.

---

[22] California Business and Professions Code section 4999.24
[23] California Business and Professions Code sections 4980.09, 4996.18, and 4999.12.5.
[24] Technically, this allowance comes from regulations that were pending at publication time for this book. But the BBS said publicly it would not punish anyone who was acting within those proposed regulations even before they were formally adopted. They were expecting formal adoption in March 2018. http://www.bbs.ca.gov/pdf/regulation/pending/app_proc_plf.pdf
[25] California Business and Professions Code sections 4980.43(h) and (i), 4996.23(l), 4999.47(b)

Associates and trainees must also be especially mindful of their scope of competence. While the law may allow them to do largely the same range of clinical activities as licensed practitioners, they are still subject to the limits of their training, education, and experience – and they bump up against those limits much more regularly. Indeed, when you are early in your career, the only way to get the experience needed to expand your competence is by working (under supervision) with client and problem types that are new to you.

Consider the example of an Associate Clinical Social Worker working with a teenage client who is self-injuring. There is nothing in the CSW scope of practice to prohibit the associate from doing such work. However, if the associate does not have experience in working with self-injuring clients, it is *essential* that they be closely supervised as they develop that experience. A good supervisor will recognize the limits of their supervisees' competence and work closely with them, providing guidance, consultation, support, and resources, to aid in the development of that competence.

When you complete your supervised experience and pass your clinical exam, you become **Licensed**. Licensed professionals can work in private practice without supervision.

These are not the only licensure statuses. The state also has provisions for those who want to retain their licensure but plan to stop seeing clients on either a temporary or permanent basis.

If you stop seeing clients but plan to eventually return, you can put your license on **Inactive** status. Therapists may do this for a number of reasons, including taking time off to start a family, moving temporarily out of state, or going on an extended military deployment. While your license is on Inactive status, you cannot see clients, but you also are exempted from continuing education requirements and pay a reduced license renewal fee.

If you stop seeing clients and do *not* plan to start again, but are interested in retaining recognition from the state, you can put your license on **Retired** status. While you can keep your license on Retired status as long as you wish, if you want to reactivate a license after more than three years on Retired status, you must reapply for licensure and retake the licensing exam.[26]

---

[26] California Business and Professions Code sections 4984.41, 4997.1, and 4999.113

▸ Licensing requirements

While there are meaningful differences in the licensing requirements for the master's-level mental health professions in California, the BBS has been gradually working to eliminate differences that do not have a clear reason behind them.

General requirements of all mental health professionals

Licensure as a mental health professional typically involves three major requirements:

(1) **Education:** A qualifying graduate degree
(2) **Experience:** Practicing under a supervisor for a specified amount of time to build skills
(3) **Exams:** Successful completion of exams related to the license

This section will detail those requirements for each of the three professions for whom this book is designed.

While we think of these as licensed professions, not everyone performing the tasks of an LMFT, LPCC, or LCSW needs a license to do so. We will also address exceptions to licensure later in this chapter.

Additional requirements for all mental health professionals

It is important to bear in mind that completion of the requirements for licensure only makes you *eligible* for a state license; it does not *obligate* the state to give it to you. The BBS can refuse to grant a license application for a number of reasons other than failure to complete requirements.

Background checks. The BBS may choose not to grant licenses to individuals who have prior criminal convictions that it views as related to the functions of a clinician. They interpret that language broadly, which is why applicants are expected to disclose *any* past crimes when applying for licensure or associate registration.

Substance-related convictions (like DUIs) are among the ones the BBS sees most commonly. For these and most other offenses, the BBS will review factors like the severity of the crime, the time since the conviction, and any evidence of rehabilitation since then. Violent crimes and crimes against children, no matter how old, will be examined especially carefully if they appear in your record. In addition, actions against a license in another state or field could also prevent the BBS from granting a license. All license and registration applicants must undergo a background check as part of the application process.[27]

Fees. Of course, there are the fees. Any application for a license, registration, renewal, or exam eligibility will have a fee attached to it. These fees are not designed to be profitable for the state, but rather to provide sufficient funding for the BBS to run without taxpayer support. That is correct: your licensing board is fully supported by the fees paid by licensees and registrants. They do not use any general tax funds.[28]

License renewals. When you are initially licensed, the length of time before your first renewal could be anywhere from 12 to 24 months, depending on when you get that license. While of course you can apply for a license any time, licenses *expire* at the end of your birth month, to help balance out renewals through the calendar year. During that first renewal period, you must complete 18 hours of continuing education, including six hours in law and ethics.

---

[27] California Code of Regulations section 480
[28] It's admittedly a bit of a tangent here – hence putting it in a footnote – but California's fees are actually pretty average, or even a bit low, compared to mental health practitioner licensing fees in other states. There's a good case to be made that our application and renewal fees should be *higher*, to enable the BBS to hire the additional staff it would take for them to be faster in reviewing applications and more responsive to phone calls and emails.

After that first renewal, you renew your license every **two years.** During each two-year license period, **you need to complete 36 hours of continuing education, including six hours in law and ethics. Those supervising prelicensed MFTs and PCCs must also include six hours of CE on supervision within their 36 hour CE requirement for each renewal period.**

Exemptions from licensure

While a professional license is generally required to provide the services of a Marriage and Family Therapist, Clinical Social Worker, or Professional Clinical Counselor, the law includes a number of exemptions from licensure. These allow certain individuals, or individuals working in specific settings, to do so without being licensed by the state. The exemptions from licensure include:

Individuals working toward licensure. Of course, trainees and registrants who are under supervision and working toward a license do not need to hold that license. Such a restriction would mean that no one could ever get the experience they needed to become eligible for licensing exams! They are still bound to all of the requirements of the law for responsible practice, however, and their supervisors must be appropriately qualified.

Clergy. The laws for LMFTs, LCSWs, and LPCCs specifically indicate that they do not apply to religious leaders performing services as part of their religious duties.[29] Any priest, rabbi, minister, or other religious leader may offer counseling services to the religious organization's members without a state license.

Other professionals. While there are meaningful differences between the BBS-governed mental health professions, there are also areas of overlap. This overlap is not meant to restrict professionals from being able to do work within their own scopes of practice.

---

[29] California Business and Professions Code sections 4980.01(b), 4996.13(f), and 4999.22(c)

For example, what the law defines as "client-centered advocacy" for LMFTs is quite similar to the practice of social work, but an LMFT does not need to also get an LCSW license in order to do client-centered advocacy. For all the mental health professions, their ability to perform psychotherapy doesn't mean that Psychologists can't do so. Scope of practice for any one profession will typically specify that it is not meant to restrict the scope of practice of any other profession.

Employees and volunteers at exempt settings. State law also defines a number of work settings as exempt from licensure requirements. These settings include schools, nonprofit charitable organizations, and government agencies.[30] However, many settings that are officially license-exempt choose to require their workers to meet licensure or registration standards anyway, either as a function of their reimbursement process or simply to demonstrate that they are upholding high standards for clinical work.

Education

Each of the master's level mental health professions requires a qualifying graduate degree of at least 60 semester units (90 quarter units). If you are seeking licensure with an older degree, you may still qualify, depending on the age of the degree and what content was covered within it.

Marriage and Family Therapists

California's curriculum requirements for graduate degrees leading to LMFT licensure are the most specific in the country.[31] While

---

[30] California Business and Professions Code sections 4980.01(c), 4996.14, and 4999.22(d)

[31] California's standards for graduate education leading to LMFT licensure changed significantly for students beginning their education on or after August 1, 2012. The discussion here is based on the current requirements. Those who began their degrees earlier than August 2012 can qualify under the old requirements if they complete their degrees by 2018. Some schools

many other states include basic curriculum requirements or defer to standards set by the Commission on Accreditation for Marriage and Family Therapy Education (COAMFTE), California requires a list of specific topic areas to be covered, and includes specific content requirements within each of those topics. For this reason, if you are currently studying outside of California but are wishing to eventually license as an MFT within California, it is vital that you make sure your degree program will meet all of California's many requirements.

Graduate degree title. In order to be licensed as an MFT with a graduate degree from within California, your degree must not only meet all of the content requirements below, but also be specifically titled "marriage, family, and child counseling," "marriage and family therapy," "couple and family therapy," "psychology," "clinical psychology," "counseling psychology," or "counseling" with an emphasis in either marriage, family, and child counseling or marriage and family therapy.[32] Degrees from out of state are evaluated as to their equivalency with California's content requirements, but may not need to have one of the specific titles listed here.

Graduate degree content. Your masters or doctoral degree must include all of the following content to be a qualifying degree for MFT licensure. Note that within many of these content areas are more specific content requirements spelled out in the law.[33]

- 60 semester units (90 quarter units) in total
- 12 semester units (18 quarter units) in "theories, principles, and methods" of psychotherapy directly related to the MFT profession and family systems work
- 6 semester units (9 quarter units) of practicum coursework (more on that below)
- Diagnosis, assessment, and treatment of mental illness, including psychological testing and psychopharmacology

---

adopted the new requirements early, so check with your university if you are unsure which set of requirements applies to you.
[32] California Business and Professions Code section 4980.36(b)
[33] California Business and Professions Code section 4980.36(d)

- Developmental issues across the life span
- Family relationships and related issues, including abuse assessment and reporting, parenting, marriage, divorce, blended families, end-of-life care, grief, and more
- Cultural competency and sensitivity
- Multicultural development and cross-cultural interaction, including how this impacts the therapy process
- How socioeconomic status impacts available treatment and resources
- Personal and community resilience
- Human sexuality
- Substance use disorders and co-occurring disorders
- California law and ethics

There are several additional content areas that must be included in a qualifying graduate degree, though these can be met through credit-level coursework or through extension programs (one-day workshops or similar events that do not result in course credit). Note that the language here is simply quoting the law itself, and the law does not further specify what these content areas must include:[34]

- Case management
- Systems of care for the severely mentally ill
- Public and private services and supports available for the severely mentally ill
- Community resources for persons with mental illness and for victims of abuse
- Disaster and trauma response
- Advocacy for the severely mentally ill
- Collaborative treatment

---

[34] California Business and Professions Code section 4980.36(e)

Professional Clinical Counselors

California's curriculum requirements for graduate degrees leading to LPCC licensure are drawn largely from the Core Content areas required by the Council for Accreditation of Counseling and Related Educational Programs (CACREP). However, California also adds a number of specific requirements on to the CACREP standards. For example, California requires a master's or doctoral degree of at least 60 semester units (90 quarter units), while many other states require 48 or fewer. California also requires specific course content not required by CACREP.[35]

Graduate degree content. Counseling degrees can carry a variety of different titles. Degrees for LPCCs are evaluated on their content and not their name.[36] Your master's or doctoral degree must be at least 60 semester units (90 quarter units) in total, and must include at least three semester units (4.5 quarter units) in each of the following to be a qualifying degree for LPCC licensure. Note that within each of these courses are more specific content requirements spelled out in the law:[37]

- Theory and techniques of counseling and psychotherapy
- Development across the life span
- Career counseling
- Group counseling
- Testing and assessment measures
- Multicultural counseling
- Diagnosis
- Research and evaluation
- California law and ethics
- Psychopharmacology
- Addiction counseling

---

[35] California's standards for graduate education leading to LPCC licensure changed significantly for students beginning their education on or after August 1, 2012. The discussion here is based on the current requirements.
[36] California Business and Professions Code section 4999.33(b)
[37] California Business and Professions Code section 4999.33(c)(1)

- Crisis and trauma counseling

If your degree is lacking in up to three of these areas, it is possible to make up the missing pieces through postdegree education. Any classes you take to make up for deficiencies in your degree must be at an accredited or approved graduate school, and must be at least three semester units (4.5 quarter units).[38]

The qualifying degree must also include at least 15 semester units (22.5 quarter units) in advanced coursework, focused on specific populations or treatment issues.[39] It must also include at least six semester units (nine quarter units) of practicum, which is further discussed in Supervised Experience below.[40]

There are several additional content areas that must be included in a qualifying graduate degree, though they do not require separate courses; they simply must be included somewhere in the curriculum within a credit-level class:[41]

- Human behavior within the context of socioeconomic status and other contextual factors
- Human behavior within the social context of a variety of California cultures
- Cultural competency and sensitivity
- Understanding of the impact of socioeconomic status on available treatment and resources
- Multicultural development and cross-cultural interaction, and how these impact therapy
- Human sexuality
- Intimate partner violence assessment and intervention
- Child abuse assessment and reporting
- Aging and long-term care, including assessment and reporting of abuse

---

[38] California Business and Professions Code section 4999.33(f)
[39] California Business and Professions Code section 4999.33(c)(2)
[40] California Business and Professions Code section 4999.33(c)(3)
[41] California Business and Professions Code section 4999.33(d)

A qualifying degree leading to LPCC licensure must also include instruction in California's public mental health system, including information about recovery-oriented care and opportunities to meet with public mental health consumers and family members.[42]

Finally, the law requires that these additional content areas be included in a qualifying degree, though they do not need to be within credit-level coursework. They can be delivered in workshops or other formats that do not lead to course credit:[43]

- Case management
- Systems of care for the severely mentally ill
- Public and private services and supports available for the severely mentally ill
- Community resources for persons with mental illness and for victims of abuse
- Disaster and trauma response
- Advocacy for the severely mentally ill
- Collaborative treatment

Clinical Social Workers

Of the three professions covered in this text, Clinical Social Workers have the fewest licensure requirements spelled out in state law. This is because the state has largely deferred to national standards in the clinical social work profession, relying on national accreditation standards for graduate education and, as of 2016, the national social work exam.

Clinical social workers must possess a master's degree from an accredited school of social work.[44] The Council on Social Work Education (CSWE) is the national accrediting body for social work programs, and as of December 2017, it recognized 22 master's degree programs in California as accredited.[45]

---

[42] California Business and Professions Code section 4999.33(e)
[43] California Business and Professions Code section 4999.33(d)(6)
[44] California Business and Professions Code section 4996.2(b)
[45] CSWE Directory of Accredited Programs

The social worker must also have training in the following areas, though these can be either within the degree program or taken separately.[46] Note that state law includes more specific content requirements within some of these training areas:

- Chemical dependency
- Intimate partner violence assessment and intervention (minimum 15 contact hours)
- Human sexuality (minimum 10 hours)
- Child abuse assessment and reporting (minimum 7 hours)

Supervised Experience

There are a number of standards for supervised experience that are common across the three license types described in this book. Regardless of whether you are seeking licensure as an LMFT, an LPCC, or an LCSW, the following minimums and maximums apply:[47]

- The 3,000 hours of experience (3,200 for CSWs) must be gained over at least a total of 104 weeks. At least 52 of those weeks must include at least one hour of individual supervision.
- No more than 40 total hours may be gained in a week.[48]
- No more than 6 hours of supervision will be credited in any given week.[49]
- **For CSWs only:** Of the 52 weeks of individual supervision, at least 13 weeks must be under the supervision of an LCSW.[50]

---

[46] For LPCCs: California Business and Professions Code section 4996.2
[47] California Business and Professions Code section 4999.46 and California Code of Regulations title 16 section 1820(e)
[48] California Business and Professions Code sections 4980.43(a)(2), 4996.23(a)(5), and 4999.46(a)(2)
[49] California Business and Professions Code sections 4980.43(d)(2), 4496.23(d)(3), and 4999.46(g)(1)
[50] California Business and Professions Code sections 4996.23(a)(4) and (c)(5)

The requirements for the supervised experience necessary to become an LMFT or LPCC changed significantly on January 1, 2016.[51] With the active support of CALPCC, CAMFT, and AAMFT-CA, the BBS sponsored a bill to eliminate some of the specific minimums and maximums that had been associated with different categories of hours of experience for each license.[52] The bill included a five-year implementation period, so **anyone who applies for licensure between January 1, 2016 and December 31, 2020, can come in under *either* hour-counting system, old or new, whichever one works better for them.**

While the LCSW experience requirement was not changed in that 2016 law, there is an effort underway to reduce the required hours of experience for LCSW licensure from 3,200 to 3,000, to be more consistent with the other professions.[53]

The supervised experience requirements for each license are summarized in Table 1.2. (Since most readers will come in under the new systems for LMFTs and LPCCs, tables describing the old structures are in the Appendix.) While the differences are not drastic, the new system is expected to meaningfully speed up the path to licensure for many counselors.

Under both the old and new systems, supervisors have some discretion in what will qualify under specific types of experience. For example, supervisors determine what is appropriate to count as "Workshops, trainings, and seminars."

---

[51] As I noted in the section describing MFT experience requirements, I am proud to have been personally involved in this change. CALPCC's support was instrumental in ensuring that counselors also benefitted from this streamlining of experience requirements.
[52] Senate Bill 620 (Block), 2015.
[53] Assembly Bill 93 (Medina), 2018.

Table 1.2: Supervised experience requirements

Licensure	Clinical hours	Non-clinical hours
LMFT[54]	**Minimum 1,750 hours.** Of these, a **minimum of 500 hours** must be with couples, families, and children.	**Maximum 1,250 hours.** This category includes the "old" categories of supervision, workshops, reports/notes, and client-centered advocacy.
LPCC[55]	**Minimum 1,750 hours.** Of these, a **minimum of 150 hours** must be in a hospital or community mental health setting.	**Maximum 1,250 hours.** This category includes the "old" categories of supervision, workshops, reports/notes, and client-centered advocacy.
LCSW[56]	**Minimum 2,000 hours**, including a **minimum of 750 hours providing individual or group psychotherapy.**	**Maximum 1,200 hours.** This category includes client-centered advocacy, consultation, evaluation, and research, and does not include supervision.

Marriage and Family Therapists

Practicum. MFTs begin seeing clients during their graduate degree programs. When a student is completing required hours of clinical experience as part of their graduate degree, they are considered to be an MFT Trainee.[57] The experience they are completing is called a practicum. One key difference from the other mental health professions covered in this text is that **MFTs can count**

---

[54] California Business and Professions Code section 4980.43(a)
[55] California Business and Professions Code section 4999.46(a)
[56] California Business and Professions Code section 4996.23(a). The "clinical" cell in this row might be confusing at first, but that's simply because of how the LCSW law defines clinical experience. It includes "Clinical psychosocial assessment, diagnosis, and treatment, *including* therapy or counseling" (emphasis mine).
[57] California Business and Professions Code section 4980.42(a)

experience gained during practicum – up to 1,300 hours – toward the 3,000 total hours required for licensure.[58]

Some universities have students complete their practicum at university-run clinics, while others partner with community agencies to place their students in the field for practicum. In either case, the school and the practicum site must have a written agreement that details how supervision is provided and ensures that the school will receive regular reports on the trainee's performance.[59]

California law requires MFT students to complete at least 225 hours of direct client contact during practicum, though up to 75 of these hours can be satisfied with "client-centered advocacy" (this term is defined specifically in the law; it essentially involves efforts to link clients with resources outside of a therapy session).[60]

No student can begin seeing clients as part of practicum before they are enrolled in a practicum class. Once students have started the practicum, they must continue to be enrolled in practicum as long as they are seeing clients (the law allows for enrollment breaks of up to 90 days to account for gaps between quarters or semesters). When a student has completed their final academic term of practicum, they can continue completing their client contact hours so long as they complete all degree requirements (including hours) within 90 days of their last practicum enrollment.[61]

Students are, of course, required to be under supervision while in practicum. The BBS considers one "unit" of supervision to be either one hour of individual supervision or two hours of group supervision, in a group of no more than eight total supervisees, Trainees are required to receive at least one unit of supervision in every week they gain experience for licensure. Over the total time a trainee is at a practicum site, the trainee must receive at least one unit of supervision for every five hours of client contact they completed at that site.[62] Every hour gained outside of that ratio will not be counted towards licensure.

---

[58] California Business and Professions Code section 4980.43
[59] California Business and Professions Code section 4980.42(e)
[60] California Business and Professions Code section 4980.36(d)(1)(B)(vi)
[61] California Business and Professions Code section 4980.42
[62] California Business and Professions Code section 4980.43(c)(1)

Most trainees are not paid while completing their services, but there is nothing prohibiting payment. Trainees can be employees of a clinic or agency, or can work as volunteers. They cannot be utilized as independent contractors. Trainees also may not work in a private practice setting.[63]

Associate experience. Once they graduate, an MFT-in-training applies to the BBS to become a Registered Associate Marriage and Family Therapist until they move ahead to licensure. (The title used to be Intern, and so you may still see job listings for prelicensed experience that label the job as an "internship." The title changed to Associate in 2018.[64])

As with MFT trainees, associates can either be employed or work as volunteers, but cannot serve as independent contractors. Unlike MFT trainees, associates *can* work in private practice settings, so long as they are on their first associate registration.[65]

Like trainees, associates must receive at least one unit of supervision in each week they gain hours of clinical experience for licensure. Because they have completed their graduate education and gotten some supervised experience already, associates are considered by the law to need less supervision than trainees. Each week an associate gains experience for licensure, how much supervision the associate needs depends on how much client contact they had. **If the associate saw clients for 10 hours or fewer, one unit of supervision is all that is needed that week. If the associate saw clients for more than 10 hours, a second unit of supervision is necessary in the same week.** There is no overall ratio that associates must meet in regard to their total time at a particular site.[66]

---

[63] California Business and Professions Code section 4980.43(d)(1)(C)
[64] For more on this change, visit www.psychotherapynotes.com/california-change-counseling-mft-intern-title-associate/
[65] California Business and Professions Code section 4980.43(e)(2)
[66] California Business and Professions Code section 4980.43(c)

Professional Clinical Counselors

In total, a PCC needs 3,280 hours of qualifying supervised experience to become eligible for their licensing exams: 280 hours of client contact during the practicum, and 3,000 additional hours of qualifying experience as an associate.[67] None of the experience gained as a trainee can count toward the 3,000 hours required after the degree.[68]

Practicum. PCCs begin seeing clients during their graduate degree programs. When a student is completing required hours of clinical experience as part of their graduate degree, they are considered to be a PCC Trainee.[69] The experience they are completing is called a *practicum*. While this experience does *not* count toward the 3,000 hours required for licensure, the state still has a number of laws that govern the practicum experience.

California law requires PCC students to complete at least 280 hours of direct client contact during practicum.[70] Some universities have students complete their practicum at university-run clinics, while others partner with community agencies to place their students in the field for practicum. In either case, the school and the practicum site must have a written agreement that details how supervision is provided and ensures that the school will receive regular reports on the trainee's performance.[71]

Students are, of course, required to be under supervision while in practicum. As you might expect, trainees need more supervision than associates do. The BBS considers one hour of individual supervision or two hours of group supervision, in a group of no more than eight total supervisees, to be one "unit" of supervision. Trainees are required to receive at least one unit of supervision in every week they gain experience for licensure. Over the total time a trainee is at a

---

[67] California Business and Professions Code sections 4999.33(c)(3)(K) and 4999.46(b)
[68] California Business and Professions Code section 4999.36(e)
[69] California Business and Professions Code section 4999.36(a)
[70] California Business and Professions Code section 4999.33
[71] California Business and Professions Code section 4999.36(b)

practicum site, the trainee must receive at least one unit of supervision for every five hours of client contact they completed at that site.[72]

Most trainees are not paid while completing their services, but there is nothing prohibiting payment. Trainees can be employees of a clinic or agency, or can work as volunteers. They cannot be utilized as independent contractors. Trainees also may not work in a private practice setting.[73]

Associate experience. Once they graduate, a PCC-in-training applies to the BBS to become a Registered Associate Professional Clinical Counselor until they move ahead to licensure.

As with clinical counselor trainees, associates can either be employed or work as volunteers, but cannot serve as independent contractors. Unlike PCC trainees, associates can work in private practice settings.[74]

Like trainees, associates must receive at least one unit of supervision in each week they gain hours of clinical experience for licensure. Because they have completed their graduate education and gotten some supervised experience already, associate are considered by the law to need less supervision than trainees. Each week an associate gains experience for licensure, how much supervision the associate needs depends on how much client contact they had. **If the associate saw clients for 10 hours or fewer, one unit of supervision is all that is needed that week. If the associate saw clients for more than 10 hours, a second unit of supervision is necessary in the same week.** There is no overall ratio that associates must meet in regard to their total time at a site.[75]

Clinical Social Workers

Clinical Social Workers typically begin seeing clients during their graduate degree programs. Unlike MFTs and PCCs, the pre-

---

[72] California Business and Professions Code section 4999.36(f)
[73] California Business and Professions Code section 4999.34(c)
[74] California Business and Professions Code section 4999.45(a)(2)
[75] California Business and Professions Code section 4999.46(g)

degree work of CSWs is not governed by state law, which instead defers to the degree requirements imposed by CSWE.

Once a social worker has completed their graduate degree, they must register with the BBS as an Associate Clinical Social Worker. This registration is necessary before gaining any of the required postdegree supervised experience for licensure.[76]

In total, a CSW needs 3,200 hours of qualifying postdegree supervised experience to become eligible for CSW licensing exams.[77] This does *not* include any experience gained as part of the degree. Of those 3,200 hours, at least 1,700 must be supervised by an LCSW (more on this below).[78] Like members of the other mental health professions who have completed their degrees and are gathering hours of experience toward licensure, Associate CSWs are allowed to work in private practice settings.[79]

The 90-day rule for MFTs and PCCs

Regardless of which profession you are in, the first time you submit paperwork to the BBS will likely be your application for associate registration. If you're an MFT or PCC, as long as the BBS receives[80] your application for associate registration within 90 days of the degree posting date on your transcript, you can count any hours of experience gained between graduation and the time your registration is granted toward the hours needed for licensure. Otherwise, any

---

[76] California Business and Professions Code section 4996.18
[77] The BBS is planning to pursue legislation in 2017 that would reduce this number to 3,000 and make a number of additional changes to the rules surrounding supervised experience for CSWs. If the legislation is signed into law, it would take effect January 1, 2018. For more information on the proposed changes, see the materials for the November 2016 meeting of the BBS (the specific proposal begins on page 235 of the PDF): www.bbs.ca.gov/pdf/agen_notice/2016/not1116_bdmtg.pdf
[78] California Business and Professions Code section 4996.23(a)
[79] California Business and Professions Code section 4996.23(g)
[80] Key word here is "*receives*." The application of this rule is not based on the *postmark* date for your application, but rather when it actually *arrives* at the BBS office. For this reason, I would recommend submitting that application well ahead of the 90-day limit, and using some form of package tracking.

hours of experience gained in that gap between graduation and registration *cannot* be counted.[81]

The six-year rules

Once an MFT, PCC, or CSW on their way to licensure registers with the state as an associate, they can keep that registration number for up to six years.[82] Associates who wish to continue accruing hours after six years must obtain a second registration number from the BBS. It is not unusual for an associate who has taken time off to raise children, care for family members, or complete a tour of duty in the military to obtain a second registration number once their original number expires. The only thing that changes with a second registration number is that the associate can no longer work in a private practice setting.[83]

That's the first six-year rule: Registrations are good for up to six years. There's actually *another* six-year rule that also applies, which can make things a little confusing.

When considering an application for license exam eligibility, the BBS will review the applicant's experience for the six years immediately before the application date – even if that experience was gained under two different registration numbers.[84] In other words, when you get a second associate registration number, your hours don't start back at zero. **This is the *second* six-year rule: Your most recent six years of supervised experience as an associate, even if under two different registrations, are countable toward licensure.**

For MFTs, clinical hours from practicum – *not* any non-clinical hours, *just* clinical hours, up to 500 – are countable forever.[85]

---

[81] California Business and Professions Code sections 4980.43(h) and 4999.46(d)

[82] California Business and Professions Code section 4984.01(c), 4996.28(b), and 4999.100(c)

[83] California Business and Professions Code section 4984.01(c), 4996.28(b), and 4999.100(c)

[84] California Business and Professions Code section 4980.43(a)(7), 4996.23(a)(5), and 4999.46(c)

[85] California Business and Professions Code section 4980.43(a)(7)

Exams

In each of the three master's level professions, you must pass two exams to reach licensure. You begin with the California Law & Ethics Exam in your first year of registration as an Associate, and then take a Clinical Exam after all of your required hours of supervised experience have been completed.

Law & Ethics Exam

The California Law & Ethics Exam must be taken in the first year of associate registration. Each profession has its own separate Law & Ethics Exam. While the legal requirements are largely the same across professions, there are meaningful differences in the professions' ethics codes.

You only need to *pass* this test once. If you pass the exam, you will not need to take another test until you have completed the rest of your supervised experience.

If you fail the Law and Ethics exam, you can take it again after 90 days. For this reason, it may be advisable to take the exam *as early as possible* in that first year of associate registration – even if you fail the first time, you can take it again three months later without yet having to worry about renewing your registration.

If the time comes for you to renew your registration and you have *not* yet passed the Law and Ethics exam, you can still renew as long as you have attempted the exam at least once in the past year. But you will need to take a 12-hour continuing education course in California Law and Ethics before you schedule your next exam attempt.[86] Once your registration renews, you will repeat the process – again needing to attempt the Law and Ethics exam at least once during the year, and again needing to take another CE course if you do not pass by renewal time. This process can be repeated as many times as it takes for you to pass the Law and Ethics test, up to the six-year maximum length of associate registration.

---

[86] California Business and Professions Code section 4980.399(d), 4992.09(e), and 4999.55(d)

Each profession's California Law & Ethics Exam consists of 75 four-option multiple-choice questions, administered via computer. Of the 75 questions, 25 are non-scored items that are being tested for possible inclusion as scoring items in later exams. These do not impact your results, but you do not know which items are non-scoring. Once you start the test, you have 90 minutes to complete it.[87]

It may help you to know that the vast majority of those taking their Law & Ethics Exam for the first time are able to pass. For the 2016 calendar year, 73% of prelicensed MFTs taking the law and ethics exam for the first time passed it, as did 69% of PCCs and 74% of CSWs.[88]

Clinical Exam

When you complete your required hours of supervised experience, you apply to the BBS for eligibility to sit for your Clinical Exam. This application is sometimes referred to as "Submitting your hours" because it is when you send in the most paperwork, and may have to wait the longest for the BBS to complete its review of your application. Once approved for exam eligibility, you schedule your exam.

The MFT Clinical Exam (also known as the CCE, for California Clinical Exam) is the only clinical exam among the three professions covered in this book that is state-specific. California is the only state in the country that does not use the National MFT Exam as the clinical examination for MFT licensure. However, the new clinical test does appear to be very similar in content to the National MFT Exam. The BBS has been working collaboratively with the Association of Marriage and Family Therapy Regulatory Boards[89] (the group behind the national exam) to determine whether California may be able to transition to the national

---

[87] PSI licensure:certification (2015). *California Law and Ethics Examination Candidate Handbook.* Las Vegas, NV: PSI. (They provide parallel handbooks for each of the three professions.)

[88] California Board of Behavioral Sciences (2017). *Examination statistics 2016.* Available online at http://www.bbs.ca.gov/pdf/exam_stats/examstats_2016.pdf

[89] www.amftrb.org

exam in the future. The California MFT Clinical Exam is administered via computer and is made up entirely of four-option, multiple choice questions. There are 150 scored questions on the test, and up to 20 non-scored items (though, again, there's no way for an examinee to know which items are non-scored). Examinees have four hours to complete the test.[90]

For counselors, California recognizes the National Clinical Mental Health Counseling Exam (NCMHCE) as the clinical examination for licensure as an LPCC. This exam, which is developed by the National Board for Certified Counselors, consists of 10 case vignettes that assess a counselor's ability to gather necessary information and make appropriate clinical decisions. One vignette is not scored, as it is being evaluated for use in future exams. Each case is divided into five to 10 sections. Some questions accept multiple responses, while others ask the examinee to choose the best option from the choices presented. Unofficial scores on the NCMHCE are typically provided immediately after the examinee finishes the test.[91]

California uses the ASWB Clinical Level Exam as the clinical exam for social work licensure. It is made up of 170 four-option multiple-choice questions, 150 of which are scored. The other 20 are being tested for possible inclusion in later exams. The exam is administered on computer, and you have four hours to complete the test.[92]

---

[90] PSI licensure:certification (2015). *Marriage and Family Therapist California Clinical Examination Candidate Handbook.* Las Vegas, NV: PSI.
[91] National Board for Certified Counselors (2016). *Candidate Handbook for State Credentialing.* Greensboro, NC: NBCC.
[92] General information on the test can be found here: www.aswb.org/exam-candidates/about-the-exams/

▸ Life coaches, consultants, and other unlicensed professions

As you can see, there are a lot of rules governing licensure, and making the task of getting licensed quite a challenge. Some who want to make a career of helping others choose to avoid the licensure process entirely, and instead to build a career as a "life coach."

Life coaching is understood by its practitioners as a process of helping people achieve personal and professional goals and fulfill their potential. **Life coaching is distinct from psychotherapy in that it does not involve any effort to diagnose or resolve mental illness.** When a reputable life coach has a client who begins exhibiting symptoms of mental illness, they will refer that client to an appropriately trained mental health professional.[93]

There are a number of voluntary training and certification programs available for life coaches, consultants, and other unlicensed professions. But the terms "life coach," "consultant," and the like do not have title protection in California law. So anyone – regardless of training or experience – can advertise themselves under these titles. That's right: Your 18-year-old nephew could set up an office and call himself a life coach if he wanted to.

Because these professions are not licensed or otherwise defined under California law, they do not have a legal scope of practice defining what they can do. They also do not have a mechanism for consumers to complain about unethical or incompetent work. Practitioners in these unlicensed professions run the full gamut, from those who have had years of high-quality training to those who have had no training whatsoever.

As noted above, those who are responsible professionals will recognize the limits of their knowledge and experience, and make

---

[93] The International Coach Federation is one of several coaching organizations that has a Code of Ethics for members and additional information about the profession. They distinguish therapy from coaching nicely at http://coachfederation.org/about/landing.cfm?ItemNumber=844&navItemNumber=617

referrals to licensed mental health professionals when appropriate. However, many lack the training to even know when the behavior a client is displaying suggests a possible mental health disorder. And one recent study noted that a number of trained psychotherapists who had their licenses disciplined or even revoked by their state licensing boards were continuing to see clients by simply changing their title – to life coach.[94] These issues raise important consumer protection concerns.

Some licensed mental health professionals choose to use the term "life coach" *in addition to* their license title when advertising. The official license title is de-emphasized, in hopes that this will bring in prospective clients who are interested in receiving help with important life decisions but are unwilling to come to "therapy" if it is called that. There is nothing stopping therapists from doing this. However, unlicensed professions (and the titles and terminology associated with them) are sometimes looked down upon by licensed mental health professionals who would rather fight the stigma associated with psychotherapy than try to market their way around it. So you might risk losing a bit of respect among your peers when pursuing that marketing gain. For some therapists, the trade-off is worth it.

---

[94] Coy, J. S., Lambert, J. E., & Miller, M. M. (2016). Stories of the accused: A phenomenological inquiry of MFTs and accusations of unprofessional conduct. *Journal of Marital and Family Therapy, 42*(1), 139-152.

Room for debate: Support animals

Emotional support animals (ESAs) are different from the trained and certified service animals used by individuals with disabilities. Unlike service animals, ESAs do not need any kind of training or certification, and they *aren't* allowed everywhere. They are primarily legally recognized in two contexts. Under federal law, ESAs can fly for free, with their owner, on commercial flights.[95] And under both state and federal law, ESAs also can accompany their owners in housing situations, even ones that do not normally allow pets or that would charge pet rent.[96]

Individuals can have ESAs if they have obtained a letter of support from a therapist. There are very few rules or restrictions on how a therapist can determine whether to issue such a letter, or what the appropriate justification for allowing an ESA should be. This is a surprisingly loose system, and in the past 10 years, the use of ESAs has grown much faster than the use of other types of service animals.[97]

Some therapists will issue ESA letters to any client who asks. Others refuse to write such letters at all. Between those extremes, others have developed their own criteria for when to issue ESA letters, though there is no standard set of criteria for decision-making in this area that therapists are required to follow.

In the absence of clear legal or ethical guidelines, is it appropriate for therapists to issue ESA letters at all?

---

[95] Duffly, Z. (n.d.). Psychiatric Service Dogs & Emotional Support Animals: Access to public places & other settings. Available at www.nolo.com/legal-encyclopedia/psychiatric-service-dogs-emotional-support-animals-access-public-places-other-settings.ht

[96] Duffly, Z. (n.d.) When California landlords must allow tenants to have service dogs and Emotional Support Animals. Available online at www.nolo.com/legal-encyclopedia/california-landlords-tenants-service-dogs-emotional-support-animals.html

[97] Herzog, H. (2016 July 19). Emotional Support Animals: The therapist's dilemma. *Psychology Today* blog.

ESAs help, and abuses are solvable

by Emma Jaegle, MS

Many studies show the benefits of being exposed to pets. Being around a cat or dog lowers blood pressure and creates a lower resting heart rate.[98] In stressful situations, a pet being present can shorten the time it takes for a person's heart rate to return to normal. Pets also provide social support much like friends and family. Having an animal present can encourage social interactions with people, reducing feelings of isolation and loneliness.[99] Taking care of an animal can also increase a sense of purpose for clients who may be feeling worthless.[100]

The lack of regulation around ESAs is certainly a problem. There is a difference between helping an autistic child to keep calm in a busy airport by ensuring they can pet their dog, and someone who just wants their dog to go on vacation with them. It is unfortunate that there is now a market for purchasing letters and certificates allowing people to have their pet be an ESA without meaningful evaluation of the client's mental health or the pet's ability to be supportive.

However, solutions to this problem are possible while still allowing therapists to act responsibly, using their best judgment and following their ethical mandates, to assist clients who will genuinely benefit from the support of an ESA. Practitioners need stricter criteria for ESAs in order to reduce public skepticism of ESAs, and to facilitate future research on the effects of ESAs over time.

---

[98] Allen K., Blascovich J., & Mendes, W.B. (2002). Cardiovascular reactivity and the presence of pets, friends, and spouses: the truth about cats and dogs. *Psychosomatic Medicine, 64*(5), 727-739.

[99] McNicholas, J., & Collis, G. M. (2000). Dogs as catalysts for social interactions: Robustness of the effect. *British Journal of Psychology, 91*(1), 61-70.

[100] Raina, P., Waltner-Toews, D., Bonnett, B., Woodward, C., & Abernathy, T. (1999). Influence of companion animals on the physical and psychological health of older people: an analysis of a one-year longitudinal study. Journal of the American Geriatrics Society, 47(3), 323-329.

Therapists should not write ESA letters

by Benjamin E. Caldwell, PsyD

I'm a pet owner and an animal lover. But the labeling of pets as Emotional Support Animals has been subject to a lot of abuse. As you consider whether to issue ESA letters to clients who request them, you should consider a pair of important questions: 1, Are you trained for this? And 2, Who do you serve?

Determining whether to write an ESA letter is not simply a matter of issuing a mental health diagnosis. It *also* involves assessing whether an ESA would meaningfully help. The science supporting ESAs is surprisingly thin,[101] and therapists are typically *not* trained to make a determination about the need for or likely effectiveness of an ESA.[102] We are not trained to assess disability, or to certify a client's claim for disability benefits.[103] As such, writing ESA letters may be outside of our scope of competence.

Then the second question: Who do we serve? If our goal is simply to please our clients, then it makes sense to write ESA letters for anyone who asks. However, if our goal is to help clients better integrate into the community, then it makes little sense to place a client's convenience over the comfort and safety of others who may have allergies, phobias, or other concerns.

The current process for clients to obtain ESA letters from therapists is, unfortunately, ripe for abuse. There's little to stop a client wanting their pet to be an ESA from getting together with a therapist who wants a quick buck. That process needs meaningful change. That change should take therapists out of the process entirely.

---

[101] Resnick, B. (2018 February 23). The surprisingly weak scientific case for Emotional Support Animals. *Vox.* Available online at https://www.vox.com/science-and-health/2018/2/23/17012116/emotional-support-animal-airplane-psychology-research-dogs

[102] For a great example of a California-licensed therapist thoughtfully reviewing all of the relevant issues, and deciding that writing ESA letters was not in her scope of competence, see Spotts-de Lazzer, A. (2015 Jan/Feb). Emotional Support Animals. *Family Therapy Magazine, 14*(1), 64-67.

[103] www.edd.ca.gov/disability/Basics_for_Physicians-Practitioners.htm

2

Supervision

From the early days of Psychology, the mental health professions have worked under an apprenticeship model. While it is one thing to read about how to do therapy, and watch example recordings, it is quite another to have a more experienced therapist watching over your work as you are doing it. The supervisor can provide guidance and correction, and also emotional support. Good supervisors are often seen as mentors.

It is important to bear in mind that what makes a supervisor *good* is not necessarily the same as what makes them likeable. A great deal of research on the supervision process makes the mistake of presuming that a supervisee's *satisfaction* with their supervisor is the same as a supervisor being good at what they do.

I would urge you to think of supervision a bit differently. While you should feel safe enough with your supervisor to reveal insecurities about your work, you *also* should feel some responsibility to your supervisor to do well, and some anxiety when you know you are falling short. In other words, like any good teacher, your supervisor should do more than patting you on the back for good work. They should push you to get *better* at what you do. That doesn't always feel good, and might actually lead you to like them a little less. But in the long term, it will make you a better clinician.

▶ The role of the supervisor

The supervisor roles discussed here are not mutually exclusive. Every supervisor finds their own balance. Rather than considering the supervisor's role as an either/or proposition, it is best to think of that role as a weighing of these priorities. How much emphasis does a supervisor place on the challenging work of helping supervisees get better, versus the more routine monitoring involved in case presentations? How strict is the supervisor when it comes to supervisee conduct?

Clinical improvement

One way of thinking about the supervisor's role – a way that, as you can probably guess, I strongly believe in – is that their job is to *make supervisees more effective*. Once you are licensed for independent practice, you could easily spend the rest of your career in a solo private practice, with your work rarely (if ever) reviewed or observed by anyone other than your clients. The time you spend in supervision, early in your career, is your golden opportunity to improve your clinical skills.

A wealth of recent research is showing just how important this time is. While most therapists improve dramatically in their first year of clinical experience, the average therapist doesn't get any better after that.[104] In fact, a large recent study showed that on average, clinical outcomes get a little bit *worse* over time, after that first year.[105]

Thankfully, we also now know quite a bit about what supervisors and supervises *can* do to improve clinical outcomes. Scott Miller has done a great deal of researching and presenting on this

---

[104] I go into some detail about this line of research in the book *Saving Psychotherapy*. Suffice to say that the expected link between experience and effectiveness has been searched for many times, in many ways, over many years, and beyond the therapist's first year of experience, it just isn't found.
[105] Goldberg, S. B., Rousmaniere, T., Miller, S. D., Whipple, J., Lars Nielsen, S., Hoyt, W. T., & Wampold, B. E. (2016). Do psychotherapists' outcomes improve with time and experience? A longitudinal analysis of outcomes in a clinical setting. *Journal of Counseling Psychology, 63*(1), 1-11.

issue, and has developed recommendations for improving outcomes in a clinical setting. His recommendations include:[106]

- **Gather meaningful data for a baseline.** It's hard to know how and where to improve when you aren't sure what is and is not working. There are a number of good, low-cost and even no-cost measurements that can be used across client populations to assess in a meaningful way whether therapy is working.
- **Seek out ongoing, formal client feedback.** Many of those same no-cost and low-cost measures can be used throughout the therapy process to monitor gains. Miller and Hubble's Session Rating Scale, when used at every session, can help predict (and thus help therapists prevent) client dropout.
- **Utilize deliberate practice.** That's a specific term, relating to efforts at improving by shoring up specific micro-skills involved in expert performance. Just as you might become a better musician by practicing difficult chord transitions, or become a better athlete by drilling on very specific skills, therapists can improve by identifying specific areas of struggle and repeatedly focusing on those.[107]

When supervision is focused on clinical improvement, it can initially feel quite vulnerable. Rather than simply reporting on all cases in broad strokes, supervisees may be expected to review data, and to focus specifically on their mistakes and on cases that are *not* progressing. This "error-centric consultation"[108] places positive clinical outcomes above other supervision priorities.

---

[106] Miller, S., Hubble, M., & Duncan, B. (2007). Supershrinks: Learning from the field's most effective practitioners. *Psychotherapy Networker, 31*(6), 26-35, 56.

[107] The recent book *Deliberate practice for psychotherapists* by Tony Rousmaniere may be useful with this process.

[108] Rousmaniere, T., Goodyear, R. K., Miller, S. D., & Wampold, B. E. (Eds.) (2017). *The cycle of excellence: Using deliberate practice to improve supervision and training.* Hoboken, NJ: John Wiley & Sons.

Monitoring

Clinical improvement isn't the only way of thinking about the supervisor's role. There are also many supervisors who believe that their primary responsibility is more aligned with *monitoring*. In other words, supervision is essentially about ensuring that clients in crisis are handled appropriately, and that supervisees follow all ethical and legal standards. If the supervisee can do so for the full length of legally-required supervision, then they have demonstrated that they can be trusted to work independently.

While many supervisors say (and, I think, genuinely believe) that their role is geared toward clinical improvement, much of what is actually *done* in supervision falls more along the lines of monitoring. Case presentations, discussions of professional growth among supervisees, and review of long segments of session video are not known to improve clinical outcomes, and yet these are the bread and butter of many supervision groups.

Gatekeeping

One important component of any supervisor's role is gatekeeping for the larger profession. More than any other single person, your supervisor is in a position to evaluate the safety and effectiveness of your work. If, in their judgment, you are not ready to advance to licensure (or worse, if they believe that you would be a danger to the public), then they have a responsibility to intervene to protect your current and future clients.

Supervisors take this responsibility seriously. However, they are particularly limited in California when it comes to what they can do about a supervisee who appears to be unfit to work in mental health. Supervisors can refer supervisees to outside therapists, and when necessary, can seek to suspend or fire the supervisee. But even when a supervisor knows that their supervisee has committed legal or ethical violations with their clients, **there is no confidentiality exception in California law that would allow a supervisor to**

---

report a problematic supervisee to the BBS.[109] And even if such an exception did exist, the BBS would need those clients' permission to review records, interview the clients, and gather more information before acting on the complaint. So a problematic or even dangerous supervisee may suffer no worse consequence than being fired from their job, free to immediately begin searching for another.

Naturally, these ways of thinking about the therapist's role are not mutually exclusive. It can easily be argued that good supervision includes all of them. But when considering potential places to work, and interviewing with potential supervisors, it is worth considering (and asking about) how they perceive the balance of these roles, and what they *actually do* in support of each.

---

[109] A few caveats here. This refers to instances when such a report would require information that arose in a confidential setting. If the report would be based on other information – such as the supervisee showing up to work drunk – how that information would be handled would likely depend on the terms of the employment contract. In other words, some supervisors could report that. Additionally, I know of some employers who build a specific release of information related to unprofessional conduct into their supervision contracts and the intake documentation for clients seen by a supervisee. That release gives the supervisor permission to report unprofessional conduct to the licensing board if the supervisor believes it necessary.

▶ Requirements for supervisors

In order for any hours of supervised experience to count toward licensure, they must be done under the supervision of an appropriately qualified supervisor. Generally speaking, that means a supervisor who is a Psychologist, Psychiatrist, LMFT, LCSW, or LPCC,[110] who has been licensed for at least two years, and who has seen clients or provided direct supervision during at least two of the past five years.[111]

There are some profession-specific requirements as well. For CSW licensure, all supervisors must have taken at least a 15-hour training in supervision, including specific content requirements,[112] and at least 1,700 of your hours must be supervised by an LCSW. For PCCs, none of your hours need to be under an LPCC, and if you're an MFT, none of your hours need to be under an LMFT. However, if you're a PCC working with couples or families, those hours must be supervised by a supervisor who is themselves qualified to work with couples or families – something that, as you'll recall from Chapter 1, is *not* in the LPCC scope unless the LPCC has done additional training and experience. For PCCs and MFTs, supervisors must have taken at least a 6-hour supervision training, and must continue to take 6-hour supervision trainings in each license renewal cycle.

It is not uncommon for a well-meaning prospective supervisor to offer supervision without understanding all of the qualifications that must be met in order to supervise. Unfortunately, in such situations, it is the *supervisee* who may suffer, if their hours under that supervisor are disallowed from counting for licensure because the supervisor was technically not qualified.

As a supervisee, it is good practice to personally ensure that your supervisor meets the qualifications to supervise in your

---

[110] LPCCs must complete additional training and supervised experience to supervise MFT associates and trainees. These additional requirements are the same as those for an LPCC to work with couples and families specified in Chapter 1.
[111] Business and Professions Code sections 4980.03(g)(1) and 4999.12(h)(1), and California Code of Regulations title 16 section 1870(a)
[112] California Code of Regulations title 16 sections 1870(a)(4)(A) and 1874

profession. I also recommend that supervisees "subscribe" to their supervisors' licenses through the state's Breeze database system,[113] so that you will be automatically notified if the supervisor's license lapses – a common reason for hours to be audited or disallowed.

A supervisor cannot supervise someone who was their therapy client at any point in the past.[114] Any hours of experience earned under a supervisor who is the supervisee's spouse, relative, or domestic partner, or a supervisor will not be counted toward licensure.[115] The BBS also will not count any hours gained under a supervisor with whom the associate has had a prior personal or business relationship that undermines the authority or effectiveness of supervision.

Profession-specific requirements

Recall from the earlier discussion of scope of practice (in chapter 1) that PCCs cannot assess or treat couples or families unless they have fulfilled additional requirements for education and supervised experience. **When a PCC associate or licensee is *gaining* their supervised experience in couple, family, and child work** to comply with these requirements, they must be supervised by either an LPCC *who has already met the requirements* to work independently with couples and families, or by a supervisor of a different license type who can competently provide couple and family therapy.[116]

Associate CSWs and PCCs must work with their supervisors to develop a supervision plan for each work setting, detailing the goals of supervision. These goals have to include ongoing assessment of the associate's strengths and weaknesses, and work to ensure practice in keeping with legal requirements. Supervisors and associates can add to this whatever goals they wish, presuming they are appropriate goals for supervision. The supervision plan must be submitted to the BBS when the associate applies for licensure.[117]

---

[113] https://www.breeze.ca.gov
[114] California Business and Professions Code section 4980.03(g)(3)
[115] California Code of Regulations title 16 section 1833(b)(3)
[116] California Code of Regulations title 16 section 1820.5
[117] California Code of Regulations title 16 section 1822(b) and California Business and Professions Code section 4996.23(e)

▸ Forms of supervision

There are a lot of ways to do supervision, none necessarily any better or worse than another. Whole textbooks have been written on supervision in psychotherapy, outlining a number of different philosophical and theoretical approaches supervisors may take. When it comes to the structure of supervision, though, there are two distinct types recognized in state law.

Individual supervision

Individual supervision involves one supervisee sitting down with one supervisor, typically for an hour. Beyond this, the structure and content of supervision are largely left up to the participants.

As of the publication time for this book, the BBS was advancing legislation that would allow triadic supervision – that is, one supervisor with two supervisees – to count as individual supervision. This would make it easier for clinics to provide individual supervision, and there is some research supporting it. If the bill becomes law (which is always a big "if," the change would take effect in 2019).[118]

Group supervision

In group supervision, a supervisor meets with a group of up to eight supervisees, typically for two hours. (Some workplaces structure groups differently; two *consecutive* hours is a common practice, not a legal mandate.) As with individual supervision, the structure and content of the group are largely left up to the people in it. Some supervision groups are highly structured, with cases presented in very specific ways, and timetables for discussion. Other groups are more process-oriented, with less predetermined structure.

---

[118] Assembly Bill 93 (Medina), 2018.

▸ Responsibilities of supervisors

When supervisors in any work setting take on supervisees, they take on quite a burden of responsibility. The CAMFT Code of Ethics makes clear that the well-being of clients of a supervisee is ultimately the responsibility of the supervisor.[119] Even when this is not explicitly spelled out in an ethics code, it is likely to be considered true; certainly in the event of a complaint or lawsuit against a supervisee, the client may pursue action against the supervisor for what they perceive as inadequate supervision leading to the problem they experienced. So in a nonprofit clinic context, where a supervisor may have eight supervisees and each supervisee has 10 clients, the supervisor likely bears final responsibility *for all 80 of those cases.*

Furthermore, state law sets forth a number of additional specific supervisor responsibilities:[120]

Notify supervisees of any disciplinary actions or changes in their licensure status. This may seem obvious at first, but making it a legal requirement does give supervisees some recourse to file a complaint against their supervisor if, for example, the supervisor accidentally lets their license lapse. The BBS will not count any hours gained under a supervisor whose license is not active.

Competence in the *supervisee's* field. If supervising someone on track to a different license than the one held by the supervisor, the supervisor needs to have sufficient training and education related to the supervisee's field to supervise them. The supervisor also needs to stay up to date on changes in the supervisee's field.[121]

Competence specific to supervision. The supervisor needs to have enough training, education, and experience specifically in

---

[119] CAMFT Code of Ethics standard 4.13
[120] These requirements are summarized for supervisors on the Supervisor Responsibility Statement that each supervisor is expected to review and sign at the beginning of the supervision relationship. They're found in law at California Code of Regulations title 16 sections 1821 (PCCs), 1833 (MFTs), and 1870 (CSWs).
[121] California Code of Regulations title 16 section 1833.1(a)(2-3), (b)(3)

supervision to competently supervise. While the state sets minimum training requirements as noted above, it's worth considering the scope of competence element here. If a supervisor went through a poorly-done supervision training, it may not make the supervisor competent enough to supervise.

Complete six hours of **CE in supervision** within 60 days of starting supervision, and in every license renewal period after that, so long as they continue to supervise.

Understand the laws surrounding supervised experience in the *supervisee's* field. Many supervisors know their own field's laws well, but may not be as familiar with the laws governing their supervisees, if the supervisees are working toward a different license.

Ensure supervisee competence. The supervisor is responsible for ensuring that the clinical work performed by their supervisee is consistent with the supervisee's training, education, and experience.

Actively monitor the quality of the supervisee's work. State law sets out a number of possible ways to do so, including review of session recordings, review of client files, live observation of sessions, or whatever else the supervisor determines is appropriate. In addition, supervisors of social work associates must *formally* evaluate supervisee strengths and weaknesses at least once per year and at the end of the supervision relationship, and give copies of those assessments to the associate.

Provide at least one week of notice if the supervisor intends to stop signing for hours gained by the supervisee.

Plan with the supervisee for client emergencies. Supervisors do not need to be available to supervisees 24 hours a day, but supervisees should know what to do if a client goes into crisis and the supervisor is not immediately available.

Only supervise those pre-degree professionals whose clinical work will be in keeping with applicable law and regulation. This includes a specific limitation that supervisors only supervise employers and volunteers, not independent contractors.

In addition to those legal requirements, professional ethical codes spell out additional supervisor responsibilities. Supervisors are generally expected to avoid dual relationships with supervisees, to ensure cultural competence in their supervision, to help supervisees in need of assistance with personal issues to find that assistance, to avoid harassment or exploitation of supervisees, and to make sure that supervisees are not working beyond their competence.[122] Additional supervisor expectations can be found in each profession's ethics code.

Finally, while state law does not directly address record-keeping for supervision, keeping good supervision records offers many of the same benefits as keeping good therapy records. Supervisors with good records of supervision have a good line of defense against claims of inadequate supervision, can track supervisees' cases more effectively, can provide justification for any corrective actions that need to be taken with a supervisee, and can provide for continuity of supervision when a new supervisor takes over.[123]

---

[122] ACA Code of Ethics section F, AAMFT Code of Ethics standard IV, CAMFT Code of Ethics section 4, NASW Code of Ethics section 3
[123] Riemersma, M. (2009 September/October). Tips on supervision: Supervisor record-keeping. *The Therapist, 21*(5), 50-51.

▶ Responsibilities of supervisees

Responsibility for an effective supervision experience, and for the quality of care provided by a supervisee, does not rest solely on the supervisor. *Supervisees* also have a number of specific responsibilities spelled out in state law and professional ethics codes.

Perhaps first and foremost, all of the rules around unprofessional conduct apply equally to supervisees as they do to licensees. A supervisee who had acted unprofessional could not avoid responsibility by making the excuse that their supervisor didn't teach them properly. **Supervisees are responsible for knowing current legal and ethical standards, and acting within them.** This includes keeping up with changes in law and in ethics codes. You are responsible for following every applicable law and ethical standard for a therapist at your stage in your profession from your first day on the job.

In some cases, disciplinary action has been taken against associates and *not* their supervisors for failures in the associate's clinical care or judgment. If, in the judgment of the BBS, the supervisor was doing their job adequately, and the supervisee violated an established rule or process of the supervisor, then the supervisor may not be held responsible for their supervisee's unprofessional conduct. (The key word here is "may." It isn't a guarantee. As noted above, the supervisor does have ultimate responsibility for client welfare in *all* cases being seen by supervisees.) This is perhaps a long way of saying that while supervisors may have ultimate responsibility for client care, supervisees have *immediate* responsibility for the quality of the care they are providing.

Graduate school and the pathway to licensure can be uniquely stressful times, so just like licensees, **supervisees are expected to closely monitor their own functioning, and ask for help when they need it.**

Supervisees also need to **disclose their status** as supervisees to prospective clients, an issue we return to in chapter 8.

▶ Supervision via technology

Increasingly, supervision is being provided via technology. This has a number of potential advantages. To name just a few: Supervisors can provide immediate assistance to supervisees, even if the supervisor (or supervisee) is out of the office; one supervisor can serve several locations for a large employer with multiple offices; and supervisees can seek out specialized supervision from a supervisor in another part of the state when necessary and appropriate.

There have been a number of recent journal publications on supervision using videoconferencing, all recognizing that the practice is becoming more common as the underlying technology improves.

However, there is also risk that comes with supervision via technology. So, the BBS has adopted a handful of rules for supervision via phone or videoconference.

Supervision via telephone

There is nothing in state law to limit your ability to speak with a supervisor by phone. Indeed, this is often a critical component of responding to a client in crisis, or to a legal or ethical problem that needs a quick answer. Many supervisors go to great lengths to make sure that they or another qualified supervisor are available to supervisees whenever they might be needed.

Technically speaking, supervision by phone is probably not to be counted toward your license. The law requires that, for supervision to count, it must be "face to face."[124] Phone calls are not face-to-face. (If you're using FaceTime or other video technology, this would be considered videoconferencing rather than a phone call. More on videoconferencing below.)

It is arguable whether this is good policy. Phone calls, especially in crisis situations, can be among the most valuable supervision you get. At the same time, the BBS would understandably want to be cautious about setting rules that would allow a supervisor to quite literally "phone it in."

---

[124] California Business and Professions Code section 4980.43(d)(3)

Supervision via videoconference

Unlike phone conversations, videoconference supervision *can be* considered face-to-face in some settings. It can count toward licensure requirements if you are working in a non-private-practice setting, such as an agency.[125] In a private practice setting, supervision needs to be in person in order for it to count toward licensure.

Because supervision via videoconference often necessarily includes the sharing of private client information, it makes sense to apply the same security and privacy safeguards to supervision via technology that you would apply to therapy via technology. I like the simplicity and directness of the NASW ethical standard here:

> "Social workers should not discuss confidential information, electronically or in person, in any setting unless privacy can be ensured."[126]

Note that this standard makes no distinction between confidential information being discussed in therapy versus in supervision. The ACA code similarly requires counselors to ensure privacy and confidentiality of client information generally, without regard for the specific context. And the AAMFT code often uses the phrase "clients and supervisees" when discussing technology, indicating a similar lack of distinction.

---

[125] California Business and Professions Code section 4980.43(d)(6)
[126] NASW Code of Ethics standard 1.07(i)

▶ Serious problems in supervision

Many of the problems that arise between supervisors and supervisees are preventable. Clear expectations, set at the beginning of the supervision process in writing, and clear procedures for evaluating a supervisee's work form the basis of a productive supervision relationship.

Some of the garden-variety struggles that occur in the relationship between supervisor and supervisee are beyond the scope of this text. Our legal requirements don't address them, beyond the supervisor and supervisee requirements described above, and more useful and detailed discussion of how to address them can be found in texts geared specifically toward the supervision process.

However, two serious problems are worth addressing here, precisely because they do tie into our legal responsibilities: Addressing ineffective supervisees, and those who may be a poor fit for the field.

Ineffectiveness

Even when using the same treatment model with the same population, some clinicians are simply more effective than others. It is a bit surprising how rarely we acknowledge this in the course of therapist training. And yet, if we were better at identifying therapists who were struggling to be effective, and either helping or replacing them, therapy in general could become much more effective for the clients who seek it.[127]

Supervisors have a legal responsibility to monitor the quality of supervisees' work, as described above. Supervisees who are failing to work effectively with their clients must be addressed. Of course, no therapist has a perfect track record of effectiveness. And even when problems are identified, supervisors may have a difficult time differentiating an ineffective therapist from one who is simply having a bad week, or one who was assigned (either by design or at random) a more difficult caseload. There are two things a supervisor

---

[127] Caldwell, B. E. (2015). *Saving Psychotherapy.* Los Angeles: Author.

can do to help make the distinction: Gather client outcome data, and provide negative feedback to the therapist.

Outcome data is relatively easy to gather. There are a number of instruments available, including some at no cost, that are quick and convenient for clients and provide useful data for therapists and supervisors. Payors are also increasingly requiring agencies to gather and report on this data, so it may already be a requirement of your site.

Negative feedback is perhaps more difficult, but it is worth noting that this is often more challenging for the supervisor than it is for the supervisee. Simply put, supervisees usually want to know what they're doing wrong. They see their treatment failures but may not understand *why* treatment failed. Supervisors may understandably worry about shaking a supervisee's confidence. I would argue, however, that it is far better for a supervisee to receive specific and actionable negative feedback than it would be for them to struggle over and over with clients and not know how they can improve.

It is very rare, to my knowledge, for a prelicensed therapist to lose their job simply for being not very good at it. Supervisors are often reluctant to fire (or to recommend the firing of) an ineffective supervisee. The supervisor may hope and expect that they can guide the supervisee to improve, or that the supervisee simply will get better on their own with more experience. The supervisor may feel that the supervisee's ineffectiveness is the supervisor's fault. The supervisor also may be reluctant to fire a supervisee out of fear that they would simply be kicking the problem to another supervisor.

While these are all understandable impulses, the end result is that ineffective therapists keep working with clients who would be better served by a different therapist. One recent study demonstrated that if the least effective therapists were routinely fired and replaced, a clinic could dramatically improve its outcomes.[128] And while the human impact certainly weighs heavier in my mind than the legal one, I do wonder about the potential legal liability for a supervisor who knows that a supervisee is ineffective, and simply keeps them on board anyway, without much in the way of remedial effort.

---

[128] Imel, Z. E., Sheng, E., Baldwin, S. A., & Atkins, D. C. (2015). Removing very low-performing therapists: A simulation of performance-based retention in psychotherapy. *Psychotherapy, 52*(3), 329-336.

Fitness for the profession

Occasionally, it will come to a supervisor's attention that one of their supervisees is struggling beyond the normal struggles therapists and counselors experience on the way to licensure. If a supervisee is quickly burning out, disregarding legal or ethical standards, or otherwise far out of line with reasonable professional expectations, that supervisee may not be a good fit for the field.

Supervisors often struggle deeply with what to do in these kinds of situations. A natural first step is to guide the supervisee into their own therapy, and consider limiting their clinical workload unless you see improvement in the supervisee's conduct. If no such improvement is seen, the supervisor may move toward terminating their relationship with the supervisee. (What this looks like necessarily depends on the structure of the work setting.)

One of the reasons this can be such a difficult situation for supervisors is that ending a supervision relationship doesn't get a supervisee the help they might need. It may only increase any emotional and financial hardship that the supervisee is experiencing. And even if the supervisee truly is not a good fit for the field, there is little the supervisor can do to prevent that supervisee from simply finding employment elsewhere, and potentially engaging in the same behavior that created concern in the first place.

As discussed earlier in this chapter, supervisors have little recourse built into state law for reporting illegal or unethical actions of a supervisee, including actions that might indicate a lack of good fit for the field. In response to this concern, some supervisors put in their supervision contracts – and some agencies put in the treatment contracts for those clients being seen by prelicensed therapists – an exception to confidentiality that grants a supervisor permission to inform the licensing board when a supervisee's conduct creates concern about their fit for the profession.

▶ Employment law

You may be surprised to learn that a number of practices that are common in the mental health world, especially when prelicensed therapists are employed in private practice settings, are actually not compliant with state law. This is not (at least, not usually) because of mustache-twirling employers trying their best to exploit their employees. Instead, it happens because:

- State law changed, and the employer is unaware of the changes.
- An employer is operating from their own experience coming up in the field, and doesn't realize that what they themselves experienced was in fact illegal.
- An employer misunderstands the law's requirements.
- An employer believes that a particular element of employment law does not apply to them when it actually does.
- An employer, acting in good faith, makes a mistake.

Each of these is common, and a good reason not to demonize an employer who is violating state employment law. Your first response when you discover such a violation should be to try to work it out directly with the employer. Quite often you will find that the employer *wants* to fully comply with the law, and will appreciate that you brought the issue to their attention.

There are entire books about state employment law, and there simply isn't enough room here to go into full detail on every aspect of the law. So, as always, if you have a question about employment law and how it might apply in your specific work setting, it's good to consult with an attorney. If you have questions about the specific details of any of the laws discussed in this section, a good first stop will be the links in the footnotes; the state's Department of Industrial Relations handles enforcement of workplace laws, and their website includes a wealth of helpful information on these issues.

Here we'll cover some of the most often misunderstood elements of state employment law as it relates to mental health professionals.

Forms of employment

One key question from the moment you plan to go to work in any particular setting: What is your relationship to the employer? **If you enter into an employment agreement and will receive a W-2 form for your taxes, you are an** *employee.* Labor laws most clearly apply in this form of employment, though some aspects of law apply differently to larger companies than to smaller ones.

If you sign some form of consulting agreement and will receive a 1099 form for your taxes, you are considered an *independent contractor* **rather than an employee.** In many ways, the law puts an independent contractor on a level playing field with the person or company with whom they have contracted; an independent contractor typically has more flexibility to set their own hours and workplace policies, so long as they complete the work they have contracted to do.[129] Many elements of employment law do *not* apply to independent contractors, which is one reason why you cannot gain hours of supervised experience toward licensure as an independent contractor. **In order for prelicensed experience to count toward licensure, you** *must* **be an employee or volunteer. Hours gained as an independent contractor will not be counted.** Once licensed, of course, you are free to enter into independent contractor agreements for your work if you choose.

Finally, **if you agree to work for a clinic or agency without pay, you are considered a** *volunteer.* Nonprofit agencies have a fair amount of flexibility to use volunteers as they see fit. Labor law protections are minimal. Most trainee experience is done as a volunteer, and it is not unusual for associates to do at least some of their supervised hours as volunteers. When you apply for clinical exam eligibility, the BBS will want a letter from any clinic where you served as a volunteer, to confirm your volunteer status. This serves primarily to ensure that you were *not* acting as an independent contractor.

---

[129] Department of Industrial Relations. *Independent contractor versus employee.* Available online at http://www.dir.ca.gov/dlse/FAQ_IndependentContractor.htm

Hiring

When you are applying for a job, you have a right to know the pay scale for that job.[130] This is a recent state law, having taken effect January 1, 2018, so some employers may not be aware of it. This law applies to all employers, including nonprofits and government agencies. Note, though, that it is required that employers provide pay information to *applicants* for a position. They are not required to include the pay scale in public job postings, or to provide it to those who are curious about a job but have not yet applied for it. Still, it can benefit employers as well as potential applicants when pay is included in job announcements. Neither side then has to waste time on applications from therapists who ultimately would not accept the pay level that the job offers.[131]

Employers are not permitted to ask you about your salary history during the application and interview process. Even if you tell the employer (without their asking) how much you were paid at previous jobs, the employer cannot use that information to make a hiring decision or to set your pay in the job for which they're hiring you.[132]

While California employers generally can no longer ask about criminal history during the application process, many employers *of therapists and counselors* are likely to continue asking those questions. Exactly what can be asked about criminal history, and how that information can be used, varies by type of employer.[133] Past criminal convictions may be considered in some mental health settings to be directly related to the functions and qualifications of the job, and as we will discuss in the next chapter, past criminal history can – but doesn't always – lead the BBS to deny your application for registration or licensure.

When making hiring decisions, **employers cannot discriminate** on the basis of "race, religious creed, color, national

---

[130] California Labor Code section 432.3
[131] My company initiated a social media campaign on this issue, highlighting the benefits of posting pay scales for employers and applicants alike. See https://bencaldwelllabs.com/pages/postthepay for more information.
[132] California Labor Code section 432.3
[133] California Labor Code section 432.7

origin, ancestry, physical disability, mental disability, medical condition, genetic information, marital status, sex, gender, gender identity, gender expression, age, sexual orientation, or military and veteran status."[134] However, if you are not hired into a job that you applied or interviewed for, you are not entitled to an explanation for why you were not chosen. Many employers, as a matter of policy, will not provide any additional feedback to an applicant who was not hired.

Wages

Simply put, **if you are a W-2 employee, you must receive at least minimum wage for the hours you worked during each pay period.** California's minimum wage, as of January 1, 2018, was $10.50 per hour for employers with 25 or fewer employees and $11 per hour for larger employers.[135] Some cities have chosen to make their own minimum wages higher.

Fee splitting

In private practice settings, associate therapists often work under fee-split arrangements. For example, an associate may be hired into a private practice with the understanding that the associate's pay will equal 40% of the total client fees for the clients seen by the associate, with the other 60% going to the employer. While such arrangements are common, the question of whether they are legal and ethical is actually more than a bit gray, especially if the employer is referring patients to the associate.

California law generally prohibits health care providers from charging, receiving, or giving fees for client referrals.[136] This protection appears to be in state law to ensure that referrals from one health professional to another are based solely on the best interests of the client, and not on what is financially best for the referrer. The ACA

---

[134] California Government Code section 12940
[135] Department of Industrial Relations. *Minimum wage.* Available online at http://www.dir.ca.gov/dlse/FAQ_MinimumWage.htm
[136] California Business and Professions Code section 650

Code of Ethics specifically prohibits fee splitting,[137] and the NASW Code of Ethics prohibits social workers from "giving or receiving a payment for referral when no professional service is provided by the referring social worker."[138] In each of these cases, there is no exception given for when the referrer is the employer of the referee. However, what makes this gray is that by working in the same practice, it could be argued that both supervisor and supervisee are parts of the same business entity, and therefore a fee split between them isn't the kind of referral kickback that those standards are aiming to prevent.

The question could be settled by the Legislature through clearer statutory language, by the professional associations through clarification or interpretation of their codes, or by a court, if the court is called upon to settle a test case where someone is sued over a fee split. In the meantime, those employers wishing to stay safely out of this murky area may prefer to set wage scales based on a flat hourly rate rather than a percentage of fees collected.

Wage formulas and deductions

Meanwhile, some private practice, group practice, and agency settings use complex formulas to determine wages, deducting for things like supervision that are required in the job. Some such deductions are legal, others are not, and for others the law is murky. Employers cannot charge prelicensed therapists for office rent, furnishings, or anything else that is reasonably the responsibility of the employer.[139] But there is debate about what that last clause means in practice.

Regardless of the specific method in which pay is computed, **you should receive at least minimum wage for the hours you worked during each pay period.** If a fee-split or wage formula leaves the employee making less than minimum wage, it may be a violation of state law.

---

[137] *ACA Code of Ethics* standard A.10.b
[138] *NASW Code of Ethics* standard 1.16(c)
[139] California Business and Professions Code sections 4980.43(i) and 4996.23(l)(3). There is no similar language for PCC associates, who are simply restricted from having a proprietary interest in the employer's business (section 4999.47(f)).

Volunteering

Since the previous title for post-degree, prelicensed MFTs and PCCs was "Intern," it has been common for such therapists and counselors to be hired into unpaid "internships" as volunteers.[140] In many cases, this is perfectly legal. However, in some cases, the work done by these volunteers would actually be considered employment under the law, and would need to be paid accordingly. For example, it would be against the law to see clients as a volunteer in a private practice setting, even if the employer called the experience an "internship." In for-profit settings, there is a six-point test the government uses to determine whether an unpaid internship is legal, and any position where a prelicensed therapist is actively doing clinical work would likely fail that test.

Even in non-profit settings, it would not be legal to bring on a therapist for an unpaid "internship" if the work setting would be considered a "commercial entity." There have not, however, been test cases that would allow us to consider whether a typical nonprofit agency, charging fees for its mental health services, would be considered a commercial entity. It is likely that most nonprofit agencies would not meet that definition, making it legal for them to use unpaid volunteers.

Notably, there was one recent case where a therapist's volunteer status was challenged. A psychologist intern was hired to work at the University of California San Francisco, for a paid job that would require 17 hours per week of work. She was told at the time she was hired that any work beyond those 17 hours would be unpaid. However, once hired, she was regularly required to work 40-hour weeks. She complained to the state that this additional required time should also be paid, and she won.[141] This case was especially

---

[140] It's worth noting that state law for MFTs and PCCs carefully avoided the term "internship" for the experience gained between graduation and licensure, even when the professional title was "intern." The simple use of the term "internship" can sometimes suggest to employers and therapists alike that these positions *should* be unpaid.

[141] Zara, C. (2013 August 8). Internship debate spills into public sector: University of California, San Francisco, ordered to pay back wages to former intern. *International Business Times*. Available online at

noteworthy because the university, as a public university operated by the state, was not a for-profit business. They argued that they should be exempt from this portion of labor law for that reason. When that argument failed, non-profits and other government employers took note.[142]

Pay periods

The rules around pay period and paydays are surprisingly complex.[143] Several different structures are acceptable, but here are a couple of common ones that are technically *not* allowed:

- Monthly pay where once each month, an employee is paid for the entirety of their work the *previous* month.
- Weekly or biweekly pay where there is a delay of more than seven days between the end of the payroll period and the date when wages are actually paid.

If you are in a position where you are paid on a salary basis, you will probably be paid once or twice a month. If you are paid monthly, you must be paid by the 26th of the month for *that month's* work, including pay for the days of the month that haven't happened yet.

In you are in a position where you are paid on an hourly basis, obviously it's much harder for the employer to predict what you might be making on days that you haven't yet worked. You can be paid as follows:

- On the 10th of each month for all wages earned on the 16th through the end of the previous month, and on the 25th of

---

http://www.ibtimes.com/internship-debate-spills-public-sector-university-california-san-francisco-ordered-pay-back-wages

[142] Unfortunately, some of the specifics of this case limit the degree that the ruling can be applied elsewhere. For example, the psychologist was hired into a paid position. Had the initial employment contract specified that the entire position was unpaid, perhaps the ruling would have been different.

[143] For all of this section: California Labor Code section 204

each month for all wages earned between the 1st and 15th of that month.

- Any other weekly, biweekly (every two weeks), or semimonthly (twice a month) schedule, so long as you are paid within seven days of the end of the pay period.

Sick leave

All W-2 employees in California must be offered paid sick leave. Any employee who is employed for more than 120 days has the right to use up to three days (or 24 hours) of paid sick leave per year. Employers can cap an employee's accrued sick leave at six days (or 48 hours). Unlike paid vacation time, employees are not required to be paid for any unused sick leave when their employment ends.[144]

Sick leave calculation can get difficult if you're in a part-time work setting where you actually aren't working all that many hours. Employees must earn 1 hour of paid sick leave for every 30 hours of actual work. If you typically work four-hour days, then you are entitled to take up to *six* days of paid sick leave per year, as the law sets the maximum use of paid sick leave at three days or 24 hours, *whichever is greater*. In this case, 24 hours would equal six days of work.

Vacation

Employers are not required to provide employees with vacation time, paid or otherwise. If they *do* choose to provide vacation time, they have to follow whatever policies are in place around its use. (For example, an employer could not include two weeks' vacation time per year in an employment contract, and then tell you at the start of the year that you actually only get one week this year.)

Some companies have policies saying that unused time from one year cannot be carried over to the next year. Such "use it or lose it"

---

[144] Department of Industrial Relations. *California paid sick leave: Frequently asked questions.* Available online at http://www.dir.ca.gov/dlse/Paid_Sick_Leave.htm

policies are prohibited by state law. The law considers vacation time to be a form of wages, so those wages can't be rescinded once they are earned. However, employers can cap the total vacation time you have built up. They also can control when vacation can be taken, and how much vacation can be taken at once.

If your employer provides paid vacation leave, you must be paid for any unused leave when the employment ends, regardless of the reason for it ending. In other words, it doesn't matter whether you quit or got fired – you are entitled to be paid for unused paid vacation time.[145]

Breaks

If you work at least three and a half consecutive hours, you are entitled to at least a 10-minute break for every four hours of work. That rest period must be paid. Notably, many therapy and counseling centers pay little attention to this rule, presuming (or requiring) that their employees will take the required breaks between scheduled client sessions. However, if the employer is requiring other work during those periods (such as documentation), it may not count as a break.[146]

If you work more than six consecutive hours in a day, your employer has to provide at least a 30-minute meal break. (If you work a five-hour day, you and the employer can waive the meal requirement; if you work fewer than five hours, a meal break is not required.) If you are required to remain at the work site during the meal break, the break must be paid, even if you are otherwise off-duty.[147]

---

[145] Department of Industrial Relations. *Vacation FAQ.* Available online at http://www.dir.ca.gov/dlse/FAQ_Vacation.htm
[146] Department of Industrial Relations. *Rest periods.* Available online at http://www.dir.ca.gov/dlse/FAQ_RestPeriods.htm
[147] Department of Industrial Relations. *Meal periods.* Available online at http://www.dir.ca.gov/dlse/FAQ_MealPeriods.htm

Workplace safety

If you get hurt on the job, you may be entitled to Workers' Compensation benefits.[148] Every California employer is required to have Workers' Compensation insurance.[149] You generally have the right to a safe workplace, and the state's workplace safety rules are governed by the Division of Occupational Safety and Health, otherwise known as Cal/OSHA.[150] However, **the simple fact that a safety concern was identified, or a client presented a danger to a therapist or other staff, does not mean that a safety violation necessarily occurred.**

It is normal in working with clients struggling with mental illness that you will sometimes feel unsafe. There of course is a difference between feeling *emotionally* unsafe, as you might in a particularly difficult supervision group, and feeling *physically* unsafe. Cal/OSHA is concerned with the physical safety of employees.

Many employers provide some level of safety and health training for each worker. The extent of this training typically depends on the clientele being served where you work; if it's a more dangerous population, it makes sense for any safety training to be more extensive.

Termination

California is an "at will" employment state, which means that unless your contract specifies otherwise, you can be fired at any time, with or without notice, with or without being told why.[151] If an employer chooses to let you go, they do not owe you an explanation. Similarly, you can leave your position at any time, with or without

---

[148] Department of Industrial Relations. *Notice to employees: Injuries caused by work.* Available online at http://www.dir.ca.gov/dwc/NoticePoster.pdf
[149] Department of Industrial Relations. *Workers compensation FAQ.* Available online at http://www.dir.ca.gov/dlse/FAQ-Workers%20Compensation.pdf
[150] Department of Industrial Relations. *CAL/OSHA.* Available online at http://www.dir.ca.gov/dosh/
[151] Department of Industrial Relations. *Termination of Employment.* Available online at https://www.dir.ca.gov/dlse/TerminationOfEmployment.pdf

notice or explanation – though it's worth keeping in mind your ethical responsibility to avoid client abandonment.

If you are laid off or fired, any remaining wages the employer owes you (including accrued paid vacation) should be paid in accordance with the employment contract and state law. If there is a good-faith dispute about the amount the employer owes you, they can withhold the amount in question until the dispute is resolved. But they are required to pay on schedule any money that is not in dispute.[152]

Handling problems

As I mentioned at the start of this section, there are a number of reasons why an employer might be acting in good faith but still violating the law. Hopefully this section has given you a sense of the scope of California's labor protections, and we've barely scratched the surface. Especially in smaller clinics and in private practices, the law has so much specificity, and can change so quickly, that it can be difficult even for well-meaning employers to keep up.

With that in mind, if you believe you are observing a violation of labor law in your workplace, a good first step can be to simply bring the issue to the employer's attention. Ask questions and offer information, rather than making threats or demands. If the employer is acting in good faith, and they can see that you are as well, then resolving the concern can become a collaborative effort.

If that process does not go well, and what you believe to be violations of state law continue, then you may need to raise the issue with administrators, a human resources representative (if one exists at your workplace; most small employers will not have one), or if necessary, the state.

Complaints and retaliation

Even when having a collaborative discussion with an employer about labor law concerns, it may be worth documenting that

---

[152] California Labor Code section 206

conversation. If your employer retaliates against you for complaining about a safety hazard, filing (or threatening to file) a wage claim, refusing to perform hazardous work, or several other legal activities (like taking unpaid time off for jury duty), you can file a complaint with the state's Division of Labor Standards Enforcement.[153]

Those complaints, as well as wage claims, really do work. Pay a visit to the home page of the Labor Commissioner's office at http://www.dir.ca.gov/dlse/dlse.html and you can see many announcements of citations for wage theft. In a recent Los Angeles case, the Labor Commissioner cited the owners of six residential board and care facilities *more than $7 million* in back wages and fines.[154]

---

[153] Department of Industrial Relations. *Retaliation/discrimination.* Available online at http://www.dir.ca.gov/dlse/FAQ_Retaliation.htm
[154] Department of Industrial Relations (2018 January 9). *California Labor Commissioner cites owner of six residential care facilities in Los Angeles over $7 million for wage theft.* Available online at http://www.dir.ca.gov/DIRNews/2018/2018-03.pdf

Room for debate: Supervisor standards

What makes someone qualified to serve as a mentor to a new professional? As you've seen in this chapter, the legal requirement to supervise is actually a fairly low standard: two years of licensure, and a six-hour supervision course (15 hours for social workers).

Professional organizations offer their own certification courses for supervisors. AAMFT offers a 30-hour course, which must be followed up with 18 hours of supervision-of-supervision before a supervisor is deemed certified. In some states, supervisors of MFTs must be certified by AAMFT in order for that supervised experience to count for licensure. CAMFT also offers a supervisor certification, which is made up of 36 hours of education.

If the professional organizations believe it takes this much training to become an effective supervisor, you might be wondering, why is the state standard so low? **Can a therapist become a skilled supervisor with so little specific training on supervision?**

The answer to that question depends at least in part on your beliefs about the role of the supervisor. If the supervisor's role is primarily to help supervisees become more effective, than additional training makes sense. Not every therapist is necessarily a good teacher, and improving a supervisee's clinical skills requires effective teaching. On the other hand, if a supervisor's role is primarily monitoring, than a lower standard seems more appropriate; it doesn't take much additional skill or training to simply keep an eye on a supervisee.

Another important consideration is the availability of qualified supervisors. If you are lucky enough to live in an urban area, there may be plenty of potential supervisors available to you. But in more rural parts of the state, this simply isn't the case. In fact, many of those who ultimately don't make it through to licensure report that a significant hurdle for them was a lack of available qualified supervisors.

While California's standards will likely be increasing soon, the state has thus far attempted to err on the side of making supervision more available to those who need it.

3

Unprofessional Conduct

When you enter into the role of an LMFT, LPCC, or LCSW, you are voluntarily giving up some of your legal rights and agreeing to be held to a higher standard of behavior than the ordinary person. As one example of the rights you give up, consider freedom of speech. It is one of our fundamental First Amendment rights in the United States. As an LMFT, LPCC, or LCSW, you agree to *limit* your freedom of speech when it comes to discussing what happens in your office. If you choose to exercise what would, for an average person, be freedom of speech and reveal who your clients are to the world, you could lose your license to practice.

This is important to consider if you are early in your education as a mental health professional. One of the most controversial policy areas in the mental health field right now is whether a therapist also gives up their freedom to practice religion as they see fit within the context of their licensed mental health work. Several recent lawsuits have focused on therapists or students who refused to treat gay or lesbian clients, citing their religious beliefs.[155] Does a client's right to receive competent services regardless of their sexual orientation trump a therapist's right to act in accordance with their religious beliefs while working under their state license?

Unfortunately, the resolution of those lawsuits did little to clarify the limits of religious practice for mental health professionals.[156] What is clear is that mental health professionals operate in an area of public trust, bestowed upon us in the form of state licensure. In exchange, we agree to uphold a high standard of professional behavior that most people – even most professionals – do not need to follow.

Why the statutes exist

As is the case with any established higher standards of behavior, there will be some within the mental health professions who violate those standards. Unprofessional conduct statutes give the state the authority to discipline the licenses of those who violate accepted standards of professional behavior. For less severe violations, punishments such as probation are often sufficient. For severe or repeat violations of professional standards, the unprofessional conduct statutes allow the BBS to suspend or even revoke a practitioner's license.

It benefits the professions as well as the public for the BBS to have this disciplinary power. Making sure that the proverbial "bad apples" are prevented from continuing to work in the mental health professions increases public trust in those professionals who *do* follow the rules, and provides clients who have been harmed by their therapists an important avenue for justice.

---

[155] Caldwell, B. E. (2011). The dilemma: Can a religious therapist refuse to treat gay and lesbian clients? *Family Therapy Magazine, 10*(5), 50-52.
[156] I wrote on the resolution of two key cases here: www.psychotherapynotes.com/education-2/eastern-michigan-settles-julea-ward-case/

How unprofessional conduct differs from ethical standards and from other laws

By defining an act in law as "unprofessional conduct," the state allows a licensing board to discipline the license of a person who engages in that act. For example, when Senate Bill 1172 prohibited therapists from performing "reparative therapy" with minors, it did this by defining reparative therapy (and therapies like it) as unprofessional conduct.[157]

A therapist who violates the law may be liable in three different contexts. A client may ask a court to award damages in a **civil** lawsuit, where the client alleges that the therapist's actions were outside of the standards of the profession and caused them harm. Civil awards are typically money, and judges in these cases make decisions based on a *preponderance* (essentially, a majority) *of the evidence*. In a **criminal** case, the government or district attorneys office alleges that the therapist is to have violated the public in some way deserving of punishment. These cases can result in fines, jail time, or both. In order to be found guilty in a criminal trial, a judge or jury must find the evidence against you to be convincing *beyond a reasonable doubt*. A **disciplinary action** is focused on your performance in (or fitness for) a professional role, and the actions against you that can result are *based on that role*. Your license can be put on probation, suspended, or revoked, for example. You may be required to attend classes to refresh your knowledge about particular issues that led to the complaint against you. You may have to pay the costs of the BBS investigation, and may have fines levied against you. You will not, however, have to go to jail in a disciplinary action because the BBS has no authority to put someone in jail.

Ethical standards are developed by professional associations for a variety of purposes. These standards clarify the expectations of members of that profession, but can sometimes be unclear or even contradictory. Individuals who clearly violate the ethical standards of the profession can be censured by, or even kicked out of, their

---

[157] Senate Bill 1172 (Lieu), 2012. The law took effect in 2014 after it was challenged all the way to the United States Supreme Court. The Supreme Court refused to hear the case, allowing the law to take effect.

professional association. That action by itself may have little practical impact, however. You do not need to be an active member of your professional association to practice psychotherapy in California. It is the state, and not any professional association, that ultimately controls who can practice via licensure. So the state needs its own set of clear behavioral standards that it can enforce, in order to govern licensure appropriately. These behavioral standards are known collectively as unprofessional conduct statutes.

Since the potential consequences of a professional action are not as severe as those in a criminal case, the burden of proof is lower: The BBS uses a standard of "clear and convincing evidence," which is higher than the burden of proof in a civil case but lower than what is needed to convict someone of a criminal offense. There is more detail on the process of a disciplinary action, from complaint to resolution, later in this chapter.

It may be helpful to keep in mind that these three kinds of actions relate to different kinds of damage done, and they are not mutually exclusive. Egregious acts may lead to all three actions at once: If you commit insurance fraud, you are harming the insurance company (for which they may file a civil suit), violating a public standard (which can lead to criminal charges), *and* breaking the trust given to professionals (leading to possible action against your license).

▶ Grounds for BBS action

The BBS lists 28 different types of violations that are considered unprofessional conduct under state law.[158] They are grouped into categories for easy reference here. Within each category you will find the specific violations listed in **bold italic** type. In most cases, each of the three mental health professions covered in this text (LMFTs, LPCCs, and LCSWs) are bound by the same rules. The few exceptions to this are noted in their respective categories. Violation titles here generally are in the same wording as in the BBS *Disciplinary Guidelines.*[159]

Footnotes in this section refer to the places in law where the act listed is defined as unprofessional conduct. Information on penalties is drawn from the *Disciplinary Guidelines*. When penalties are discussed here, note that the focus is on the *minimum* penalty the BBS can impose for a particular offense. They will evaluate the severity of the case and the practitioner's history of similar acts in the past, and can impose harsher penalties based on these or other factors if they wish. In the most severe instances of almost all offenses, the practitioner's license or registration can be revoked. Also, there are several additional penalties that come with any violation of the unprofessional conduct statutes; we shall discuss these further when talking about the disciplinary process later in this chapter.

---

[158] Board of Behavioral Sciences (2015). *Disciplinary Guidelines*. Sacramento, CA: BBS. Downloadable here: www.bbs.ca.gov/pdf/publications/dispguid.pdf
[159] Board of Behavioral Sciences (2015). *Disciplinary Guidelines*. Sacramento, CA: BBS. As an aside, the full name of this document is now *Uniform Standards Related to Substance Abuse and Disciplinary Guidelines*, which is a mouthful. Throughout this book, I continue referring to it as simply the *Disciplinary Guidelines* as a matter of convenience.

Sexual misconduct

Perhaps the area of professional misconduct that grabs the most attention is sexual misconduct. It certainly receives the harshest penalties – which makes sense. Therapists are in a position of both power and emotional intimacy with clients, who often come to therapy in vulnerable states. For a therapist to engage in a sexual relationship with such a client can be very damaging to the client. It also undermines the public trust in *all* mental health professionals. It is considered such a violation of the professional relationship that **if a licensee or registrant is found to have had a sexual relationship with a client, or with a former client in the two years following the last professional contact, the BBS <u>must</u> revoke the license or registration.**[160] By law they cannot impose any lighter sentence. However, sex with a client is not the only form of sexual misconduct the BBS will take action on.

There are four different types of sexual misconduct, and one other related violation, spelled out in the unprofessional conduct statutes. *Sexual contact with client or former client* requires revocation of the license or registration, as noted above. *Engaging in an act with a minor punishable as a sexual offense, even if prior to registration or licensure,*[161] also typically results in a revoking of the license or registration. This keeps pedophiles out of the mental health professions. Note the careful language here – by using the language of an "act with a minor punishable as a sexual offense," this standard does not mean that the therapist must have actually been *convicted* of the sexual offense. So, if a therapist admits as part of a plea arrangement in a criminal case that they committed an act that could be punishable as a sexual offense, and in exchange prosecutors chose to use a lighter criminal charge, the BBS could still revoke the practitioner's license because of this language. *Commission of an act*

---

[160] California Business and Professions Code sections 4982.26, 4992.33, and 4999.90(k). The LPCC law does not require license revocation, but as a matter of practice, it appears likely that a license would be revoked in such circumstances.

[161] California Business and Professions Code sections 4982(aa)(1), 4992.3(x)(1), and 4999.90(z)(1)

punishable as a sexually related crime[162] uses similar language, applies regardless of whether the crime was before or after licensure, and similarly requires the BBS to revoke the license or registration. ***Sexual misconduct***[163] is a lesser offense that covers any type of sexual misconduct except those that fall under the other types here. A therapist found to have violated this standard may have their license revoked, though not necessarily. Still, the penalties for a therapist engaging in any kind of sexual misconduct are harsh; for this last category, the minimum possible punishment includes a license suspension of at least 120 days, and 7 years of probation. The therapist also must retake, and pass, the licensing exams before they can resume practice.

As part of protecting the public from sexual misconduct by therapists, every member of the mental health professions is required to give the state-produced brochure "Professional Therapy Never Includes Sex"[164] to any client who says they have had a sexual relationship with a prior therapist. This helps the client to know that the previous therapist's actions were not appropriate, and gives the client guidance on how to report the previous therapist. ***Failure to provide the sexual misconduct brochure***[165] is punishable by the BBS with a minimum one-year probation.

The mental health professions have been getting gradually tougher on professionals who engage in sexual relationships with clients (current or former) or clients' family members. The 2014 ACA Code of Ethics has a five-year prohibition on sexual contact with former clients or their family members,[166] and the 2015 AAMFT Code of Ethics made it a lifetime prohibition.[167] The NASW Code, which does not offer a specific timeframe of prohibited sexual contact, makes it clear that such contact always poses significant risks.[168]

---

[162] California Business and Professions Code sections 4982(k), 4992.3(l), and 4999.90(k)
[163] California Business and Professions Code sections 4982(k), 4992.3(l), and 4999.90(k)
[164] California Department of Consumer Affairs: *Professional Therapy Never Includes Sex*. Sacramento, CA: DCA.
[165] California Business and Professions Code section 728
[166] ACA Code of Ethics, subprinciple A.5.c
[167] AAMFT Code of Ethics subprinciple 1.5
[168] NASW Code of Ethics subprinciple 1.09(c)

Although the timeframe for the legal standard here is shorter than the ethical standards, if you are successfully sued for sexual contact with a current or former client or a member of their family, your professional liability insurance will probably not cover you. Professional liability insurance policies routinely exclude sexual violations from coverage. They will provide for your defense in a trial, but if you admit or a court rules that you committed the act, your insurance will not pay any damages awarded to the plaintiff.[169]

Impairment

Therapists can lose their ability to practice effectively for a number of reasons. Just as we do not want drivers on the road whose driving is impaired by alcohol or other substances, we do not want therapists in practice whose behavior is so impaired as to be unsafe. *Impaired ability to function safely due to mental illness, physical illness, or chemical dependency*[170] leads to a 60-day minimum suspension, which seems at least partly to be for the purpose of assessing whether the person will be able to continue in practice at all. Medical or psychological treatment may be required, and the therapist may see their practice restricted. In cases more directly impacting therapy, categorized as *Chemical dependency or use of drugs with a client while performing services*,[171] at least a 120-day suspension is imposed, and the therapist must agree to abstain from substance use for the full term of their probation (at least 5 years) – including doing frequent blood or urine testing, which the therapist must pay for.

In 2015, the BBS adopted new disciplinary guidelines that are especially tough on substance-related violations. For more on this, see Changes to Drug and Alcohol Rules later in this chapter.

---

[169] This is the policy of CPH and Associates, one of the larger professional liability insurance providers. Most liability insurers have similar rules.
[170] California Business and Professions Code sections 4982(c), 4982.1, 4992.3(c), 4992.35, and 4999.90(c)
[171] California Business and Professions Code sections 4982(c), 4982.1, 4992.3(c), 4992.35, and 4999.90(c)

Committing a crime or bad act

The BBS conducts background checks on all license and registration applicants to determine whether the applicant has a criminal history. Once a therapist is licensed or registered with the Board, the Board then automatically receives a report if the licensee or registrant is convicted of a crime in the future. The BBS can take action against anyone who has been both charged and convicted of a crime that is "substantially related to the qualifications, functions, or duties" of a therapist,[172] and they interpret that language broadly to mean any crime that shows "present or potential unfitness" of the person to perform therapy work in a manner consistent with public safety. ***Conviction of a crime substantially related to the duties, functions, and responsibilities of a licensee or registrant*** does not always lead to BBS action, however. Each case is evaluated individually. If you had a minor criminal conviction 15 years ago and have been out of trouble since, the BBS would of course examine the circumstances of your case, but it is unlikely they would discipline your license or registration (or prevent you from obtaining one). There are exceptions, of course, for crimes that fall into the sexual misconduct categories above. These acts *will* prevent someone from obtaining (or keeping) their license or registration. ***Commission of a dishonest, corrupt, or fraudulent act substantially related to the duties, functions, and responsibilities of a licensee or registrant***[173] can result in enforcement actions against your license even if you are not convicted of a crime for that act. The minimum penalty for such an act includes 30 days suspension, 3 years of probation, and a Law and Ethics course.

---

[172] California Business and Professions Code sections 4982(a), 4992.3(a), and 4999.90(a); California Code of Regulations title 16 section 1812
[173] California Business and Professions Code sections 4982(j), 4992.3(k), and 4999.90(j)

Fraud and misrepresentation

Anyone found to be responsible for *Securing (or attempting to secure) a license by fraud*[174] – the most common example being lying to the BBS on your license or registration application – automatically has that license or registration revoked.

There are two basic ways that you can misrepresent yourself in the therapy world. You can misrepresent your own licensure status, or you can pretend to be someone else who is licensed.

Misrepresentation of (your own) license or qualifications[175] leads to a minimum 60-day suspension, 3 years minimum probation, and possibly having to retake licensing exams. This kind of punishment would be given to an associate who advertised as being fully licensed, for example. This can happen outside of marketing contexts as well – an associate who claimed to be licensed while billing insurance for a client's therapy would also be committing this offense (and others).

Impersonating a licensee[176] is the other kind of misrepresentation. It occurs when someone who is not licensed tells a client or others that they are actually someone else, when that someone else *is* licensed. This, too, can occur in the context of insurance billing, if an associate attempts to bill an insurance company by suggesting that it was actually their supervisor who provided the therapy being charged. A supervisor who supports such behavior is also committing this offense, as the language includes *allowing* impersonation. This violation is met with a minimum 60-day suspension and 5-year probation.

---

[174] California Business and Professions Code sections 4982(a), 4992.3(a), and 4999.90(a)
[175] California Business and Professions Code sections 4982(f), 4992.3(g), and 4999.90(f)
[176] California Business and Professions Code sections 4982(g), 4992.3(h), and 4999.90(g)

Assisting someone practicing without a license

If someone is practicing in California without a license, then by definition, there is no license for the BBS to act against. (The state could pursue a *criminal* case against that person, since practicing without a license is a crime.) However, if a licensed or registered person helped in the unlicensed activity, then the BBS would discipline that person for *Aiding and abetting unlicensed activity.*[177] For example, a licensee who described their colleague as being licensed when making referrals to the colleague, knowing that the colleague was not actually licensed, would be aiding unlicensed activity. This is punished with a minimum 30-day suspension and 3 years of probation. This charge could also be applied to *unregistered* activity; a supervisor who allowed a recent graduate to work in their private practice before registering with the BBS could be considered to be aiding unregistered activity. (Recall that registration is needed before working in a private practice.)

Testing-related violations

It is essential to the fairness and validity of any testing process that those who take the test are who they say they are, do not attempt to cheat on the test, and do not reveal any information about test content to those who have not yet taken the exam. This is certainly true with licensing exams, which are considered high-stakes tests because failing directly impacts one's professional standing and job opportunities. *Violating exam security or subverting a license exam*[178] occurs most commonly when someone who has just taken their exam shares its content with others who have not yet taken the exam. This is punished with a minimum of 5 years probation and retaking of classes. *Subverting*, as it is used here, means impacting the

---

[177] California Business and Professions Code sections 4982(h), 4992.3(i), and 4999.90(h)
[178] California Business and Professions Code sections 4982(ab), 4992.3(z), and 4999.90(aa)

integrity of the exam; while sharing content is perhaps the most common way this happens, it certainly is not the only way it could occur. Someone who hacks into the testing centers' computer network to give examinees extra time is also subverting the exam process.

It is worth mentioning here that violating exam security is not always an obvious thing. Of course it would be a violation to use your phone's camera to take pictures of exam questions, and then to share them with others about to take the test. That is one of many reasons why testing centers do not allow phones. But violating exam security can also happen in subtler ways.

In recent years, a number of social media groups have sprung up to help provide social support to those in various stages of their careers, including some groups specifically focused on prelicensed therapists. In those groups, people who have recently taken their licensing exams can provide very helpful social and emotional support to those who are about to test. However, I have seen several instances of group members posting questions like "What will I need to know about cognitive-behavioral interventions for my exam?"[179]

When someone who has recently taken a licensing exam answers that question, they likely have good intentions; they're trying to help a fellow professional to focus their preparation on those pieces that will be most helpful. But in doing that, they are giving the person who asked for the information an unfair advantage in testing. Licensing exams are only fair if everyone goes into them on a level playing field in terms of their awareness of specific exam content. If you are a member of such groups on any social media site, and you see specific discussion of exam content, please do all you can to prevent test information from being posted or shared. Obviously there is risk to those who are sharing test information, as they could lose their (sometimes brand new) license over it. But there is also significant risk for all those anxiously preparing for their own upcoming exams, whether members of the particular group or not: **If the BBS learns that exam content is being circulated among those who have not yet tested, one possible response would be for them to simply**

---

[179] For more detail on what seems to me to be fair to share from your exam experience, and what you should probably not share, go to www.psychotherapynotes.com/can-share-license-exam-part-2-2/

shut down that cycle of the exam, and not allow *anyone* to test until the next exam cycle starts a few months later with new exam content.

While it is not broken into a distinct category in the BBS Disciplinary Guidelines, the law also defines public disclosure of psychological tests as unprofessional conduct when the validity of the test depends upon the public being unfamiliar with it. Personality tests, such as the MMPI or the Rorschach, are among those tests that cannot be shared publicly. "Disclosure" here does not only mean sharing the test itself – even *describing* the test publicly in detail could be considered a violation.[180]

Discipline by another state or board

Some therapists maintain more than one professional license. A therapist may have licenses in multiple states. Others may have two licenses within the same state, such as a therapist who licenses as an LPCC after the completion of a master's degree and chooses to maintain an LPCC license even after completing a doctoral degree and getting licensed as a Psychologist. If the BBS learns that another state or government agency has acted against your license or registration with that other agency, of course it makes sense that the BBS would want to investigate the circumstances of that discipline. If it reflects poorly on your ability to work safely within your BBS license, then *Discipline by another state or governmental agency*[181] will also lead to discipline from the BBS. Of course, they will review the relevant laws; if you were disciplined in another state for an act that is legally acceptable in California, the BBS may choose not to take any action.

Failure to maintain confidentiality

At first glance, this may appear to be an easy problem to avoid: Keeping records secure and not revealing what clients have told you in

---

[180] California Business and Professions Code sections 4982(q), 4992.3(r), and 4999.90(q)
[181] California Business and Professions Code sections 4982.25, 4992.36, and 4990.38

therapy are clear standards. However, many violations of confidentiality occur accidentally. A therapist slips up and uses the actual name of their client in a public discussion. Cars and computers get stolen with client records inside. Or, as happened to a therapist in the United Kingdom, clients recognize themselves as the subjects of social media discussion even when the therapist never uses specific names.[182] ***Failure to maintain confidentiality***[183] is met with a minimum 60-day suspension and 3 years probation, required educational classes and retaking of licensure exams.

Supervision-related violations

As discussed in the last chapter, supervisors of trainees and associates are responsible for the conduct of those under their supervision. While the common phrasing of working "under the supervisor's license" is technically inaccurate – a trainee, or associate is working under their *supervision*, not their license – a supervisor can be held responsible in addition to the supervisee if the supervisee commits acts of misconduct, or if the supervisor does not live up to the supervisor's legal obligations.

There are two types of unprofessional misconduct in this category. ***Improper supervision of a trainee, associate, or supervisee***[184] occurs when a supervisor is failing to abide by the legal responsibility for oversight of the supervisee's work. This includes monitoring the supervisee's cases and records. It is punishable by a minimum of 30 days suspension and 2 years probation. Of course, "improper" is a somewhat vague word. Some codes of ethics provide more detail than the law does about the specific expectations of supervisors. This is important, as the BBS will often review professional ethical codes to determine whether a supervisor has failed to live up to their profession's standard of care for supervision. If it is the supervisee, instead of the supervisor, who commits an

---

[182] www.dailymail.co.uk/news/article-2755853/
[183] California Business and Professions Code sections 4982(m), 4992.3(n), and 4999.90(m)
[184] California Business and Professions Code sections 4982(r), 4992.3(s), and 4999.90(r)

unprofessional act, but the supervisor knew or reasonably should have known about the violation, this would likely fall under *Violations of the chapter or regulations by licensees or registrants / Violations involving acquisition and supervision of required hours of experience.*[185] These violations are punishable by a minimum one-year probation. Any hours of experience gained illegally are automatically revoked.

Fees and advertising

In Chapter 4, we will learn about the state requirements for what must be disclosed to clients before therapy begins. This includes a requirement to disclose what fee the client is being charged and how that fee was computed. *Failure to disclose fees in advance*[186] is a serious offense, but certainly not as serious as sexual misconduct or some of the other acts described here. For this reason, it is one of the few acts of unprofessional conduct where the maximum penalty is not revoking the license. The minimum penalty for failing to disclose fees is one year of probation; the *maximum* penalty includes a 30-day suspension and 2 years probation.

In Chapter 8, we will see that the state's laws surrounding how therapists market themselves are quite specific. *False, misleading, deceptive, or improper advertising*[187] leads to a minimum one-year probation. As with failing to disclose fees, this is not considered as severe an offense as many others; the maximum penalty here includes a 60-day suspension and 5 years probation.

Finally, if you refer a client to another health care professional, this should be an unbiased act, made solely based on the best interests of the client. For this reason, *Paying, accepting, or soliciting a fee*

---

[185] California Business and Professions Code sections 4982(e) and (u), 4992.3(f), and 4999.90(e) and (u)
[186] California Business and Professions Code sections 4982(n), 4992.3(o), and 4999.90(n)
[187] California Business and Professions Code sections 651, 4982(p), 4992.3(q), and 4999.90(p)

for referrals is met with a minimum of 3 years probation and a required course in law and ethics.[188]

Record-keeping

It seems basic that therapists would need to keep records on the services they have provided to clients. Under a law that took effect January 1, 2015, LMFTs, LPCCs, and LCSWs all must retain client records for at least seven years after the end of therapy. If the client is a minor, their records must be retained until the client's 25th birthday (that is, seven years after they turn 18).[189]

Surprisingly, surveys of therapists show a small percentage who refuse to keep any records at all.[190] *Failure to keep records consistent with sound clinical judgment*[191] leads to at least a year of probation. It seems likely that violations of the seven-year standard for retaining records would be disciplined under this category.

As we will see in Chapter 5 on Confidentiality, clients have a right to access their records (with some meaningful exceptions) – one of many reasons it is expected that you will have records in the first place. *Willful failure to comply with clients' requests for access to mental health records*[192] also leads to at least a year of probation.

The maximum penalties for violating these standards are not as harsh as those for some of the other standards. Maximum penalties in each of these areas include 30 days of suspension and 3 years of probation.

---

[188] California Business and Professions Code sections 4982(o), 4992.3(p), and 4999.90(o)
[189] Senate Bill 578 (Wyland), 2014.
[190] Surveys done by CAMFT and others over the past several years typically show about 3-5% of respondents saying they do not keep any records at all.
[191] California Business and Professions Code sections 4982(v), 4992.3(t), and 4999.90(v)
[192] California Business and Professions Code sections 4982(y), 4992.3(w), and 4999.90(ad)

Practicing beyond license or competence

As we saw in the previous chapter, the titles of "Licensed Marriage and Family Therapist," "Licensed Clinical Social Worker," and "Licensed Professional Clinical Counselor" are meaningfully distinct. Each one comes with specific requirements and limitations, and each license takes a lot of time and work to earn. It is important that the practice of psychotherapy be limited to those appropriately qualified to do it. Even within the professions, it is important that you be trained specifically to deliver the services you provide. It is not professional to try out a new type of therapy you do not know well on an unsuspecting client who has placed their trust in you to provide good care. *Performing, offering, or representing yourself as able to perform a service outside of your scope of practice or competence*[193] is a serious offense punishable with a minimum 30-day suspension and 3 years of probation. A supervisor who allows their supervisee to do such a thing is also considered to have committed this offense.

Telemedicine violations

In Chapter 9 (Technology), we will discuss the California Telemedicine Act, which sets standards for therapists and other healthcare providers who offer services via phone, Internet, or other technology. We also will review new state regulations, which took effect in 2016, surrounding therapy provided via telehealth. *Violating the state telehealth standards*[194] (most commonly, by failing to obtain or record client consent for telehealth services) results in a minimum of one year of probation and required educational coursework.

---

[193] California Business and Professions Code sections 4982(l), (s), and (t); 4992.3(m); and 4999.90(l), (s), and (t); California Code of Regulations title 16 sections 1881(g) and (h)
[194] California Business and Professions Code sections 4982(z), 4992.3(x); 4999.90(ac); and 2290.5(b) and (c)

General misconduct, negligence, recklessness, or willful harm

The categories reviewed so far will not capture every inappropriate professional act. So the BBS also has at its disposal additional categories that are less specific. These serve to prevent licensees or registrants from avoiding discipline based on technicalities or arguments about the meaning of a particular word. They also can be useful when the BBS is engaging in what is essentially plea bargaining with a licensee under investigation; we will tackle that process in the next section.

General unprofessional conduct[195] and *gross negligence or incompetence*[196] are catch-all categories for behavior that is well outside of professional standards but does not readily fit into the more specific categories listed above.

One example of general unprofessional conduct would be failing to file a mandated report of child, elder, or dependent adult abuse. Under California law, mental health professionals are required to report such abuse (more on these reporting requirements can be found in Chapter 7). The mandated reporting laws come with specific timeframes, which changed significantly for elder and dependent adult abuse in 2012.[197] Failing to file a mandated report is problematic for multiple reasons, the most troubling of which is that it potentially allows an abuser to continue to abuse the same or other victims.

Another example of general unprofessional conduct is to offer so-called reparative therapy, also known as conversion therapy or ex-gay therapy, to minors. Under a law passed in 2012 that took effect in 2014 (see Chapter 10 for more on the story of this bill), any mental health professional is committing unprofessional conduct if they attempt to change the sexual orientation of a minor through therapy.[198]

---

[195] California Business and Professions Code sections 4982, 4992.3, and 4999.90
[196] California Business and Professions Code sections 4982(d), 4992.3(d) and (e), and 4999.90(d)
[197] See Chapter 7, Working with Elders and Dependent Adults
[198] California Business and Professions Code section 865

A third example of unprofessional conduct comes when you are under investigation for another possible violation. Under regulations that took effect in 2013, it can be considered unprofessional conduct to refuse to participate in, or cooperate with, a BBS investigation. It is also now considered unprofessional conduct to refuse to turn over records to the BBS within 15 days of their request when they are conducting an investigation.[199] While there are some exceptions in these rules to protect therapists, it is noteworthy that either of these charges can result in action against your license or registration *even if* the original complaint that sparked the investigation turns out to be groundless.

General unprofessional conduct is punished with a minimum 60-day suspension and 3 years of probation; gross negligence or incompetence is punished with a minimum 60-day suspension, 5 years of probation, and having to retake the licensing exams.

***Intentionally or recklessly causing physical or emotional harm to a client*[200]** occurs when a therapist not only has violated the standards of their profession, but has done so in a such a way that a client has truly suffered as a result. This is considered a severe violation, and so even the minimum penalty is severe: 90 days of suspension, 5 years of probation, and retaking licensing exams.

***Violations of the chapter or regulations by licensees or registrants / Violations involving acquisition and supervision of required hours of experience*[201]** was mentioned above, in discussing supervision-related violations. This category (particularly its first half) also addresses in general terms any violations of the licensing acts of each of the professions covered in this text. These violations are punishable by a minimum one-year probation. Any hours of experience gained illegally are automatically revoked.

---

[199] California Code of Regulations title 16 sections 1823, 1845, 1858, and 1881
[200] California Business and Professions Code sections 4982(i), 4992.3(j), and 4999.90(i)
[201] California Business and Professions Code sections 4982(e) and (u), 4992.3(f), and 4999.90(e) and (u)

▸ The disciplinary process

Most actions against a license or registration are initiated by either a consumer complaint or a law enforcement report of a therapist's arrest or criminal conviction. The process is designed to give the professional a fair hearing, but it is not like a civil or criminal trial.

For the three-month span of July through September 2016, the BBS received 285 consumer complaints against its licensees and registrants.[202] At first that number may sound high, but it is actually fairly low when you consider that there are more than 100,000 licensed and registered mental health professionals under BBS jurisdiction in California.[203] Consider as well that a majority of complaints are closed without the need for a field investigation or hearing. The number of therapists who commit an act so outside of accepted professional standards as to warrant action against their license or registration is actually quite low.

One way to look at this is through raw frequency numbers; in the first quarter of the 2016-17 fiscal year there were a total of 643 issues presented to the BBS (285 consumer complaints plus 358 arrest or conviction reports of licensees and registrants), and in that same time, just 22 final disciplinary orders were adopted.[204] Another way to look at this is through the lens of how much it costs you to purchase professional liability insurance; mental health professionals actually pay less than many other health care professionals, because of both a lower frequency of complaints and lower monetary awards when lawsuits are either won by complainants or settled before going to trial.

---

[202] Materials for the November 2016 meeting of the Board of Behavioral Sciences, page 67.

[203] Board of Behavioral Sciences: Licensee and Registrant Statistics

[204] Materials for the November 2016 meeting of the Board of Behavioral Sciences, page 67. This is not a perfect apples-to-apples set of data, since most of the cases closed would have originated in earlier months. However, the numbers of licensees and registrants disciplined in any given year is similarly low compared to the total population of professionals.

Few therapists ever want to be the subject of a complaint. But if you *are* ever the subject of an investigation, or if a client wants your help as they prepare to file a complaint against a previous therapist, it will help you to know how the process works. It can be roughly broken down into four stages: Complaint, Investigation, Hearing, and Resolution. The BBS web site describes the entire process, from complaint to resolution, as taking about two years,[205] though their own data suggests that it often takes longer.[206]

Complaint

The BBS accepts complaints against licensees or registrants through its web site or via mail. While complaints may be made anonymously, doing so sometimes makes it more difficult for the BBS to conduct a proper investigation. For example, an anonymous complaint about a therapist's advertisement can still be investigated; the BBS would be interested in the content of the ad, not the identity of the complainant. But if an anonymous complaint is received about something that took place in a therapy session, the BBS cannot go on a proverbial "fishing expedition" through a therapist's records without knowing which client was potentially harmed.

When the BBS first receives a complaint, it is reviewed by their staff to determine whether it is against a person who is actually licensed or registered with the BBS. If not, there is no license or registration to discipline; the BBS might keep the complaint on file in case the subject of the complaint ever applies for a license or registration in the future, and it might forward the complaint to another enforcement agency if appropriate. For example, if the BBS receives a complaint about someone practicing without a license, then (assuming the complaint is accurate) there isn't a license for the BBS to discipline. They would forward the complaint to the office of the state Attorney General.

If the subject of the complaint *is* a licensee or registrant, then the complaint is evaluated based on whether it would be actionable *if*

---

[205] Board of Behavioral Sciences: *Complaint Process*
[206] Materials for the November 2016 meeting of the Board of Behavioral Sciences, page 67.

everything in the complaint were true. A client complaint about the color of paint on your walls will not be pursued. A client complaint about therapy that was simply ineffective will also not be pursued, so long as the therapist's actions were within all legal and ethical boundaries and in keeping with the standard of care for the profession. Therapy does not always work, and a therapeutic failure in and of itself is not a reason for a therapist to be disciplined. If the complaint is against a current licensee or registrant, *and* is something that would be actionable if true, it is typically forwarded to the BBS's investigative unit.

Investigation

Investigations can take a very long time. In an average case, it takes more than two years from the time a complaint is received for a disciplinary order to be finalized. Some take months or even years longer. Most cases are investigated by the BBS Division of Investigation (DOI), though allegations of misconduct that would also be criminal offenses may be investigated through other agencies. Partly because the DOI investigators have such heavy caseloads, it may be months between a complaint being filed and that same complaint being actively investigated. The investigation often involves interviews with the person filing the complaint and the therapist accused of wrongdoing, as well as others relevant to the issue. Depending on the nature of the complaint, it may also involve a review of the therapist's records for the case being investigated. Other records may be brought in as needed, such as the therapist's educational transcripts.

During the time a complaint is being investigated, therapists typically can go on practicing as usual. Not all investigations lead to discipline, of course, and a therapist should not be restricted from practice while a complaint is being investigated in case it turns out that the complaint is groundless. Exceptions are made in the case of therapists who may present an immediate danger to their clients; for example, a therapist who is in the throes of a substance abuse problem may be immediately suspended from practicing while an investigation is ongoing.

Therapists are required to cooperate with the investigation process and to produce records when requested, as noted earlier in this chapter. However, the investigator should not be viewed as a friend to the therapist. The investigator's role is to determine the facts of the case so that the BBS can decide whether the therapist poses a danger to the public requiring disciplinary action against the therapist's license.

Therapists accused of wrongdoing often bring in a lawyer early in the investigation process. Legal counsel, typically provided for the therapist by their professional liability insurer, can help ensure that the therapist is cooperating with the investigation while also protecting the therapist's own interests.

Many cases are not pursued past the investigation stage. If the investigation confirms the allegations in the original complaint, the BBS may forward the case to the office of the state Attorney General to begin formal disciplinary action. A formal **Accusation** is then filed against the therapist, who has the right to request a hearing to fight the charges.[207]

Before a hearing is held, the BBS will often work with those formally accused of misconduct to see whether they can reach a settlement, or a **stipulation**. In a stipulation, the therapist accused of unprofessional conduct admits to certain specific violations and agrees that a particular set of disciplinary actions can be imposed.[208] If you are familiar with the process of plea bargaining in criminal cases (fans of TV crime shows like *Law & Order* will know this process well), the process of reaching a stipulation can be similar, if less dramatic. The state may agree to pursue a lesser punishment if the accused person simply admits that the alleged act took place rather than continuing to fight the charges. When a case is settled through stipulation, there is no formal hearing. The case skips ahead to the resolution phase.

Hearing

Disciplinary hearings take place in the presence of an Administrative Law Judge. In some ways these hearings look like criminal trials, with the state and the accused person each presenting their case and calling witnesses. However, recall from the beginning of this chapter that a disciplinary hearing does not require a therapist to

---

[207] Board of Behavioral Sciences: *Complaint Process*
[208] Board of Behavioral Sciences: *Complaint Process*

be proven guilty beyond a reasonable doubt. The burden of proof here is *clear and convincing evidence*, which is something of a lower bar. The Administrative Law Judge weighs the facts as presented, and writes a *proposed* decision on the matter. This judge does not have the final say, however. The judge's proposed decision is forwarded to the BBS for their consideration.

The BBS – and here, I refer simply to the 13 members who actually make up the Board,[209] not the full staff of the organization – can choose to adopt or not adopt any proposed decision in a disciplinary action. This applies to both Administrative Law Judge proposed decisions that result from hearings, and stipulations that result from negotiations between an accused therapist and the state. In most cases, the BBS will accept the proposed decision or stipulation. In some cases, they review the case and instead issue a different decision or different discipline. Either way, the therapist can appeal for reconsideration of the case or appeal through the state court system.[210]

Resolution

If a licensee or registrant is disciplined, the suspension and probation periods noted above are not the only elements of the therapist's punishment. Standard terms and conditions include cost recovery (that is, the therapist must pay for the costs of the BBS investigation of them), notifying all employers and clients of the disciplinary action, and filing quarterly reports with the BBS regarding probation compliance. Licensees or registrants on probation also cannot supervise any associates or trainees, and cannot serve as instructors for continuing education. Those on probation also must maintain their license or registration, and commit to obeying all laws.[211]

The BBS also has several additional optional requirements that they may choose to impose as part of a disciplinary order. These include requiring the therapist to retake licensing exams, take a law and ethics course, hire an outside monitor or auditor for their billing

---

[209] California Business and Professions Code section 4990(a)
[210] Board of Behavioral Sciences: *Complaint Process*
[211] Board of Behavioral Sciences: *Disciplinary Guidelines*

system (common when the discipline is for billing-related issues), undergo psychological or psychiatric examinations, participate in psychotherapy, have their practice supervised or otherwise restricted, and pay the costs of their own probation. Any therapist disciplined for issues surrounding drug and alcohol use will also be required to abstain from substance use and submit to regular testing – at the therapist's expense – to verify that they are not using.[212]

As you can see, any disciplinary action has a major impact on a therapist's practice. Thankfully, avoiding such actions is not simply a matter of hoping for the best. There are many proactive steps a therapist can take to protect their practices.

---

[212] Board of Behavioral Sciences (2015): *Disciplinary Guidelines.* See Changes to drug and alcohol rules (next page) for additional information.

▶ Changes to drug and alcohol rules

The BBS has strict rules surrounding drug and alcohol-related violations. Those rules are called the *Uniform Standards Related to Substance Abuse*, or more simply known just as the Uniform Standards.[213] The Uniform Standards are intended to protect consumers from potentially dangerous professionals. As you will see, the penalties required by the Uniform Standards can be tough. The BBS has very little leeway to deviate from them.

In 2015, the Uniform Standards became a part of the BBS's Disciplinary Guidelines.[214] Under the new rules, certain penalties are automatic with all substance abuse violations. Other penalties, if applied, cannot be reduced based on specific circumstances of the case. The punishments for substance-related violations can include:

- **A clinical diagnostic evaluation** to determine whether the therapist has a substance use disorder. Notably, even if this evaluation results in a finding that the licensee or registrant does *not* have a diagnosable substance use problem, other penalties can remain in effect.

- **Mandatory drug and alcohol testing** to ensure the therapist is not continuing to use substances. No licensee or registrant put on probation for a substance use violation is allowed to return to practice until they have at least 30 days of negative drug tests. For the first year of probation, the therapist will be randomly drug tested between 52 and 104 times each year; they must make *daily* contact with a testing center to see whether they have been randomly selected to test that day. In years 2-5, testing is reduced to between 36 and 104 times per year. Any planned vacations or absences must be pre-approved by the BBS, who will approve alternative drug testing locations close to where the therapist will be. Failure to report for required testing, or testing positive for alcohol or any controlled

---

[213] Department of Consumer Affairs (2011). *Uniform standards regarding substance-abusing healing arts licensees.* Sacramento, CA: DCA.
[214] www.bbs.ca.gov/pdf/publications/dispguid.pdf

substance, will be punished with *automatic and immediate* suspension of the license or registration and referral back to the BBS for additional disciplinary action. The therapist's employer will be immediately notified of the suspension.

- In addition to the above, the BBS can mandate supervised practice, restricted practice, participation in chemical dependency support or recovery group meetings, and other standard terms and conditions of probation. Perhaps most significantly, those who are on probation are typically required to pay for the costs of the investigation into their violation and the costs of probation. As you can imagine, the costs of drug testing alone – **up to 520 tests over five years of probation** – can easily reach tens of thousands of dollars for those therapists who commit substance use violations.

▶ Protecting yourself

The purpose of this chapter is not to make you fear for your license. It is to make you familiar with the disciplinary rules and the disciplinary process, so that you are best aware of the rules that apply in the state of California. Both the standards themselves and the disciplinary process may vary in other states. Following California's standards is not a guarantee that you will avoid ever having a complaint or lawsuit filed against you, but it *can* help prevent that complaint or lawsuit from damaging or even ending your career. This section focuses on five common-sense things you can do that will help ensure that your practice is as safe as possible.

A reminder here is in order: **I am not a lawyer, so please do not interpret any of this as legal advice.** I am a therapist, and so this is intended as common-sense advice on running a sound and clinically-appropriate therapy practice. If you are interested in more specific advice on risk management and risk avoidance from a legal perspective, I would strongly encourage you to consult with a lawyer. In many cases, you can obtain qualified legal advice for free through your professional liability insurance or your professional association membership.

1. Maintain familiarity with professional standards

California's state laws for mental health professionals change every year, often significantly. It is vital to remember that laws are not set in stone. They are living documents, meant to adapt to changing social and professional conditions. You cannot simply carry on in your career presuming that your profession's rules are still the ones that were in effect when you went to graduate school, or when you first obtained your license.

It is for this reason that California requires licensees to take a six-hour continuing education course in Law and Ethics in each two-year license renewal period. Ideally, this keeps practitioners up to date with the great many changes in state law and ethical standards that can occur, even in a short timeframe. In addition, membership in professional associations (listed at the end of this book) and attendance at their conferences and events can help you stay in the loop on changes in law or policy that directly impact your work.

If you are a supervisor, you have specific additional obligations to your supervisees to remain current in your understanding of state law and professional ethical standards, and to supervise accordingly. Directing a supervisee to work in a manner that is inconsistent with current state law could be considered "improper supervision," one of the types of unprofessional conduct detailed above.[215]

2. Maintain professional liability insurance

This may be the single most important purchase you make as a professional. For a relatively low price – some professional associations will even give student members professional liability insurance for free – you can have easy access to attorneys and professional support in the event of complaints or lawsuits against you. You may go through your entire career never *needing* your liability insurance, but it will provide a great deal of peace of mind to know that you have it just in case.

Professional liability insurers offer multiple types of protection. Most commonly, they will insure you against claims made against you for actions taken in your professional role, so long as those actions were not intentionally harmful. Depending on the type of practice you have and the physical location of your practice, you may require general liability insurance (called "slip-and-fall" coverage) for your office. You may also want coverage for the costs of legal defense during a licensing investigation. As with other types of insurance, professional liability insurance companies offer various options and add-ons that may increase or decrease your premium.

As mentioned earlier, policies make exclusions for sexual acts with clients, since those are presumed to be intentional. But if a client sues you or complains about you because they did not like the outcome of your work, and you have acted responsibly and professionally, your liability insurance can feel like a lifesaver.

---

[215] California Business and Professions Code sections 4982(r), 4992.3(s), and 4999.90(r)

3. Address potential complaints

If you have clients who you know are unhappy with the service they have received from you, or if you become aware that you have accidentally committed a violation of the unprofessional conduct statutes, potential complaints can sometimes be addressed informally and resolved to the client's satisfaction. Working with clients to minimize any harm they might experience because of inadvertent violations is consistent with the mental health professions' ethical values of beneficence and nonmalfeasance, and may convince a dissatisfied client that a formal complaint is not needed.

Research in the field of medicine shows that when doctors apologize and take responsibility for medical mistakes, rather than taking a defensive posture, their patients are more satisfied and less likely to sue.[216] Of course, you should not try to use force to prevent someone from filing a complaint against you, and it is against the law to include a "no-licensure-complaint" clause in a settlement agreement that avoids or ends a civil lawsuit.[217]

4. Keep excellent records

As detailed above, keeping records consistent with sound clinical judgment is a requirement for licensed mental health professionals. Such records also can be especially useful in defending yourself from an accusation of improper conduct.

If a client makes a claim that an intervention from your session on November 16 harmed them and was not professional practice, simply telling the BBS, "No, I did not do that!" is not likely to be considered a full or adequate defense. You are likely to be much better off if you have thorough records from that day's session that detail what interventions you did use and how the client responded to them. It also can be helpful if records from sessions after that day showed the client's continued engagement in therapy without any noticeable worsening of symptoms. In any situation where it is a client's word

---

[216] Robbennolt, J. K. (2009). Apologies and medical error. *Clinical Orthopaedics and Related Research, 467*(2), 376-382.
[217] California Business and Professions Code section 143.5

against that of the therapist, naturally one of the first places the BBS would look for additional information is in the therapist's documentation. If a client claims that they experienced harm as a result of the therapy, can they document that harm? Or instead, can you show that your actions in therapy were well within accepted professional standards? For more on how to do this, see Chapter 5.

5. Follow the law, even in non-professional contexts

You may have noticed at the beginning of this section that the BBS receives arrest and conviction reports on its licensees and registrants. It receives roughly as many of these as consumer complaints. While consumer complaints necessarily involve your professional conduct, arrest and conviction reports go to the BBS regardless of whether the crime you were charged with had anything to do with your professional role.

As described earlier in this chapter, conviction of a crime related to the duties, functions, and responsibilities of a therapist is cause for disciplinary action. There are also several acts that do not require criminal convictions in order for the BBS to act against your license, if the arrest report suggests that you may not be able to function safely in your professional role. Recall as well that the BBS takes a broad view of what may reflect on your fitness for your professional role, and you can see that your responsibility to abide by a higher standard of behavior than the average person does not only apply while you are in the office.

Among the most common offenses the BBS disciplines its licensees and registrants for are substance use offenses, particularly driving under the influence of alcohol or other drugs (DUI). The impact of a DUI conviction will last for years on your professional life as well as your personal life. As you have read, the penalties that took effect in 2015 for substance use violations can be quite severe.

Simply put, one of the best things you can do to protect your practice is to take a cab if you've been drinking.

Room for debate: Accusations

In early 2016, a bill was proposed in the California legislature that would have required law enforcement to inform licensing boards any time there was an accusation to police that the licensee had been accused of certain crimes.[218] These crimes included sexual crimes, elder abuse (including failure to report elder abuse), child abuse (including failure to report child abuse), and hate crimes against those with disabilities.

From a public protection perspective, this proposal makes sense. In some cases, accusations may not lead to quick arrests. And a great deal of time can go by between an accusation and a conviction. Allowing licensing boards to access and act on initial police reports would enable them to act more quickly against therapists whose behavior had potentially become dangerous.

The professional associations argued strongly against the proposed law. The associations expressed concern that false reports might prompt BBS action against a licensee who had actually not committed any crime. Sometimes people accused of crimes are not arrested because police cannot find any immediate evidence that the person had committed the crime, and needs time to investigate. But sometimes people accused of crimes are not arrested because police simply don't believe the accuser.

None of the professional organizations dispute that the role of the BBS is to protect the public from abuses by professionals. In other words, and as mentioned previously, the BBS does not exist to serve us; it exists to protect the public *from* us. However, there is still a balance to be struck between protecting the public and protecting the presumption of innocence when therapists are accused of criminal behavior.

The legislation was amended to address only crimes related to child and elder abuse, but that was not enough to move it forward. With opposition from many organizations, the bill died in committee.

---

[218] Assembly bill 2606 (Grove), 2016.

4

Confidentiality

For several years, the treatment contract I used in my private practice included this statement: "The therapy office is like Vegas. What happens here stays here." I've switched to using a bit more formal language these days, but the underlying idea is the same: The therapy room must be a private setting, to allow clients to feel safe in sharing parts of their lives that they might otherwise be embarrassed or ashamed to discuss. This, like informed consent, is a fundamental principle of ethical psychotherapy.

While there is meaningful overlap between the two, the terms *confidentiality* and *privilege* mean somewhat different things. **Confidentiality is a broad term that refers to your responsibility as a therapist to keep the process of therapy private**. This is the term used in professional codes of ethics. **Privilege is a specific legal term, and refers to a client's right to keep information about their therapy from being shared as part of a court proceeding.**

To you, to your client, and to most of the outside world, confidentiality is usually the key concept. Normally, therapists keep all information from therapy confidential, including even the fact that someone *is* your client.[219] As we will see, there are several exceptions to this general rule.

---

[219] Leslie, D. (1989 July/August). Confidentiality. *The Therapist.*

In a court proceeding, privilege is often the more relevant concept. Communications between a client and therapist are considered *privileged communications* under the law.[220] For this reason, a court cannot force a therapist to share information about therapy in a court proceeding, except in limited circumstances. If a therapist receives a subpoena (a request for information as part of a court proceeding), professional associations typically advise that the therapist consult with the client to see whether the client will consent to releasing the information. If not, the therapist may formally refuse to give information to the court, which is known as *asserting privilege*. Then a judge would need to determine whether an exception to privilege applies.

---

[220] California Evidence Code section 1014

▶ Confidentiality and its exceptions

Confidentiality is recognized across the mental health professions as a cornerstone of ethical psychotherapy. All California psychotherapists are required to learn about confidentiality,[221] and failing to uphold a client's confidentiality can result in action against your license or registration (see Chapter 3, Unprofessional Conduct), as well as civil liability.[222]

There are a number of exceptions to confidentiality defined in the law. **While many therapists are aware of the most common exceptions, you may be surprised at some of the exceptions to confidentiality that come up less often.**

As a general rule, any time you reveal/disclose confidential information, you should share *just enough information to resolve the problem at hand.*[223] If you are dealing with a threat and need to break confidentiality, you should not reveal any more information about your client than what is necessary to address the immediate threat. If you are reporting abuse, the information you share should only be the information necessary for the abuse report; you would not offer additional information on someone's course of therapy, their treatment goals, or other parenting issues if that information is not relevant to the specific incident of abuse being reported. In this way, we make safety the highest priority but provide as much confidentiality as possible while addressing safety needs. This can be a challenging balance.

Danger to self

Most mental health clinicians will work with at least one patient who is actively considering suicide at some point in their

---

[221] California Business and Professions Code sections 4980.36(d)(2)(J)(iv) and 4999.33(c)(3)(I), and Council on Social Work Education 2015 Educational Policy and Accreditation Standards Competency 1
[222] California Business and Professions Code sections 4982(m), 4992.3(n), and 4999.90(m)
[223] ACA Code of Ethics subprinciple B.2.e

careers. State law requires mental health professionals to receive training in suicide assessment and intervention so that such clients can be properly assessed and treated, ensuring that they do not ultimately hurt themselves.[224]

Bellah v. Greenson

Before this court case, it was actually unclear what a therapist's responsibility was to a client who was contemplating suicide. In the case of *Bellah v. Greenson*, the parents of a young woman who had committed suicide by overdosing on pills sued her psychiatrist. The parents argued that the psychiatrist had not taken adequate action to prevent the suicide even though he knew their daughter was a suicide risk. The parents argued that the same principles at work in the *Tarasoff* case (discussed below) applied here.

An appeals court disagreed. They refused to extend the specific provisions of the *Tarasoff* case, which would have required therapists to warn authorities if a client was actively suicidal. However, the court did determine that because of the special relationship between therapist and client, **a therapist does have a responsibility to take reasonable steps to prevent a threatened suicide**. The court ruling did not say what those "reasonable steps" would be, leaving that question up to the standards of "good medical practice" – that is, the standard of care.[225]

---

[224] California Business and Professions Code sections 4980.36(d)(2)(J)(iv) and 4999.33(c)(3)(I). For social workers, the Council on Social Work Education 2015 Educational Policy and Accreditation Standards requires training consistent with the NASW Code of Ethics, and that Code demands appropriate intervention in risk (subprinciple 1.02).
[225] *Bellah v. Greenson*, 81 Cal. App. 3d 614 (1978)

Intervening with a suicidal client

Depending on the immediacy and severity of the threat, and the location of the client, you have a number of interventions available to you; note that our focus is on laws, so **this is not a complete list**. Remember too that in any threat situation, you want to use the least intrusive means you can use that will actually resolve the threat. This requires seeking out a careful balance between safety and confidentiality, granting as much confidentiality as is possible while keeping the person safe.

Suicide assessment. Today, there are a number of well-developed and commonly used suicide assessment protocols available. Most focus on issues like the presence and detail of a suicide plan, the intent to follow through with that plan, and the availability of means to carry out the plan. If you determine in assessing your client that they pose a danger to themselves, you must intervene in an effort to help them. This can involve breaking confidentiality if necessary.

Safety planning. For clients who are thinking about suicide but assessed to be low risk, therapists are often now using **safety plans**.

A safety plan is a written agreement where the client commits to taking a number of specific actions before doing anything that would be harmful to themselves. While safety plans come in many forms, these actions often follow a stepwise progression; for example, a client who starts thinking about suicide while at home might have agreed to first reach out to a friend or family member. If that friend or family member is not available or contacting them is not helpful to the client, the client has agreed to then call the therapist or therapist's clinic. If the therapist or another person from the clinic is not available, or if that contact is insufficient, the client might commit to then calling the local crisis hotline.

It is important to note that such safety plans are typically used with clients who pose low suicide risk. In essence, they are a protective measure just in case a client's symptoms worsen. If the client does wind up making use of any part of the safety plan, the therapist is likely to thoroughly reassess at the next session whether a more intrusive level of intervention is needed.

In the past, many therapists have used written agreements with clients where the client agreed not to hurt themselves in any way prior to the next meeting with the therapist. Such agreements, often referred to as "no harm contracts," have largely fallen out of favor in the field. For one thing, they are not contracts in any legally enforceable way; if your client completed such a contract and then went on to attempt suicide anyway, it is not as though the therapist would then sue the client for breach of contract. Another reason these have fallen out of favor is that they may actually hurt a therapist's defense if the therapist is alleged to have not acted sufficiently to prevent a suicide. If you believed your client was at risk for suicide – which the mere presence of a no-harm contract would suggest – and you made no additional effort to ensure their safety beyond having them sign a form saying they would not harm themselves, you might be seen as not having done enough.

Increased frequency of contact. If a client is low risk for the moment, but the therapist believes there is a chance that the client will become higher risk in the days ahead, that therapist may encourage more frequent phone contact, office visits, or both. This can help ensure that if a client's symptoms worsen, the therapist will be aware of the change and able to intervene more quickly than they would if a week or two went by between regularly scheduled contacts.

As with safety plans (which may be used in conjunction with more frequent contact), the therapist should continue to carefully assess changes in the client's symptoms and risk level at each contact.

Care of a loved one. If a client is not a severe enough risk to warrant hospitalization, but enough of a concern that you feel they should be in the presence of other people, you may want to ask the client's friends or family members for assistance. While the *Bellah v. Greenson* ruling would suggest that breaking confidentiality is acceptable when informing a client's family members of a suicide risk can help them protect the client, clients are often willing to either make contact with family members themselves, or voluntarily grant permission for you to do so, such that there is no breach of confidentiality.

Voluntary hospitalization. If a client's suicidality poses such a risk that they are an imminent danger to themselves, hospitalization is necessary. Once it has been established that hospitalization is needed, the choice for your client comes down to whether this hospitalization will be voluntary or involuntary. Clients are likely to prefer voluntary hospitalization.

Involuntary hospitalization. If a client poses an immediate threat to themselves, and is unable or unwilling to receive appropriate care, a psychotherapist may initiate the process of involuntary hospitalization described in section 5150 of the California Welfare and Institutions Code.[226] (You might have heard therapists using that number as a verb. A person who is involuntarily hospitalized is sometimes referred to as having been "fifty-one-fiftied.") Note here that a therapist can begin the process, but in most counties, therapists cannot actually *invoke* an involuntary hospitalization. Only a licensed physician or another professional (mobile crisis team, police officer, etc.) specifically authorized by their county can make the final determination as to whether someone will be hospitalized against their will.

Once a person has been admitted to the hospital under section 5150, they may be initially held for up to three days. That is why involuntary hospitalizations are also referred to as "72-hour holds." Most 72-hour holds are actually much shorter; a person hospitalized against their will may be discharged as soon as they have met with a physician who has determined the patient is no longer a threat. In many instances, a 72-hour hold actually lasts less than a day before the patient is released. At the same time, a 72-hour hold can actually be longer than three days if it occurs over a weekend or holiday at facilities permitted by the state to not count weekends and holidays toward the 72-hour limit.[227]

If, however, the 72-hour hold has elapsed and the patient still poses a threat to themselves, the patient can be held for up to 14 more days.[228] If the patient is still an active danger to themselves at the end

---

[226] California Welfare and Institutions Code section 5150
[227] California Welfare and Institutions Code section 5151
[228] California Welfare and Institutions Code section 5250

of that 14-day hold, they may be hospitalized for up to 14 *more* days.[229] Beyond that time frame, they must be released unless they have voluntarily agreed to continued treatment, have been recommended to be placed on conservatorship, or present an active danger to others.[230]

Danger to others

Clients regularly come to therapy expressing feelings of anger or a desire for aggression – indeed, that is often what clients come to therapy to resolve. It is vital to understand the difference between a client who is simply expressing anger and one who presents a risk of violence.

Tarasoff v. California Board of Regents

If you are reading this text as part of a Law & Ethics class, you may already be familiar with the *Tarasoff* case. It involved a young woman, Tatiana Tarasoff, who was studying as an undergraduate at the University of California-Berkeley when she met Prosenjit Poddar, a graduate student. Poddar pursued a romantic relationship with Tarasoff, and gradually became obsessed with her. When she attempted to break off their relationship, he began having violent fantasies about her. He sought therapy through the university while Tarasoff was spending the summer with a family member, and he told the therapist about his violent fantasies. The therapist notified campus police, who picked up Poddar and then released him when he promised to stay away from Tarasoff. He dropped out of therapy, and when Tarasoff returned that fall, he stabbed her to death.[231]

Tatiana's parents sued the psychologist who had provided Poddar's therapy and the university, arguing that their daughter should have been warned of the danger she faced upon returning to campus. California courts ruled that **therapists have a duty to protect reasonably identifiable victims of a dangerous or**

---

[229] California Welfare and Institutions Code sections 5257(b)(2) and 5260
[230] California Welfare and Institutions Code section 5260(b)
[231] *Tarasoff v. Regents of the University of California*, 17 Cal. 3d 425, 442 (1976)

threatening client. The court famously wrote, "The protective privilege ends where the public peril begins."[232]

Intervening with a dangerous client

As with suicidal clients, it is vital to effectively assess the potential danger posed by your client and respond appropriately to that level of danger. If a client merely expresses anger at another person, but no intent to harm them, their assurances may be all you need. If they do not appear dangerous during session but you worry that they may become dangerous, a safety plan may be appropriate. You also may want to consider increasing the frequency of contact as discussed above. But if the client leaves your office presenting an imminent danger of severe bodily harm to reasonably identifiable others, you must act to resolve the threat.

Your available options for intervening are different if your client poses an imminent danger to *specific, reasonably identifiable others* as opposed to presenting a *general danger* to anyone who happens to be nearby. Again, remember that our focus is on California law, so the list below is not a complete list of possible interventions for a dangerous client.

However you choose to intervene, remember that any time a therapist breaks confidentiality, even when the law allows or requires the therapist to do so, the therapist should only provide the minimum information necessary to meet their legal requirement. Do not share any details of the client's therapy that are not relevant to the immediate threat.

Reasonably identifiable victims. If your client poses an imminent danger to reasonably identifiable victims, then you must act to protect those victims in accordance with the *Tarasoff* ruling. This may mean warning the victims directly, contacting law enforcement, and any other steps necessary to eliminate the threat. It is important to remember here that **yours is a duty to *protect*, not a "duty to warn."** While warning the potential victim typically is a necessary step

---

[232] *Tarasoff v. Regents of the University of California*, 17 Cal. 3d 425, 442 (1976), p. 10

in protecting them from a dangerous client, it is not always possible or helpful. Consider the example of a client who is known to be a gang member, and tells you of his plans to kill a rival gang member. If you warn the potential victim of this threat, you may actually *provoke* violence from the rival gang. Legislation passed in 2012 clarified that therapists' duty in such cases is the *protection*, and not necessarily the warning, of potential victims. Therapists must take "reasonable efforts" to notify intended victims *and* law enforcement when a client poses a threat to reasonably identifiable victims. This matched instructions that California courts had been giving to juries in such cases for years.[233] The statute notes that if you make reasonable efforts to warn the victim and communicate with law enforcement about the threat, you are immune from liability.[234]

In a 2004 California ruling in the case of *Ewing v. Goldstein*, the court found that a therapist should treat communications from a client's family member (about the client posing a threat) similarly to how they would treat such statements coming directly from the client.[235]

Following mass shootings in Newtown, CT, and Isla Vista, CA, legislators re-examined the laws surrounding when potentially dangerous clients of mental health professionals should be allowed to buy or possess guns. A California law that took effect January 1, 2014, specified that a person who communicated a "serious threat of physical violence against a reasonably identifiable victim or victims" to a licensed therapist should not be allowed to possess a gun for five years unless a court grants permission for them to do so.[236] **A licensed therapist whose client communicates such a threat must report that threat to local law enforcement within 24 hours,** so that local law enforcement can inform federal authorities and the gun possession ban can take effect.[237] Since this law is written in such a way that it applies only to communications from the client of a *licensed* therapist, you should consult your supervisor and an attorney if you are a

---

[233] Senate Bill 1134 (Yee), 2012
[234] California Civil Code section 43.92(b)
[235] *Ewing v Goldstein*, 15 Cal Rptr. 3d 864 (Cal. Ct. App. 2004). An APA brief on the case can be read at www.apa.org/about/offices/ogc/amicus/ewing.aspx
[236] California Welfare and Institutions Code section 8100
[237] California Welfare and Institutions Code section 8105(c)

registrant or trainee dealing with such a threat. In light of the *Ewing v. Goldstein* ruling noted above, you should also consult an attorney if you learned about the threat through a third party such as the client's family member.

General danger to others. If your client is in such a distressed or aggressive state that they pose a general danger to others, but there is no reasonably identifiable victim to protect, then you may act to intervene with the client in accordance with section 5150 of the Welfare and Institutions Code. As is the case with a suicidal client, **those who pose a general danger to others may be involuntarily hospitalized for up to 72 hours.**[238] Once the 72-hour hold has elapsed, the patient can be held for up to 14 more days if they still pose a danger to others.[239] If the patient remains a danger to others at the end of that 14-day hold, they may be hospitalized for up to 180 *more* days for additional treatment if they are determined by a court or jury to present a continued risk.[240] At the end of that 180 days, the process can be renewed with a new court certification that the patient continues to present a danger to others.[241]

Gun Violence Restraining Orders

On January 1, 2016, a state law took effect regarding Gun Violence Restraining Orders (GVROs). While this law does not directly impact therapists' rights or responsibilities, it is helpful for therapists to be aware of it when working with clients who may pose a risk of violence or who may become victims of violence.

Under the law, concerned family members or law enforcement officers may petition a court for a GVRO. A GVRO is a court order that temporarily prohibits someone from purchasing guns or ammunition.

---

[238] California Welfare and Institutions Code section 5150
[239] California Welfare and Institutions Code section 5250
[240] California Welfare and Institutions Code section 5300
[241] California Welfare and Institutions Code section 5304(b)

Perhaps more importantly, it *also* authorizes law enforcement to remove any guns or ammunition that the person already owns.[242]

If you're wondering who might qualify as a "family member," the law is written to apply broadly. It includes partners, blood relatives, and anyone who has regularly resided in the person's house within the past six months.[243] While a therapist could not directly petition for a GVRO pertaining to a client, if a client makes a threat and the therapist notifies law enforcement, then law enforcement may pursue a GVRO against the client.

This law does not change our responsibilities relating to confidentiality or the reporting of threats. However, many clients who are connected to potentially dangerous individuals may not be aware of this new legal option that can help protect their safety. If you are working with clients who are concerned about potential threats posed by others, you may want to make them aware of this option.

Danger to property

Section 1024 of the California Evidence Code states that the therapist-patient privilege does not apply if a client, because of a mental or emotional condition, poses a threat to threat to themselves or the person *or property* of another.[244] This has been interpreted to mean that psychotherapists are allowed, but not required, to communicate with law enforcement or others to reduce or remove the threat.[245] However, it is worth recalling here the difference between confidentiality, which broadly applies in therapy, and privilege, which is specific to court proceedings. This section of law is written as an exception to *privilege*, not as an exception to confidentiality. That leaves therapists in a gray area when considering whether to break confidentiality over a threat to property. As with any situation where

---

[242] For more information on the multiple types of GVROs, why the law is not considered to conflict with the Second Amendment, and additional background information, there's good detail here: smartgunlaws.org/californias-new-gun-violence-restraining-order-law/
[243] California Penal Code sections 422.4(b)(3) and 18150
[244] California Evidence Code section 1024
[245] Pelchat, Z. (2001 July/August). Legal issues in treating suicidal patients. *The Therapist*.

you are aiming to balance your obligations under the law with the protection of threatened people or property, you should consult with an attorney.

One of the strongest arguments in favor of breaking confidentiality over a threat to property is the risk that when property is damaged, destroyed, or stolen, a person might accidentally be hurt in the process. If your client were a burglar and they told you what house they would be robbing tonight, the simple fact that the client does not intend to harm any person does not mean that either the client or those living in the house are safe. If the client was wrong about the house being empty, and a physical confrontation occurred, you may wish you had intervened.

If you do choose to break confidentiality to prevent a danger to property, the law is not specific as to who you should share information with. It would make sense to disclose information about the threat – as minimally as possible, remember – to whomever is best positioned to resolve the threat. This could mean the property owner, a family member of the person making the threat, law enforcement, or anyone else you identify as needing to be informed in order to eliminate the danger.

Child, elder, or dependent adult abuse

California law protects vulnerable populations from abuse. Therapists are required to break confidentiality if they develop reasonable suspicion of child, elder, or dependent adult abuse. For more information on abuse reporting, see Chapter 7.

Releases of information

You are allowed to break confidentiality if you have been given permission by the client to do so. A written request from a client to share information from therapy with a specific third party is called a *release of information*. Most agencies have release forms for their employees, and mental health professional associations make sample release forms available as well.

If you work in a setting that is covered under HIPAA, you may be interested in knowing that HIPAA allows health care providers across multiple settings to share information about a client even without a written release for the purposes of treatment planning.[246] As a practical matter, however, most settings still require the written form. If nothing else, this provides assurance that the person who would be receiving the information actually is actively involved in the client's treatment.

Other exceptions to confidentiality

In addition to the common exceptions outlined above, state and federal law define several additional exceptions to confidentiality. While these are not commonly used, it is helpful to know them and to share with your clients that these are additional instances where disclosure of information may be required. **Other situations where therapists are <u>required</u> to break confidentiality if asked to do so include those on the following list:**[247]

- Court order
- Investigation by a board, commission, or administrative agency
- Subpoena from a court (i.e., from a judge – see "Responding to a subpoena" in Chapter 5)
- Lawful request from an arbitrator or arbitration panel
- Search warrant
- Coroner's investigation, when the person whose death is being investigated is the client
- Request for records from a client or client's representative (there are limited times when you can justify not turning over records; see "Client requests for records" later in this chapter)

In addition to these, **there are other instances where a therapist is <u>allowed</u>, but not mandated, to break confidentiality:**[248]

---

[246] Code of Federal Regulations title 45 section 164.506. A useful summary of the HIPAA privacy rules can be found at www.hhs.gov/ocr/privacy/hipaa/understanding/summary/index.html
[247] California Civil Code section 56.10(b)
[248] California Civil Code section 56.10(c)

- Communicating with other providers, health plans, or facilities for the purposes of diagnosis or treatment
- Determining responsibility for payment and for payment to be made
- To a billing, claims management, medical data processing, or other administrative process
- To an official review group for quality control
- To a licensing or accreditation body for the health care provider
- As part of a coroner's investigation when the person whose death is being investigated is not the client
- For research purposes
- Related to employment, if the information comes from employment-related health care services, such as when a client has made their mental condition the focus of a lawsuit against their employer or if the client's fitness for their job is impacted

These are just a sampling. There are a total of 21 instances where a therapist is allowed, but not required, to break confidentiality in this section of state law. While you may initially think these don't matter – after all, your ethics codes still require you to maintain confidentiality – bear in mind that ethics codes usually include an exception for times when breaking confidentiality is required or allowed by law.[249] You can then use your professional judgment and consultation with colleagues, supervisors, and an attorney, as you see fit, to determine whether disclosure of confidential information is warranted. As previously mentioned, when disclosure is allowed but not required, therapists tend to prefer upholding confidentiality.[250]

---

[249] AAMFT Code of Ethics subprinciple 2.2; ACA Code of Ethics subprinciple B.1.c; CAMFT Code of Ethics subprinciple 2.1; NASW Code of Ethics subprinciple 1.07(e)
[250] Leslie, D. (1989 July/August). Confidentiality. *The Therapist.*

▶ Privilege

Communications between a client and a therapist are considered to be privileged communications under the law.[251] This essentially means that the state considers the privacy of these conversations to be of the utmost importance, so much so that the content of therapy cannot even be used in most court proceedings unless the client, or a judge, allows it.

Just as there are exceptions to confidentiality, there are also exceptions to privilege. As we discussed above, client threats to property are not considered privileged communications. Other exceptions apply as well.

Note that the discussion here applies to situations where it is your *client* who is involved in a court proceeding. If *you* are the person being sued, the rules are a bit different, and you should utilize the services of an attorney regarding issues of privilege.

Holders of privilege

Clients generally are holders of their own privilege.[252] That is, they can determine on their own whether they would like to allow for confidential information from their therapy to be revealed in a court process. This is particularly important for therapists to be aware of with minors; **even minors are typically holders of their own privilege**, though as we will see below, minors are not always free to choose on their own whether to waive it.

In some instances, the court may appoint someone to be responsible for the client's decisions regarding privilege, particularly if the client is a minor. This person is called a *guardian ad litem*.

---

[251] California Evidence Code section 1014
[252] California Evidence Code section 1013

Asserting privilege

As a mental health provider, you can refuse to release information on the grounds that any communications between a client and a psychotherapist are considered privileged communications under the law. This is called "asserting privilege," and you can assert privilege without revealing even whether the person involved in the court case is a client of yours. However, you cannot assert privilege if your client asks, or a judge demands, that privilege be waived.

Asserting privilege cannot be done passively, though. It does not mean simply failing to respond to a request for records. It must be done formally, and is often necessary if you receive a request for records from a judge or an attorney. For more on this, see "Responding to a subpoena" in Chapter 5.

Waiving privilege

Most clients can choose to *waive privilege*, thus allowing a therapist to discuss their therapy in a court proceeding, if they wish. However, courts do not always defer to the client who wants to waive privilege. Judges may block a client's request to waive privilege if the judge believes doing so is not in the client's best interest, particularly if the client is a minor.

In any case, **it is never up to the therapist to determine whether privilege should be waived**. It is always the choice of the client, the client's guardian (including guardians appointed by the court), another court appointee, or a judge. If a client instructs you that they are waiving privilege, you should document and follow their instruction.

Exceptions to privilege

The law defines a number of exceptions to psychotherapist-client privilege, including (among others):

- If a client, anyone making a claim on the client's behalf, or a beneficiary of the client raises the client's mental or emotional state as an issue in a court proceeding.[253]
- If the client sought the therapist's services for the purpose of planning or committing a crime, or to avoid being arrested for a crime after the fact.[254]
- If the client is a danger to themselves, to others, or to property, and disclosure of that information is necessary to prevent the threat.[255] See "threats to property" above.
- If the client is under age 16 and is the victim of a crime, and the therapist believes that disclosing that information is in the child's best interest.[256]

A client's death does *not* create an exception to privilege, as the client's representative can still claim privilege on their behalf. However, once a client has died, any information the client told their therapist about how they wanted their property distributed is not subject to privilege.[257]

---

[253] California Evidence Code section 1016
[254] California Evidence Code section 1018
[255] California Evidence Code section 1024
[256] California Evidence Code section 1027
[257] California Evidence Code section 1021

▶ Maintaining confidentiality

Now that you are familiar with all of the exceptions to confidentiality, let us return to your core responsibility: maintaining it. In spite of the high number of specific exceptions to confidentiality under state law, those are still exceptions; unless one or more of them clearly apply, you must keep all information from therapy sessions confidential.[258]

Confidentiality with couples and families

As you can imagine, issues of confidentiality are more complicated when you work with couples or families. While you have a legal responsibility to maintain your clients' confidentiality, they have no such responsibility to each other. Furthermore, you have to make difficult decisions as a therapist when it comes to keeping what one family member tells you confidential from another.

When working with couples or families, some therapists choose a *no-secrets policy*. With this understanding with the clients, everyone agrees that any information any individual in the family shares with the therapist – even if other family members are not around at the time – is "fair game" for the therapist to bring up in a future family session. This keeps the therapist from being put in an awkward position if one family member, speaking with the therapist by phone or on an individual basis, acknowledges an affair, substance use, or some other issue that is impacting the family but that other family members may not be aware of.

Other therapists prefer a *limited-secrets policy*, where the therapist does keep some information learned from individuals secret from the others, even when the focus of treatment is the couple or family. Some therapists prefer this kind of policy because they feel it allows for clients to be more open in the assessment stage of therapy, particularly around issues like intimate partner violence that may be

---

[258] California Business and Professions Code sections 4982(m), 4992.3(n), and 4999.90(m)

easier to discuss when a family member is alone with the therapist than when in front of an abusive partner or the couple's children.

Neither of these policies is inherently right or wrong; this has been an issue of debate for some time in family work, and state law appears to allow either kind of policy. Whatever policy on secrets you choose for couple and family work, **each member of the couple or family should agree to that policy in writing.** Confidentiality is an individual right, and the ethics codes of many of the major mental health associations covered in this text specifically require addressing the confidentiality of each individual client within a couple or family treatment context.[259] As part of this policy, you may ask family members to commit to keeping each other's confidentiality outside of the therapy room, though there is no legal requirement for them to do so.

Confidentiality in group therapy

As with couples and families, members of a therapy group are not bound to maintain each other's confidentiality outside of the group setting. Indeed, it is common for the sharing of personal information in session to lead group members to become friends outside of the therapy room. While this can be good for clients in building their social support, it also can raise questions about group boundaries.

You do have a responsibility as a therapist to maintain the confidentiality of all group members. If you are running a therapy group, it may be helpful to regularly review the expectations of group members, including boundaries on sharing anything from the group with outsiders. Some professional ethics codes encourage regularly revisiting issues of confidentiality in any therapy setting,[260] and some specifically address the importance of clarifying confidentiality in a

---

[259] AAMFT Code of Ethics subprinciple 2.2; ACA Code of Ethics subprinciple B.4.b; NASW Code of Ethics subprinciple 1.07(f)
[260] AAMFT Code of Ethics subprinciple 2.1; ACA Code of Ethics subprinciple B.1.d; NASW Code of Ethics subprinciple 1.07(e)

group treatment setting.[261] You may even choose to set a policy where those who violate the confidentiality of the group may be asked to leave the group.

Confidentiality and the Internet

Maintaining confidentiality can become far more difficult if you are working with clients via phone or videoconference, issues we will tackle in Chapter 9 (Technology). Even when you are providing services in person, the Internet has created new concerns about client confidentiality.

Web sites like Yelp, Angie's List, and Health Grades allow consumers to post their reviews of professionals in a variety of fields. This can make for difficult decision-making where confidentiality is concerned. What happens if a client posts a negative review of you on one of these sites? Even worse, what if the person posting about negative experiences with you in therapy isn't a client, and never was?

Remember from the beginning of this chapter that it is typically *your* responsibility to maintain confidentiality, even as it applies to something as basic as whether a person has been your client, and even if the client does not seem concerned about keeping therapy confidential. When someone posts about your clinical work online, regardless of whether they are a client or just pretending to be, that should not be taken as their permission for you to talk openly about them or to respond to their comments.

Most therapists presented with such a situation will choose simply to not respond. Some, however, choose to be a bit more proactive. By registering with such sites and controlling their directory information (basic information like your address and phone number), therapists sometimes have the opportunity to add a statement to their listing outlining the limits of confidentiality and explaining that they cannot respond to any comments posted there, even to say that someone wasn't actually their client.

---

[261] AAMFT Code of Ethics subprinciple 2.2; ACA Code of Ethics subprinciple B.4.a; CAMFT Code of Ethics subprinciple 2.7; NASW Code of Ethics subprinciple 1.07(f)

Room for debate: Privacy and stigma

by Jeffrey Liebert, MA

The legal and ethical standards surrounding confidentiality provide structure for much of the work psychotherapists do. By adhering to these rules, psychotherapists provide clients a sense of security, which may be necessary for clients to feel comfortable enough to honestly express themselves.

It can also have unintended consequences. Confidentiality can reinforce the stigma that many of us believe surrounds mental health care: The notion that if you're going to therapy, you should *want* privacy, because therapy (or needing it) is embarrassing. In this way, confidentiality may have the *opposite* effect from what is intended. Rather than protecting clients, it leaves them feeling like seeking help confirms that they are deeply troubled.

Interestingly, the stigma that surrounds psychotherapy is one that appears to be largely a concern of psychotherapists – *and not clients.* While stigma is certainly real and linked to history in some underserved communities, it is consistently at the bottom of the list when people are surveyed about why they don't go to therapy even when they know they have mental health needs.[262]

Given that clients seem far less embarrassed about going to therapy than therapists expect them to be, it may be time to rethink the role of confidentiality in therapy. Perhaps confidentiality could be a right of the client – something they could opt in to if they wanted, preserving the privacy that many clients do still agree is important – rather than a blanket obligation of the therapist.

The impact of such a change could be far-reaching. Clients may experience greater control and autonomy over their experiences in mental health care. Those who still value privacy would be no less entitled to it than they are today, but those who value sharing their experiences in their communities may feel more emboldened to do so. We could have real, research-driven discussions about where privacy boundaries begin and end, and who should be in charge of placing those boundaries.

---

[262] Caldwell, B. E. *Saving Psychotherapy.* Los Angeles: Author.

5

Documentation

You might be familiar with the expression often used online: "Pics or it didn't happen." When it comes to mental health services, a parallel saying applies: Documentation or it didn't happen. A current, complete, and accurate client file is your first stop when seeking out a client's contact information, your first point of reference when preparing for an upcoming session, and your first line of defense against accusations of wrongdoing.

Given the critical role of documentation in mental health care, you may be surprised to learn just how few documentation requirements actually exist in state law. For the most part, the state has seen fit to leave standards for clinical record-keeping up to the professions themselves, through professional ethics codes, and up to the standard of care.

We'll talk in this chapter about common components of a client file, starting with informed consent. We'll also talk about what to do when clients or others request copies of clinical records.

▸ Informed consent

It is a longstanding principle across the healthcare professions that patients should know what they are getting into with any medical treatment, so they can make an active choice whether to receive that treatment. While state law does not provide much guidance for what needs to be included in an informed consent agreement, a therapist who fails to engage their client in an informed consent process can have their license disciplined for unprofessional conduct (see Chapter 3, Unprofessional Conduct).

In basic terms, an informed consent process involves describing for your client what treatments will be performed and for what purposes. Clients are also informed of the "ground rules" for therapy, including confidentiality and its exceptions (see Chapter 5, Confidentiality, Privilege, and Exceptions). Informed consent also includes information about fees and billing practices, as we will see below.

Ultimately, the larger idea of informed consent is every bit as important as the more specific requirements. Every professional ethics code in mental health emphasizes the importance of client autonomy and **self-determination**, the right of clients to choose for themselves what treatment to take part in and what goals to pursue in therapy. The more information a client has about the therapy process before it begins, the better position they are in to act from a place of autonomy and self-determination.

In this section, we discuss primarily the state requirements for informed consent. It is important to understand, however, that your ethical code is likely to describe specific required elements of informed consent in more detail, and you are obligated to the specific requirements of your ethical code as well as state law.

Disclosure requirements

In *Cobbs v. Grant*, the California court case that defined health care providers' informed consent obligations, four principles of informed consent were outlined:[263]

1. Clients do not usually have the same expert knowledge as health care providers.
2. A client has the right to control their participation in treatment, including the right to choose whether to participate in treatment.
3. A client needs information, particularly about the benefits and risks of treatment, to make an effective decision about whether to participate in treatment.
4. A client relies on the health care provider to give them that information in terms the client can understand.

However, state law offers little in the way of more direct guidance on what an informed consent agreement should include. State law specifies surprisingly few things that a client must be informed of prior to mental health care; those requirements are described below. However, the standard of care for such agreements within your profession may include additional information, which we will cover in the next section.

Any disclosures made to the client as part of an informed consent process should be in easily understood language. Informed consent documents or conversations that are in language too complex or sophisticated for clients to understand do little good in actually informing them.

Fees

The state requires that clients be informed, prior to the beginning of mental health treatment, of what the fee for that treatment will be. Clients also must be informed about how the fee

---

[263] *Cobbs v. Grant*, 8 Cal. 3d 229 (1972)

was computed.[264] For example, is yours a standard fee charged to all clients for each hour of service? Or is it set on a sliding fee scale, based on the client's income? Either of these is allowed, of course. The client simply must know before treatment begins how much they will be paying for it, and how that fee was set.

Fee disclosures should not simply be limited to how much you charge per session. You can (and many therapists do) charge for client no-shows, testifying in court, and for any number of other non-clinical tasks you may engage in on a client's behalf. But these fees should be clearly disclosed at the beginning of treatment. Even collaborating with a referring therapist or another current treatment provider is something you can charge for, so long as that fee was disclosed in advance.[265]

Licensure status

All licensees and registrants are required to post their licenses or registrations in a clearly visible place in their offices.[266] This helps ensure that clients will be aware of the licensure of their therapist before treatment. The law is a not clear as to whether this information actually needs to be part of informed consent, but given the disclosure requirements for all therapist advertising (see Chapter 8, Advertising), it seems like good sense to ensure in any informed consent agreement that clients are at least made aware of your license or registration title and number.

If a therapist is operating a private practice under a fictitious business name (for example, if I called my practice the "Anytown Counseling Center"), the client must be informed of who actually owns the business, and what their licensure status is.[267]

---

[264] California Business and Professions Code sections 4982(n), 4992.3(o), and 4999.90(n)
[265] California Business and Professions Code sections 4982(o), 4992.3(p), and 4999.90(o)
[266] California Business and Professions Code sections 4980.31, 4996.7, and 4999.70
[267] California Business and Professions Code sections 4980.46, 4992.10, and 4999.72

Any trainee or associate providing therapy must inform the client, prior to the beginning of treatment, of their licensure status and that they are under licensed supervision. They also must provide the name of their employer.[268]

Technology

If you will be using technology as part of the delivery of services, California law requires that you obtain and document the client's *verbal* consent for telehealth services. This applies to therapy by videoconference, telephone, texting, or any other technologies that allow services to be provided in some way other than face-to-face.[269] Regular check-ins and phone calls for the purposes of scheduling would likely not qualify as service delivery.

I will admit, I sometimes find this requirement a little laughable. It is not as if clients who are receiving therapy by phone are not aware that they are using the phone. But, the underlying reason for the law makes sense: clients need to understand the risks and limitations of the technology being used. We are likely to understand those risks and limitations as they relate to mental health service delivery far better than the clients do. So, as the *Cobbs v. Grant* ruling described, clients need information from us to make a truly informed decision as to whether to participate in technology-assisted services.

While we're on the topic of technology, it is important to note that, with the exception of confidentiality, clients cannot waive the therapist's ethical or legal responsibilities through the informed consent process. So even if a client agreed to video-based therapy through an unsecured platform, the therapist would still likely be violating their ethics code as well as California's new telehealth standards (see Chapter 9, Technology, for more on this).

---

[268] California Business and Professions Code sections 4980.44(c), 4980.48(a), 4996.18(h), 4999.36(d), and 4999.45(a)(3)
[269] California Business and Professions Code sections 2290.5(b) and (c)

Privacy practices

For those therapists and organizations covered by HIPAA (and not all are – see Chapter 9), all clients must be given a copy of the provider's Notice of Privacy Practices, detailing how the therapist safeguards the client's private information. The client should acknowledge in writing that they have received that documentation.[270]

Other common elements of disclosure

There are a number of other commonly-included elements of informed consent. While these are not directly required by state law, the law does require that all mental health professionals practice in keeping with the standards of their professions – so most professionals choose to follow common practices within their professions. There are several sample Informed Consent agreements available through professional associations, and they tend to include the elements below. Note that in many instances, these are required by professional Codes of Ethics.

Limits of confidentiality

While the "big four" exceptions to confidentiality are commonly known, there are also a number of additional exceptions to confidentiality in California (see Chapter 5, Confidentiality, Privilege, and Exceptions) that should be acknowledged in some form. Some therapists prefer to use general language for these other exceptions (for example, my own informed consent agreement notes that there are "other, rare instances where disclosure is required or permitted by law") while others choose to specifically list them. The first option may be better for the therapist if laws regarding confidentiality change, while the latter may be helpful for clients in understanding that these instances are truly not commonly used.

---

[270] Office of Civil Rights, U.S. Department of Health and Human Services: Notice of Privacy Practices

Defining who is the client

In couple and family work, it is important for both the therapist and those attending therapy to be clear as to who is the client. Is the therapist aiming to produce the best outcome for the couple or family, or for a specific person (or people) within it? These can be very different aims. The ACA Code of Ethics specifically notes that "In the absence of an agreement to the contrary, the couple or family is considered to be the client."[271] There are also implications here regarding confidentiality. Therapists do not share individual confidences without written consent to do so. If the therapist has made clear in the informed consent agreement that the couple or family is considered to be the client, and that individual statements to the therapist may be shared with the person's partner or family, an individual could not claim later that their confidentiality had been breached by such sharing. For more on this important issue, see Confidentiality with Couples and Families in Chapter 4.

Cancellation policy

Clients sometimes need to reschedule or cancel planned sessions. Therapists have a variety of policies for such instances, and having your policy agreed to in writing at the beginning of treatment can spare you from awkward conversations later. Many therapists will charge their full fee if a session is cancelled without enough advance notice (24 or 48 hours are common policies, though some therapists require more or less; there is not a uniform standard here).

My private practice is in Los Angeles, where many clients are in some way tied to the entertainment industry. Here, therapists will sometimes provide added flexibility for clients who may not know whether they are working on a given day until they get a call that morning. Some therapists here choose to charge only a nominal fee for late cancellations if the client reschedules (and attends the rescheduled session) within the same week.

---

[271] ACA Code of Ethics, subprinciple B.4.b

Procedures to be used

An Informed Consent document for an individual practitioner can be fairly specific about the techniques the therapist uses, especially if that therapist has a specialized practice. Clinics and other settings where the same Informed Consent agreement is used for many therapists have to be more general in their descriptions of the services to be offered. In either case, though, the Informed Consent often makes clear that clients always have a right to know what procedures are being used with them and why they are being used. You may also want to have a more specific discussion in person with each client about the procedures being used, revisiting that conversation whenever appropriate, and document that discussion in the client's record.

The informed consent may be a good place to include discussion about the expected length of treatment. Obviously, some treatment methods allow for more specific prediction of treatment length than others.

Risks and benefits

While a general discussion of the risks and benefits of psychotherapy can be included in a written informed consent document, some therapists also will have more detailed conversations with clients about the specific risks and benefits of that particular therapist's type of treatment for the client's particular problem. Such a discussion, if it occurs, should be documented in the client's file.

Of course, not every possible risk can be known ahead of time for any health care procedure. Your discussion of the potential risks of therapy simply needs to cover those risks that are reasonably foreseeable.

One risk of therapy that *is* foreseeable is simple ineffectiveness. No form of therapy is 100% effective. Clients may benefit from knowing before therapy begins that neither you nor any other therapist can guarantee that treatment will work.

Right of refusal

Clients have complete freedom of choice when it comes to their health care. They are under no obligation to start (or, once started, to continue) treatment with a specific therapist. Even a person ordered by a court, their employer, or another outside entity to receive mental health treatment typically can choose their treatment provider. An Informed Consent document will often specify that a client can discontinue treatment at any time and for any reason.

Communication and emergency practices

Can your clients call you between sessions if they feel it necessary? What about in emergencies? If so, how do you charge for this service? What about email, or texting? In our technological age, it may be easier than ever for clients to reach you, which raises concerns about both confidentiality and professional boundaries. You may want to spell out in your Informed Consent agreement precisely how you handle issues like between-session calls, emails, texts, and the like. You may also want to spell out how the client should proceed in a mental health emergency, particularly those where you are not immediately available.

Some therapists who maintain presences on Facebook, Twitter, or other social media use their informed consent documents to describe the nature of their social media relationships. The ACA Code of Ethics requires therapists who use social media to discuss social media as part of informed consent.[272] Clients will naturally be curious about you and your life, but the ACA Code of Ethics requires counselors to keep their personal and professional social media presences separated, so as to avoid confusing clients about the nature of the therapeutic relationship. For all mental health professionals, becoming Facebook "friends" with clients, following clients on Twitter, or connecting with clients through LinkedIn, Instagram, and other social media can raise concerns about confidentiality and multiple relationships, and so is generally discouraged.

---

[272] ACA Code of Ethics, subprinciple H.6.b

Any discussion of communication practices also provides you an opportunity to discuss your rules and practices regarding requests for records (see later in this chapter).

Billing practices

In order to bill a client's insurance for services, a therapist must send the insurer information about the service provided, the client's diagnosis, and sometimes, additional information. While it is possible to make arrangements for this through a separate Release of Information (see Chapter 4), many therapists include information on their interactions with insurance companies in the Informed Consent agreement.

This is also a convenient place to include some information about what happens when clients are unable to pay their fees. The NASW, ACA, and CAMFT Codes of Ethics all specifically addresses this issue, noting that it is ethical to terminate for nonpayment as long as this is done in a manner that is clinically appropriate.[273] However, a therapist should make reasonable efforts to address the issue first. Offering a payment plan, or even reducing the fee, may help the client to remain in therapy. If this is not possible, the client should be referred to any available local low-fee clinics. A therapist cannot refuse to make referrals or withhold treatment records simply because a client has an unpaid balance. As a last resort, therapists may make use of collection agencies to collect unpaid balances from clients. Therapists who do so may want to make note of this in their informed consent agreement.

Therapist background

State law encourages, but does not require, LMFTs to provide clients with detailed statements of their "experience, education, specialties, professional orientation, and any other information deemed appropriate."[274] This does not need to be prior to the

---

[273] ACA Code of Ethics subprinciple A.11.c; CAMFT Code of Ethics subprinciple 1.3.4; NASW Code of Ethics standard 1.17(c)
[274] California Business and Professions Code section 4980.55

beginning of therapy. This encouragement is *not* included in state law for the other mental health professions.

Wilcoxon et al. similarly advocate the use of a "Professional Disclosure Statement" that can include a great deal of additional information on a therapist's training, background, philosophy, treatment model, and any other relevant information.[275] While that text is also focused on LMFTs, providing clients with such information is in keeping with the general principles of informed consent. It would qualify as a best practice for therapists of all types.

Expectations of clients

The discussion of a client's rights and responsibilities in therapy does not need to be limited to their legal rights and responsibilities. You may also want to include discussions about your clinical expectations of the client. These may include expectations regarding the frequency of sessions, client behavior in session, and the client's role relative to the therapist (that is, do you as a therapist take on an expert role with the client, or do you expect the therapy relationship to be more collaborative in nature?).

Verbal versus written consent

California law generally does not specify whether consent for mental health treatment should be in writing or whether verbal consent is sufficient. While the ACA Code of Ethics specifies that counselors need to review the rights and responsibilities of clients and therapists "in writing and verbally,"[276] the codes of ethics of AAMFT, CAMFT, and NASW are not specific as to whether the informed consent process should be verbal or in writing. This would seem to allow for a verbal consent process, which is necessary for those clients who cannot read or who need information about therapy to be translated to their native language. (It can easily be argued that the

---

[275] Wilcoxon, A., Remley, T. P. Jr., & Gladding, S. T. (2012). *Ethical, Legal, and Professional Issues in the Practice of Marriage and Family Therapy (updated 5th edition)*. Upper Saddle River, NJ: Pearson Education.
[276] ACA Code of Ethics subprinciple A.2.a

ACA Code also does allow for this when appropriate). Still, most practitioners generally use a written consent form that each client signs, so there will be no dispute later about what a client was informed of prior to the beginning of treatment. Regardless of how consent is obtained, it should be documented in the client's file.

There are some instances where written consent *is* necessary. For example, any person bringing a minor in for any form of medical care who is not the minor's parent or guardian but is consenting to the minor's treatment must complete a Caregiver's Authorization Affidavit.[277] This form is not an informed consent agreement by itself, but rather is a way for the adult to attest in writing that they are legally able to consent for the minor's treatment.

Marriage and family therapists should note that the professional ethics codes of counselors and MFTs specifically require **written** informed consent prior to audiotaping or videotaping clients, or allowing third parties to observe sessions.[278] (The NASW code simply requires that informed consent be obtained in such instances, not that it be in writing.[279]) The ACA Code of Ethics also includes some instances where written informed consent is needed, such as when transferring records to third parties.[280]

Informed consent with minors

In California, minors as young as 12 can independently consent to their own mental health care, so long as the practitioner determines that the minor is mature enough to participate intelligently in treatment.[281]

---

[277] I've provided a sample Caregiver's Authorization Affidavit for you here: http://www.bencaldwell.com/extras/caregivers-authorization-affidavit.pdf
[278] AAMFT Code of Ethics subprinciple 1.12; ACA Code of Ethics subprinciples B.6.c and B.6.d; CAMFT Code of Ethics subprinciple 1.5.4
[279] NASW Code of Ethics standard 1.03(h)
[280] ACA Code of Ethics subprinciple B.6.g
[281] California Health & Safety Code section 124260(d). This law inadvertently excluded social work associates. Under Assembly Bill 1808 (Wood), 2016, which took effect on January 1, 2017, social work associates can treat minors who are independently consenting.

One of the ways a therapist might assess whether a minor is capable of consenting to treatment on their own is by going through the informed consent agreement with the minor and evaluating whether the minor is adequately understanding what each part means. If the minor cannot make sense of the limits of confidentiality, for example, the therapist may want to consider whether the minor is capable of participating intelligently in treatment.

Even when the minor shows the maturity needed to consent to treatment on their own, the therapist is required to make contact with the minor's parents unless the therapist can document reasons why that would be detrimental to the minor. (A law that took effect January 1, 2017, clarified that trainees can treat minors consenting on their own. In such instances, the trainee needs to notify their supervisor within 24 hours after treating the minor. If the minor is a danger to self or others, the trainee must notify the supervisor immediately.[282])

Minors with divorced parents

When a minor's parents are divorced, separated, or never married, therapists often have questions about whether one parent's consent is sufficient to begin treatment. It can be considered a best-practice standard to obtain a copy of a written custody agreement, if one exists. This will *sometimes* clarify the conditions under which each parent can consent for mental health treatment for their child. Even agreements in which parents share joint legal custody may require parents to jointly select treatment providers or to consult with one another regarding mental health care.[283]

At treatment intake, it is unlikely that a therapist would run into difficulty for simply taking a parent at their word that they have the legal authority to consent to their child's care (especially if the parent signs something to that effect, which is why you'll see language about this in many agencies' informed consent agreements). However, where such situations sometimes get messy is when the other parent

---

[282] Assembly Bill 1808 (Wood), 2016
[283] Montgomery, A. (2016 July/August). Know your LEBs like you know your ABCs. *The Therapist, 28*(4), 72-76.

becomes aware of the therapy, and seeks to immediately terminate the child's treatment. This places the therapist in a difficult position. It may be possible to avoid this by getting clarity at the beginning of therapy on who truly has the authority to provide – or revoke – consent.

Assent agreements

For minors too young to consent to treatment on their own, or who legally could do so but are nonetheless covered by a consent form signed by a parent, therapists still engage in an informed consent process. In doing so, they sometimes make use of "Assent agreements." These are not legally binding, but do describe for children (in age-appropriate language) what the therapy process is and how it works. This can alleviate their fears of coming to a therapist's office, and help them understand their role in therapy.

Even when children are too young to read an assent agreement, a therapist can work with the parent or guardian to ensure that the child has an age-appropriate understanding of where they are, who the therapist is, and what they have come to therapy for. Regardless of the process, it is important to clearly document what was done to explain informed consent to the child.

▸ Documenting treatment

In addition to an initial Informed Consent document (many places will call it a treatment contract), therapists are obligated to keep adequate records of treatment on an ongoing basis. There is great diversity among workplaces and client populations when it comes to the kinds of documentation that would be considered adequate, but there are some common practices that can be identified in clinical work.

Types of records

Most settings will require that, early in the therapy process, a **treatment plan** be developed. This document outlines the goals and methods of treatment that the client and therapist have agreed upon. Some agencies even require that the client sign the treatment plan, though this is not a requirement of state law.

After each session or clinical contact, the therapist typically makes notes about that meeting. These might be called **progress notes,** session notes, or something similar. (There's a specific legal definition of the term "psychotherapy notes," which is different from this. We'll get to that in a moment.) This book does not contain any guidance on the specific content of progress notes. This is because state law simply requires that you keep treatment records consistent with "sound clinical judgment [and] the standards of the profession,"[284] and the standard of care for record-keeping changes over time. Recall from our earlier discussion of the *standard of care* that books and journal articles, in addition to the practices of colleagues, can offer strong guidance on the standard of care within your field. For information on how to document therapy, a number of popular texts are available, including *The Psychotherapy Documentation Primer.*[285] Specifically for LMFTs, *Mastering*

---

[284] California Business and Professions Code sections 4982(v), 4992.3(t), and 4999.90(v)
[285] Wiger, D. E. (2012). *The Psychotherapy Documentation Primer (3rd edition).* Hoboken, NJ: John Wiley & Sons.

Competencies in Family Therapy: A Practical Approach to Theory and Clinical Case Documentation[286] also offers useful examples.

In settings where payment is provided on a per-session basis – which is to say, most treatment settings – the client file will also include meaningful **financial records** indicating past payments and any current balance.

Client files generally also include things like **records from other providers, correspondence with the client, and other records** relevant to treatment.

Under federal law, there is a type of record called **"psychotherapy notes"** that is different from the progress notes described above. Psychotherapy notes are usually made during session, and document content of a therapy session and nothing else – if a note includes information like a client's symptoms, diagnosis, medications, or even the start and stop times of the session, it *cannot* qualify as a psychotherapy note. Psychotherapy notes also must be stored separately from the client's file.[287]

While some therapists appreciate having a distinct category of records for their immediate reflections about conversations occurring in session, it should be noted that California law does *not* recognize a distinction between psychotherapy notes and other kinds of mental health records. So when a client requests a full copy of their record, or when you are required by a court to produce the complete record of a case, it is at best arguable whether you could hold back psychotherapy notes. If you maintain psychotherapy notes separate from client files, a client (or third party, with the client's or a court's authorization) requests access to all of a client's record, and you would like to hold back the psychotherapy notes, consult with an attorney.

---

[286] Gehart, D. R. (2014). *Mastering Competencies in Family Therapy: A Practical Approach to Theory and Clinical Case Documentation*. Belmont, CA: Brooks/Cole.

[287] Welty, K. (2016). Psychotherapy Notes and HIPAA. *Psych Central*. Available at https://psychcentral.com/lib/psychotherapy-notes-and-hipaa/

Session recordings

In training settings, sessions with clients may be recorded for educational or supervisory purposes. Workplaces have different policies as to whether these recordings are to become part of the client file. In a very literal sense, an audio or video recording is a *record of the session*, which would support making it part of the client file and retaining it for the legally-required seven years. However, many agencies argue that the sole purpose of these recordings is training, and some even put in the consent form for taping that clients understand the recording will *not* become part of their file.

Regardless of the stance of your particular employer on this specific question, of course the recording will contain clients' private information. As a result, it is critical to follow workplace (and, if applicable, university) policy for securely transporting and disposing of recordings of client sessions.

Workplace expectations

It is common for employers to have their own specific requirements and expectations where record-keeping is concerned. Employers may have standards for additional required paperwork, additional signatures on certain pieces of the client file, or timeliness in completing paperwork after sessions. Failure to live up to those standards *usually* is not a violation of law – although even that can get muddy if you're working in a public system under standards set by local or county government – but even so, it can endanger your good standing with your employer. When you agree to go to work for an employer, you are agreeing to abide by their internal policies and requirements.

Record retention, storage, and disposal

Therapists are expected to retain treatment records for at least 7 years after the last professional contact with clients who are adults. If treatment involved a minor, the therapist should retain the records until the minor turns 25 (that is, 7 years after their 18th birthday).[288] You can choose to retain records for longer than this if you wish; the law simply provides a *minimum* amount of time for which records must be kept.

The current *statute of limitations* – that is, the amount of time the BBS has to take action against you based on an act you are alleged to have committed in your therapy practice – is 7 years for most violations, and 10 years for violations involving sexual misconduct. For acts involving sexual contact with a minor, the BBS can act for 3 years *from the time that they first learn about the act* – no matter how long it has been since the act occurred – as long as there is corroborating evidence. For other violations involving minors, the clock does not start on these time periods until the minor turns 18.[289]

In today's digital age, records can be retained for much longer periods of time if the therapist or therapist's employer chooses. State law does not define a *maximum* length of time to retain records. Since treatment records can be important in a therapist's defense against charges of wrongdoing, many therapists choose to retain their records for 10 years following the conclusion of treatment. Some therapists who work with minors retain their records for at least 10 years following the time the minor turns 18.

For as long as records are maintained, they must be secured to prevent the disclosure of confidential information. **State law specifies that health care records must be secured, but does not specify *how* records must be secured.** As we will discuss in Chapter 9 (Technology), federal laws also purposefully do not specify methods of securing files, because the digital technology for creating and securing files is changing so quickly. Federal law instead requires that security practices be adequate and that they be *regularly reviewed and updated*, understanding that the needs of different providers will vary.

When the time comes for records to be disposed of, you cannot simply throw paper files in the trash. As is the case with any California business, you must dispose of records by shredding or other means that protect clients' confidentiality.[290]

---

[288] California Business and Professions Code sections 4980.49(a), 4993(a), and 4999.75(a)
[289] California Business and Professions Code sections 4982.05 and 4990.32
[290] California Civil Code section 1798.81

▶ Access to records

Clients are typically entitled to review or receive a copy of their treatment records if they wish. If a client requests their records, you must comply within five days if the client simply is asking to inspect their records, and within 15 days if they are requesting a copy of their records.[291] Requests to inspect or receive copies of records must be made in writing.[292]

You cannot refuse a client's request for records simply because they owe you fees for past sessions.[293] However, you can require clients to pay for reasonable clerical costs of locating the client's file and making it available, including the cost of copies.

If a minor has consented to services on their own, the minor has a right to access their own records. Their parents do not have the right to access the minor's treatment records. Only the minor themselves can authorize the release of their own records.[294]

On the other hand, if the minor's parent or guardian provided consent for the minor's treatment, the parent or guardian has a right to access those records.[295] This is true even if the parent does not live with the child or is a noncustodial parent.

Family therapy involving a minor

If you have been working with a minor as part of family therapy, releasing records to any family member requires consent from *all* family members who provided consent for treatment originally. (After all, if you are keeping one treatment record for the family, it is impossible to release one person's records without releasing the records of others.) Typically this means all family members over the

---

[291] California Health and Safety Code section 123110(a)
[292] California Health and Safety Code section 123110(a) and (b)
[293] California Health and Safety Code section 123110(j)
[294] California Health and Safety Code section 123110(a)
[295] California Health and Safety Code section 123110(a)

age of 18, as parents usually provide consent on behalf of minors in family therapy contexts.[296]

There is some understandable confusion about this, though. State law includes two different sections related to the release of records from family therapy involving minors, and those sections provide somewhat different standards. Section 56.10 of the Civil Code incorporates a portion of the Health and Safety Code, which entitles parents to access records of treatment for which the parents had provided consent.[297] But the next section of the Civil Code, 56.11, appears to require that the minor themselves authorize the release of information from treatment they were involved in if they legally *could have* consented for the treatment, regardless of whether they actually *did*.[298] With this framework, you would need to ask anyone who had been 12 and older at the time of family treatment to consent for the release of records (assuming those minors at least 12 years old had been mature enough to participate intelligently in treatment).

When faced with questions about such a release, it is advisable to contact an attorney. There is little concern if the minors who had been involved in family therapy will authorize a release of records; getting their permission when you may not need it does no harm. But questions can quickly arise if a minor does not want to release records that their parents have agreed to release. It is not clear whether that minor has the authority to prevent the release in this situation.

Treatment summaries

In many cases, clients or others (such as the client's insurer) will request a copy of the client's record when they don't actually *need* the entire file. Whenever a client requests their file, or authorizes it to be released to a third party, it may be worth discussing the purpose of that release with the client. The client may actually be better served by your preparing and then providing a **treatment summary** instead.

---

[296] California Civil Code section 56.10
[297] California Health and Safety Code sections 123105(e) and 123110(a) define a parent or guardian as a "patient's representative" for Civil Code section 56.10(b)(7).
[298] California Civil Code section 56.11(c)

Treatment summaries must be available within 10 business days of the client's request, unless there is an exceptional circumstance that requires more time. One example would be a client who has been with the same therapist for many years, through many crises, and as a result has an extensive file running hundreds of pages in length. In those instances, the therapist needs to notify the client of the unusual circumstance, and then has up to 30 days to provide the summary.[299]

Refusing access

If you believe that your client would suffer negative consequences from seeing their treatment records, you can refuse their request to review their records. However, this rule comes with a number of additional requirements. If you do choose to refuse a client's request for records, you must (1) document within the client's record the date of their request and your reasons for refusing it, including the specific negative consequences you think would happen to the client if they were to see their records; (2) inform the client that you are refusing their request, and of their right to designate another mental health professional who could review the records on their behalf; and (3) make the records available to the licensed or registered mental health professional of the client's choosing.[300]

These same rules apply to treatment of a minor. If the therapist can document that doing so would likely be harmful to the minor or to the therapy process, they can refuse to do so. (The therapist must note the date of the request and the specific description of the negative consequences the therapist believes would occur for the minor if the records were released.[301]) If there is no such likely harm from releasing the records, the therapist must release them.

---

[299] California Health and Safety Code section 123130
[300] California Health and Safety Code section 123115(b)
[301] California Health and Safety Code section 123115(a) and (b)

Client corrections

If the client, upon reviewing their records, sees something they think is incorrect or incomplete, they have the right to submit a statement of up to 250 words that you must add to the client record.[302]

---

[302] California Health and Safety Code section 123111

▸ Responding to a subpoena

Courts and the attorneys who represent clients often request records of psychotherapy, or even request the therapist to appear in court, as part of a court case. Such a request is called a **subpoena**. (If you are not familiar with that term, it's pronounced suh-PEE-nuh.) At first, it may be difficult to tell whether the request has come from a judge or from a private attorney, but the source of the subpoena is important. If it comes from a judge, you typically *must* comply, as it has the power of a court order. If it comes from a private attorney, and you do not have your client's authorization to release records, it may actually be a *violation* of the law for you to turn over the records requested in the subpoena.

You essentially have three options when served with a subpoena:[303]

1. Assert privilege
2. Object to the subpoena
3. Comply with the request for records or court appearance

Unless you know that privilege has been waived or a judge has determined that privilege does not apply, asserting privilege is an appropriate default position for a therapist to take.[304] What you should *not* do is simply fail to respond to a subpoena. If you do not respond to a lawfully issued subpoena, you can be held in contempt of court, and fined or even jailed.

Objecting to the subpoena may be appropriate if there is something wrong with the subpoena itself or with how it was delivered. In most instances, a subpoena must be delivered to you in person. In many instances, it must come with supporting documentation. It may be useful to consult an attorney who can help determine whether it is appropriate to object to a subpoena.[305]

---

[303] Jensen, D. (2007 November/December). Diagnosing a subpoena for validity. *The Therapist.*
[304] California Evidence Code section 1015
[305] Jensen, D. (2007 November/December). Diagnosing a subpoena for validity. *The Therapist.*

When you receive any subpoena related to a client's therapy, it will be useful to consult with both your own attorney and the client (or the client's attorney or representative). The client or their attorney will determine whether to waive privilege when it comes to their treatment.

If the subpoena is valid and it either comes from a judge or your client agrees to waive privilege, your responsibility is to comply with the subpoena, by producing the requested records, appearing in court at the requested time, or both.

Room for debate: Anonymous clients

Technology is making therapy available to those who previously may not have been able or willing to come to a therapist's office. One of the largest platforms for online therapy, Talkspace, promises clients that they can remain anonymous – even from their own therapist.[306]

This raises a host of legal and ethical concerns. Without adequate basic information about the client, the therapist is not able to report suspected abuse or intervene in other dangers in any meaningful way. And of course, client anonymity makes it difficult to know where the client is – even whether they are within California.

At the same time, there are certainly clients who value the opportunity to present their problems to a therapist without having to give that therapist any other information about them. It can be easier to share your secrets when you feel like the person listening to you *can't* really know you.

Should clients have that option?

---

[306] From the Talkspace Frequently Asked Questions page at https://www.talkspace.com/online-therapy/faqs/ : "It's completely up to you whether or not you reveal your real name to anyone at any time."

Clients should not be anonymous

by Emma Jaegle, MS

Why would someone seeking the help of a therapist not want the therapist to know their name? Embarrassment for needing help is one possibility. Surely it is the reason why some people avoid therapy altogether. But research shows that it isn't the reason for very many. Providing those very few with a link to anonymous services is simply not worth the risk it creates with others.

Wanting to remain anonymous naturally insinuates that the client has something to hide. A client may have committed what they know to be a reportable act of child, elder, or dependent adult abuse. They may be an imminent danger to themselves or others. In such instances, one likely reason for wanting to be anonymous is to prevent therapists (and law enforcement) from being able to help them or their victims.

Online therapy portal Talkspace has struggled with this issue. They advertise to prospective clients that those clients can remain fully anonymous from their therapists, placing the therapists providing treatment through the platform in a very difficult position. One therapist told online magazine *The Verge* a particularly harrowing story about a client in need of immediate help – and the therapist's inability to get it to them.[307]

Most therapists would agree that an effective therapeutic process requires some openness and vulnerability on the part of the client. Both public protection and effective therapy are inhibited when the structure of therapy allows clients to remain anonymous. A client who wants to be anonymous in therapy is perhaps better thought of as a client who is not fully ready for therapy. The process requires both client and therapist to take on a level of responsibility that client anonymity actively undermines.

---

[307] Ferguson, C. (2016 December 19). Breakdown: Inside the messy world of anonymous therapy app Talkspace. *The Verge.* Available online at https://www.theverge.com/2016/12/19/14004442/talkspace-therapy-app-reviews-patient-safety-privacy-liability-online

Meet people where they are – including in the shadows

by Benjamin E. Caldwell, PsyD

California's regulations for online psychotherapy make the possibility of anonymous services a non-starter. As we will see in Chapter 9 (Technology), master's-level mental health professionals are required to obtain the client's *full name* and current location at every instance of telehealth services. Failure to gather that information can be considered unprofessional conduct.[308] Simply participating on a platform that allows client anonymity places the therapist at risk for action against their license or registration.

That's unfortunate. Many suicide hotlines and other crisis services provided by phone or text work well precisely *because* they do not require users to identify themselves. When we tell clients who would prefer to remain anonymous that we cannot work with them unless they first tell us exactly who and where they are, we are telling them not that we are *unable* to help them, but that we are *unwilling* to do so.

The concerns around crisis intervention that Emma cites are legitimate. Client anonymity does make it harder for us to get help to people in crisis. But this is not as dire a problem as it may seem. Offering anonymous services makes it *more* likely that someone in crisis will reach out to a therapist who can provide help – and who, quite often, will be able to convince the client to provide the information necessary to get that help to them.

It seems unlikely that clients who want anonymity are still coming to therapy, grudgingly providing their personal information. More likely is that they are not coming to therapy at all. So instead of getting help from a mental health professional, they get help from whatever untrained, unlicensed people are willing to help them – or from no one at all. Each person who makes that choice is a missed opportunity for therapists to do exactly the kind of work we train for.

---

[308] California Code of Regulations Title 16 section 1815.5(d)-(f)

6

Families and Children

Clinical work with families and children is inherently complex. In addition to the possibility that you will discover competing needs and expectations among various family members, you also may find that simply complying with state law around issues like consent for treatment becomes difficult.

Thankfully, state law is actually fairly forgiving of therapists who act in good faith to serve couples, families, and children who are in need of emotional support.

▶ Family Law

At the risk of taking some of the romance out of family life, the state of California doesn't much care how much you love your partner and, if you have any, your children. Family law focuses on the specific responsibilities you take on in various family roles, from birth through old age.

Marriage and domestic partnerships

I'm fairly recently married, so in my eyes, marriage is a wondrous and magical thing made of unicorns and fairy dust. As far as the state is concerned, it is a binding legal contract.

When couples marry in California, they contract with one another for "respect, fidelity, and support."[309] That "support" piece in the law doesn't refer to emotional support. It means that if your spouse needs your assets, you will spend those assets for your spouse's benefit.[310]

Any assets you owned prior to getting married are considered *separate property*, for which you maintain individual ownership. Any assets you or your spouse acquire while you are married are considered *community property*, meaning that each of you owns half of it.[311] You have a duty to your partner to manage those assets responsibly. (That half-ownership does not necessarily mean that all assets would be split 50/50 in a divorce; we'll cover that below.)

Laws around property and ownership in marriage are complex. For that reason, before they get married some couples will enter into a *premarital agreement* (sometimes referred to as a *prenuptial agreement*, or more simply as a *prenup*). That agreement clearly defines in writing what assets are to be considered separate property versus community property.

Married couples have inheritance rights, meaning that unless a person's written will specifies otherwise, upon death their spouse

---

[309] California Family Code section 720
[310] California Family Code section 4301
[311] California Family Code section 1100

inherits at least one half of their property.[312] Communications between married partners are considered privileged under the law, so spouses typically do not have to testify against one another in court.[313] Married couples can (but are not required to) file taxes jointly.[314]

When spouses injure each other, the injured spouse can sue the other for damages.[315] Spouses also can press charges against each other for marital rape.[316]

So, like I said. Unicorns and fairy dust.

In a handful of states, a couple may be recognized as *common-law married* even if they never sought out a marriage license or had a wedding. In the few states where this is recognized, the couple must meet specific criteria, such as living together for a certain length of time, and presenting themselves to the world as spouses. **California has no legal criteria or recognition for common-law marriage.** So except perhaps in the very rare instance where a couple becomes common-law married in a state that recognizes it, and then *moves* to California, *and then seeks a divorce,* the state does not legally recognize any couples as being common-law married. Even in that rare instance, there would be a lot of legal questions that courts would have to handle.

For several years before same-sex marriage was first legalized in California, the state recognized *domestic partnerships*. Even though same-sex couples can now legally marry across the country, **California is one of several states that have maintained their domestic partnership provisions.** A California domestic partnership consists of "two adults who have chosen to share one another's lives in an intimate and committed relationship of mutual caring," in the dry language of statute.[317] Domestic partnerships provide many, but not all, of the legal benefits and obligations that come with marriage.[318] For

---

[312] California Probate Code section 6401
[313] California Evidence Code section 970
[314] California Revenue and Taxation Code section 18521
[315] California Family Code section 781-782
[316] California Penal Code section 262
[317] California Family Code section 297
[318] *State* law treats domestic partnerships as essentially equal to marriage; see California Family Code section 297.5. However, *federal* law does not provide the same equivalency, so domestic partners do not receive the same treatment as married couples on federal issues, such as federal taxes.

example, domestic partners are treated as spouses under various public assistance programs, have inheritance rights if a partner dies, and are protected by community property laws. However, domestic partners are also responsible for each other's debts in the same way spouses are.

Couples wishing to make their relationship a domestic partnership simply file paperwork with the Secretary of State. Current law limits who can register. Both partners must be at least 18, unless a partner under 18 has requested and received a court order allowing them to enter into a domestic partnership. Neither partner can be currently married or in another domestic partnership. Same-sex couples of any age (within the limits just discussed) can register as domestic partners. For an opposite-sex couple to register, one partner must be at least 62 years old.[319]

Ending a marriage or domestic partnership

California is a "no-fault divorce" state, meaning that you do not need to show that your partner did something wrong in order to end a marriage. You simply need to report to the court that you and your spouse have "irreconcilable differences."[320] To get a divorce, at least one spouse must have lived in California for six months, and in the county where they are filing for divorce for at least three months.[321] The person filing for divorce must attend a court hearing. If there is an agreement in place for the division of assets, child custody, and other related issues, or if the non-filing spouse does not attend the court hearing, the divorce is considered uncontested.[322]

Once one spouse files for dissolution of a marriage, the other spouse is served with paperwork indicating that the first spouse intends to divorce them. A divorce *can* become final six months after the other spouse has been served with that paperwork, but it isn't automatic. The spouse who filed for divorce has to request a final

---

[319] California Family Code section 297
[320] California Family Code section 2310
[321] California Family Code section 2320
[322] Office of the Attorney General. *Ending your marriage.* Available online at https://oag.ca.gov/publications/womansrights/ch6#6_2

judgment from the court. The divorce is not final until that final judgment has been entered.[323] If a divorce is contested, the legal process can take years before it reaches final judgment.

Some couples can avoid the court process altogether by requesting "summary dissolution." In order to meet criteria for this process, they must have been married fewer than five years, have no children, have agreed on how their assets will be distributed, agree that neither will receive spousal support after the divorce, and meet a variety of other requirements.[324]

A couple can legally separate without getting a divorce. The two processes are largely similar in terms of the process, and just like a divorce decree, a decree of legal separation will address issues like child custody and distribution of assets.[325] Importantly, though, a legal separation does *not* actually end the marriage. Neither partner can marry anyone else. This can be important to couples who wish to end their relationship but believe that divorce is not an option, for religious or other reasons.

There is one other way to fully end a marriage, outside of divorce. It can be *declared void* by a court if for some reason it should not have been granted in the first place. For example, a marriage may be voided if one partner was underage, if the marriage is incestuous (one family member marrying another) or bigamous (one spouse was already actively married to someone else), or for a handful of other reasons.[326] These options are rarely used, and typically are applied very early in a marriage once the problem is discovered.

Ending a domestic partnership often requires court action similar to a divorce proceeding. Much like with summary dissolution of a marriage, some couples with no children, limited assets, and an agreement about division of assets can simply file a Notice of Termination of Domestic Partnership to end the legal recognition of their relationship.[327]

---

[323] California Family Code section 2338
[324] California Family Code sections 2400-2406
[325] California Family Code sections 2330-2348
[326] California Family Code sections 2200-2255
[327] California Family Code section 299

Child custody

When a couple with one or more children divorces, child custody is often the main driver of ongoing conflict between the couple. Therapists who have been approved by the relevant court can serve as child custody evaluators, but should keep in mind the risks associated with that role: **ethics codes keep the role of evaluator and treatment provider separate;** parents who lose custody proceedings may file complaints or lawsuits against any therapists involved in the evaluation process; and there is high likelihood that the court will request all records, so they should be in great condition.

Ultimately, child custody following a divorce typically falls into one of four categories:

- **Sole custody.** One parent has full authority to make decisions for the child, who is with that parent all (or almost all) of the time. The other parent may or may not have visitation rights, but does not have any authority to make legal decisions on behalf of the child.
- **Primary custody.** Some families have one parent who is with the children most of the time, while the other parent maintains some time in charge. An example would be when children spend the school year with one parent, and then go to live with the other parent for the summer each year. In these arrangements, the parent who is with the children at the time typically has legal decision-making authority for them, but that is not always the case.
- **Joint custody.** In this setup, also known as shared custody, both parents have legal authority to make decisions for the child. This usually requires good communication and coordination between parents. Actual physical custody may not be evenly split, especially if the children are in school and the parents live in different school districts.
- **Split custody.** In a split custody arrangement, one or more children go to one parent, while the other children go to the other parent. Typically, each parent has legal decision-making authority for only the children who live with them. Split custody arrangements are uncommon, as courts (and families too) typically want to keep siblings together when

possible. However, this is the preferred arrangement for some divorcing families, and courts may be reluctant to impose a different structure on a family than what the family says they want.

You may sometimes hear or read about "physical custody" as opposed to "legal custody." Physical custody simply refers to who the child lives with. Some caution is warranted here, because physical custody and legal custody are not always in sync. You cannot safely presume that a parent has legal decision-making authority just because the child is with that parent on that day.

Indeed, custody orders can sometimes be quite specific as to which parent has what kinds of authority and responsibility for which children at which times. Unfortunately, as a therapist, you cannot make assumptions about the specifics of a custody order simply based on the type of custody it sets forth. Some custody orders add specific requirements for the parents to collaborate on health care decisions. Even a parent who is in charge of their children most of the time does not always have complete and independent decision-making authority when it comes to mental health care.

In a few pages, we'll talk further about consent for treatment in divorced, separated, and never-married families.

Guardianship and adoption

There are a number of situations where parents may be temporarily or permanently unable to care for their children. In those instances, courts may step in to ensure that children's safety and legal rights are protected.

A *guardianship* is when someone other than the child's parent has been appointed by a court to care for the child. There are two kinds of guardianships: Those supervised by a Juvenile Court, and those supervised by a Probate Court. Juvenile Court guardianships are often used when a child has been removed from their home following an accusation of abuse or neglect, when the county has found evidence supporting that accusation.[328] Guardians in a Juvenile Court proceeding may be relatives, or they may be foster parents who have no relation to the child. In all Juvenile Court cases where children have been placed in the care of foster parents or other relatives, there will be a court hearing to review the case at least once every six months. The guardian is notified before the hearing, and can submit to the court any information they think will be helpful.[329]

The most common reason for Probate Court guardianship is when a child is living with an adult who is not their parent, and the parent needs the legal authority to make decisions (like health care decisions) on the child's behalf. For example, if a single parent is in the military and is deployed overseas, they might ask a court to turn care of their young child over to an older, adult sibling so that the child can remain in their home and school.

Once appointed by a court, a guardian (of either type) has legal authority and responsibility for the child. They can make medical decisions and are responsible for the child's behavior and well-being. However, the parents do *not* give up their parental rights. They can request reasonable contact with their child, and seek to have the guardianship be ended if they become able to care for the child. A guardianship can be supervised or ended by the court as the court sees fit.[330]

In other words, guardianship is designed to be temporary. **Adoption is the process where an adult or couple becomes responsible for a child who is not their own, on a permanent basis.** The relationship between an adopted child and their adoptive family is treated in law as being the same as a child's relationship to their birth family. Birth parents' rights are permanently ended. In an *open adoption*, an adopted child knows about the identities and backgrounds of their birth parents, and may even visit with them on

---

[328] It's important to note here that most accusations of abuse or neglect, even ones supported by evidence, do *not* result in children being removed from the home. We return to this issue in Chapter 7 on Abuse Reporting.

[329] Judicial Council of California (2000). *Caregivers and the Courts.* San Francisco: Author.

[330] Some information on guardianship and adoption here is drawn from the California Courts Guardianship page. www.courts.ca.gov/selfhelp-guardianship.htm

occasion. In a *closed adoption*, information about a child's birth parents is purposefully withheld from them. While there can be good reasons for either kind of adoption, fully closed adoptions have become somewhat controversial, as some adopted children have sought information about their birth parents, such as cancer history, that would be relevant to medical choices.

Conservatorship

One of the biggest challenges for elders and dependent adults, as well as their families, is managing their legal rights and responsibilities. While less intrusive methods are preferred whenever possible, elders and dependent adults who lack the ability to care for themselves or make sound decisions may have their legal rights scaled back by a court in a process known as conservatorship.[331]

In a conservatorship, a court appoints someone (the conservator) to care for the adult who is unable to care for themselves or manage their own money (the conservatee). California has two types of conservatorships: Probate conservatorships and Lanterman-Petris-Short (LPS) conservatorships.

Probate conservatorships are much more commonly used. In probate conservatorships, the conservator may be responsible for the conservatee (including their living arrangements, health care, and general well-being), the conservatee's finances (including paying bills, responsibly investing, and budgeting), or both, depending on the conservatee's needs. A spouse, relative, other interested party, or even the person needing conservatorship can file a request for conservatorship with the court.

LPS conservatorships are much less common. They are only used when an adult has a serious mental health problem that requires extensive care and the person is unable or unwilling to receive that care. A family member or caregiver cannot apply for this kind of conservatorship on their own; the process must be started by a local

---

[331] The information in this section is drawn from the California Courts Conservatorship page, which offers a wealth of additional resources for anyone considering asking the court to appoint a conservator for themselves or a loved one. www.courts.ca.gov/selfhelp-conservatorship.htm

government agency. These conservatorships only apply for one year, and only can be used when someone is gravely disabled due to mental illness.

In either instance, because a conservatorship by definition involves taking some of the adult's legal rights away, courts will prefer less-intrusive means of ensuring that the adult is properly cared for if at all possible. Someone who is initially unwilling to appropriately care for themselves may change their mind when faced with the possibility of being placed in conservatorship. For financial issues, courts may prefer that the client voluntarily set up a power of attorney arrangement, giving a trusted person control over financial decisions, rather than using the more-intrusive conservatorship route.

If you are working with a client under conservatorship, obtaining a copy of the court order appointing the conservator may help you determine what rights the client has and what rights the conservator has. For example, the order may clarify who has the ability to consent for mental health treatment on the client's behalf, and who can authorize a release of confidential information.[332]

---

[332] Kashing, S. (2015 Nov/Dec). What therapists need to know when working with conservatees and their conservators. *The Therapist, 27*(6), 59-62.

▸ Restrictions on work with minors

Providing psychotherapy to minors (individuals under age 18) is within the scope of practice of all the psychotherapy professions, including clinical social work, professional clinical counseling, and marriage and family therapy. However, there are two key restrictions in state law for working with minors.

Ban on sexual orientation change efforts

As you learned in Chapter 3 (Unprofessional Conduct), it can be considered general unprofessional conduct for a licensed or registered therapist to attempt to change a minor's sexual orientation through therapy. This law was very carefully worded so as to ban the therapies that seek such changes, without hindering conversations that therapists legitimately should be having with adolescent clients about their developing romantic relationships and sexual identities.

LPCC limitation on working with couples and families

Professional clinical counselors can work with minors. However, because working with minors necessarily involves working with families (see "Involving family members and others" later in this chapter), clinical counselors wishing to work with minors must be aware of the unique restrictions in their scope of practice related to assessing or treating families. These restrictions were reviewed in Chapter 1.

This law was not intended to ban typical, non-therapeutic contacts between an LPCC and the parents of a child the LPCC is working with in therapy. Such contacts to simply *inform* the parents of what is happening in treatment, or to handle termination and aftercare, would not qualify as assessing or treating the family.[333]

---

[333] California Code of Regulations section 1820.5(d)

▶ Consent for treatment

In most cases, if you are working with a minor, you will be doing so under consent from the minor's parent or guardian. If the minor has two parents with legal custody, typically, *either* parent may provide consent for the child's treatment.

When working with children whose parents are divorced or were never married, matters of consent become more complicated. Specific custody arrangements vary in how they handle children's health care decision-making. Some custody agreements allow either parent to provide consent, while others specify a particular parent as having authority over health and medical care. Getting a copy of the custody agreement can be considered a best practice. In cases where a parent is incapacitated or unavailable, consent becomes even more complex.

Fortunately, you are not required to get a DNA swab, a copy of the divorce decree, or other hard proof of guardian status from every person who claims to be able to provide consent for a child's mental health treatment. The law offers protection for clinicians who provide treatment under a good-faith belief that the person who claimed to be able to consent for a child's therapy is actually legally able to do so.[334] For the therapist to get this protection, the person who brings a minor in for therapy must be a relative (the term is broadly defined, and includes stepfamily, half-siblings, cousins, grandparents, and so forth), they must live in the same home as the child, and they must complete a "Caregiver's authorization affidavit."[335] It is important that the affidavit follow the very specific content and structure requirements defined in law.[336] If you have the person providing consent for the minor complete that affidavit, you are not required to do any investigation of the accuracy of the claims of the person claiming to be a caregiver, and are not liable if the person was lying.[337]

---

[334] California Family Code section 6550(c)
[335] I've provided a sample Caregiver's Authorization Affidavit for you at www.bencaldwell.com/extras/caregivers-authorization-affidavit.pdf
[336] California Family Code section 6552
[337] California Family Code section 6552

Minors consenting on their own

Any minor age 12 or older can independently consent for their own psychotherapy, as long as the therapist determines that the minor is mature enough to participate intelligently in therapy. In such cases, the minor is responsible for paying for therapy (the parents cannot be forced to pay for therapy for which they did not provide consent).[338]

When minors do consent for treatment on their own, it is important to remember that the therapist still must attempt to involve the parent or guardian unless the therapist can document why doing so would likely be detrimental (see "Involving family members" later in this chapter). It is also important to remember that parents do not have a right to access records for a minor seen under the minor's independent consent (see "Access to records" later in this chapter).

Emergencies

Parental consent is generally not required to treat a minor in life-threatening emergency situations, such as an immediate risk of serious physical harm to self or others.[339] However, this general rule comes with some meaningful cautions.

First of all, while there is some room in the law to provide emergency mental health care to a minor 12 or older in emergency situations (indeed, it even need not be an emergency, as you have read), it is not absolutely clear in the law when a child *under* 12 could be given emergency mental health treatment without parental consent. The law tends to defer to the judgment of professionals when acting on a good-faith belief that someone's life is in danger, and that

---

[338] California Health & Safety Code section 124260(d)

[339] California Business and Professions Code section 2395 exempts *physicians* from liability when acting in an emergency situation on patients of any age, though this law likely would not be considered to extend to master's-level mental health professionals. California Family Code section 6924 allows for the mental health treatment of minors 12 and older without parental consent in emergency situations by master's level professionals, with the cautions noted above.

would seem to reasonably include actively suicidal or homicidal clients. But if a minor under 12 is having some other kind of mental health emergency – a psychotic break, for example – and they do *not* appear to pose an immediate physical danger, it is less clear whether that minor could be given mental health treatment without parental consent under the emergency care rules.

In addition, the California Family Code statute that allows for emergency treatment of minors 12 and older without parental consent is written to apply to licensees and MFT and PCC associates only, and leaves out associate social workers and trainees from all three professions.[340] In any situation involving emergency treatment of a minor without parental consent, trainees and social work associates should proceed with caution.

However, if a minor client's life is on the line, it would be sensible to place a higher priority on protecting that life than on technical concerns about legal compliance. As long as you obtain consent to the degree possible, provide competent care to the best of your ability, and involve the parents and any other needed caregivers (and your supervisor, if you are not yet licensed) as quickly as possible, it would likely be challenging for a reasonable person to argue that you had made a mistake by intervening with a minor who presented immediate and life-threatening danger.

Parental disagreement

What happens when two parents each could consent for treatment, and one wants their child in therapy while the other does not? Recall that if parents are married, or if a custody agreement gives both parents the right to make health care decisions for their child, then you only need the consent of *one* parent to provide treatment. The other might object, but unless given this right in a custody order, cannot revoke consent that was provided by the other parent.

While of course such situations present a good time to consult with an attorney, they may primarily represent a need for clinical decision-making. It may be legal for you to continue to treat a child over the objections of a non-consenting parent. But will that treatment

---

[340] California Family Code section 6924

ultimately benefit the child, given the tension and conflict it is creating in the family? And do you want to be in the difficult position of treating a child against one parent's wishes?

▶ Involving family members and others

Working with any minor will mean doing at least some systemic conceptualization (that is, considering the family as a whole, and weighing the impact of other social systems). Children are greatly impacted by their family circumstances, and while their ability to change those circumstances grows with age, it often remains quite limited. Therapists may choose to involve family members, teachers, and other important people in a child's life in the therapy process.

When parents or guardians __must__ be involved

Even when a minor consents for treatment on their own, a minor's parent or guardian must be brought into the therapy unless there is clear reason not to do so. When a minor consents independently for therapy, as the therapist, you must document (1) whether and when you attempted to contact the parent or guardian, and (2) whether each attempted contact was successful or unsuccessful. Alternatively, you may decide it would not be appropriate to contact the parent or guardian. In this case, you must document he reason why.[341]

Notably, these rules do not mean parents must be contacted before commencing treatment. The law specifically suggests that therapists make a determination about whether and how the parents should be involved *after* consulting with the minor.

If a parent or guardian provided consent for treatment on a child's behalf, the level of involvement of the parents in ongoing treatment becomes a clinical decision. Unless there is a specific, documented reason not to involve the parents in therapy, it would be highly unusual for a therapist to work with a child without meeting with the parents at some point, typically early in the treatment

---

[341] California Health & Safety Code section 124260(c)

process. Failing to do so could be considered a violation of the standard of care, because the overwhelming majority of therapists would meet with the parents. How often the parents are met with and how much information is shared with them are up to the clinical judgment of the therapist, but typically a therapist would meet with the parents of younger children more often, and the parents of older children less often. Regardless of the child's age, parents should be included in treatment in some way unless there is good reason not to.

Involving other important adults

In assessing a child's behavior and their progress in therapy, it can be useful to discuss the minor and their treatment with other adults. For example, teachers can be very helpful in determining whether a minor's troubling behavior is limited to the home, or occurring at school as well.

In order to make contact with any other important adults in a child's life, and share information with them about the minor's treatment, you must have a signed Release of Information that allows you to disclose information that would normally be confidential. If the minor consented for therapy on their own, the minor must be the one to authorize this release. If a parent, guardian, or legal representative consented for the minor's treatment, that person must also be the one to sign the release.[342]

Minors hold their own privilege

Recall from our discussion in Chapter 4 that under California law, minors typically hold their own privilege.[343] However, minors generally cannot make legal decisions, so minors are only allowed to waive privilege in some instances. Ultimately, if a minor wishes to waive privilege, the decision will be up to a judge, who will weigh the minor's age and maturity among other factors.

---

[342] California Welfare and Institutions Code section 5328, California Civil Code sections 56.10 and 56.11
[343] California Welfare and Institutions Code section 317(f)

Room for debate: Following up

Under a law that took effect in 2016, California set up a pilot program for counties looking to bring their process of child abuse reporting online.[344] The pilot program was designed to be small, limiting the reports that can be submitted online to only some mandated reporters. Clinical social workers can participate, but professional clinical counselors and family therapists are not included.

One section of the law establishing the pilot program should be cause for concern. It requires that those submitting reports of suspected abuse online "shall, as soon as practically possible, cooperate with the agency on any requests for additional information if needed to investigate the report, subject to applicable confidentiality requirements."[345] For clinical social workers, this statement contradicts itself.

Mandated reporters have previously *not* typically been obligated to cooperate with requests for more information from investigators. Once we file our report, we have discharged our responsibility under the law. While we can clarify information already submitted, we do not gather additional information on the investigators' behalf. To do so would make us investigators, and change the nature of the therapist-client relationship. As such, the mandate for additional cooperation presented in this law could lead reporters to choose not to participate.

On the other hand, that last part – "subject to applicable confidentiality requirements" – might be enough to make reporters more comfortable with internet-based reporting. Those applicable requirements are arguably sufficient for an LCSW to politely decline any requests for additional information related to their report.

---

[344] Senate Bill 478 (Huff), 2015. Note that some counties have already been working on online reports of suspected child abuse; if your county allows reports to be filed online, that does not necessarily mean it is as part of this specific pilot program.
[345] California Penal Code section 11166.02(b)(1)

7

Abuse Reporting

Mental health professionals in California are mandated reporters of suspected child, elder, and dependent adult abuse. These laws place important limits on confidentiality, and place a high priority on the protection of vulnerable populations.

While such mandated-reporter laws are now common around the country, they were controversial when first put into place. And as we'll see, many practitioners remain frustrated by California's reporting laws to this day.

It's also notable that California law does *not* create an exception to confidentiality for most instances of intimate partner violence discussed in a therapist's office.[346] If the victim is a child, elder, or dependent adult, then this would be reportable as abuse. And as we will discuss, if children are present when IPV occurs, this too is often reported. However, in instances where neither of those applies, the therapist is required to keep their knowledge of the violence confidential, leaving IPV victims as a vulnerable population that our state law has chosen *not* to protect through mandated reporting.

---

[346] It is worth noting here that mental health practitioners have different rules than medical practitioners, who *are* expected to report to law enforcement any time they treat a patient for injuries that result from "assaultive or abusive conduct." See California Penal Code section 11160

▶ Key definitions

Knowing the specific meanings of the terms "child," "elder," and "dependent adult" is essential to appropriate abuse reporting. California's definitions of these terms may differ from those of other states. In fact, differences in abuse reporting standards are among the key reasons why many states (including California) have a state-based law and ethics exam on the pathway to licensure – the licensing board wants to make sure that you know *that specific state's* rules for reporting abuse.

Child

California law defines anyone under the age of 18 as a child for the purposes of abuse reporting.[347] If you are working with an 18-year-old who you believe has developmental delays or other issues that impact their functioning, you *could not* report the abuse of that client as child abuse – but you may want to examine whether they would qualify as a dependent adult under the law.

Elder

Under California law, an "elder" is anyone age 65 or older *residing in the state of California*.[348] That last part is important – a 67-year-old who lives out of state and is simply in California on vacation is *not* an elder under the law. If such a person were to suffer abuse while in the state, a therapist is *not* required to report that abuse. In fact, such a report could be considered a breach of confidentiality.

So what does it mean, exactly, to reside here? California tax law defines a resident as anyone in the state "for other than a temporary or transitory purpose." Those who live in California and are outside of the state temporarily are also considered residents for tax purposes.[349]

---

[347] California Penal Code section 11165
[348] California Welfare and Institutions Code section 15610.27
[349] California Revenue and Taxation Code section 17014; California Code of Regulations title 18 section 17014

Ultimately, determining residency can be a surprisingly complex factual question; if you have a client whose residency status you are not sure of, you may want to consult with an attorney.

Dependent Adult

Any California resident (the same residency requirement applies here as in the above definition of "elder") who is age 18-64 and cannot carry out their normal activities or protect their own rights because of physical or mental health issues is a "dependent adult" in the eyes of the state. This includes the physically or developmentally disabled, and those whose physical or mental abilities have diminished with age. It also includes anyone who has been admitted as an inpatient to a hospital or other 24-hour health care facility.[350]

It is important to note that a person does not need to have had their legal rights restricted (under conservatorship, for example) to be considered a dependent adult. By including those not able to carry out their typical activities of daily living, the definition is fairly broad. It is also common for people to fit the definition only temporarily, and then to recover from whatever condition had kept them from engaging in typical activities for an adult. One does not need to be permanently disabled to be a dependent adult.

Reasonable suspicion

Under state law, if you are a mental health professional and develop a "reasonable suspicion" that child, elder, or dependent adult abuse has taken place, it must be reported. Often therapists will ask what exactly "reasonable suspicion" means: Do you need to have seen physical evidence? Do you need to be absolutely sure?

The law defines reasonable suspicion of child abuse to mean that **it is objectively reasonable for a person to entertain a suspicion, based upon facts that could cause a reasonable person in a like position, to suspect abuse or neglect.**[351] The definition of reasonable suspicion for elder and dependent adult abuse is essentially

---

[350] California Welfare and Institutions Code section 15610.23
[351] California Penal Code section 11166(a)(1)

the same.[352] Reasonable suspicion does not require certainty that abuse or neglect has occurred, nor does it require a specific medical indication of abuse or neglect.[353]

This description answers both of the questions above, and also provides a clear avenue therapists can use to check and see whether their suspicion level meets the "reasonable suspicion" standard: Consult. Without revealing identifying information about the specific clients, **consulting with colleagues and supervisors you know and trust will help determine whether a report is appropriate.**

It is important to note that the law does not require therapists to take on the role of investigating potential child abuse. **You are not an investigator.** Reporting should be determined based on information gained in the normal process of therapy – you do not need to gather information you would not normally gather in order to determine whether a report should be made.[354] For more information on a possible recent exception to this, see the "Room for Debate" sidebar at the end of this chapter.

---

[352] California Welfare and Institutions Code section 15610.65
[353] California Penal Code section 11166(a)(1)
[354] *People v. Stockton Pregnancy Control Medical Clinic*, 203 Cal. App. 3d 225, 1988

▶ Reporting suspected child abuse

All mental health professionals in California are categorized as mandated reporters for known or suspected child abuse.[355] However, this only applies when you are acting in your professional capacity. When you are outside of your therapist role, you are not a mandated reporter. For example, you are not required by law to report a mother you observe physically abusing her child in a grocery store.[356] Of course, even when you are outside of your mandated-reporter role, you are still *allowed* to make a report of suspected child abuse – you just are not required to do so.[357]

What is reportable

The following types of suspected child abuse **must** be reported:

- **Physical abuse**
- **Sexual abuse**
- **Willful harm or endangerment**
- **Neglect**
- **Abuse in out-of-home care**

In addition, **emotional abuse operates under a permissive reporting standard**, which means that mandated reporters may report the emotional abuse of a child but are not required to do so by law.[358] Children witnessing domestic violence are often reported as victims of emotional abuse.

The following are brief descriptions of what qualifies as abuse under each category. More detailed descriptions can be found in a

---

[355] California Penal Code section 11165.7(a)(21)
[356] California Penal Code section 11166
[357] California Penal Code section 11166(g)
[358] California Penal Code section 11166.05

number of documents available online.[359] While this guide is focused on the legal, rather than the clinical, aspects of reporting child abuse, there are a number of good articles and textbooks on the clinical assessment and potential indicators of child abuse.[360]

Physical abuse

Physical abuse is defined in the law as any situation where any person **willfully causes an injury to a child** or engages in cruel or inhuman corporal punishment. In practice, it can be thought of like this: If a parent disciplines their child (physically strikes them) in a way that does not leave a bruise or injury, it is likely not abusive. If the punishment *does* leave an injury on the child, it is abusive.

There are a number of specific exceptions to the standards for physical abuse. Police officers operating in the normal scope of their duties are not considered to be abusing children when they use physical force to control a situation. Similarly, school employees are not considered abusive when they use physical force to control a disturbance or to remove weapons or other dangerous objects from a child's control.[361] Finally, children fighting by mutual consent (as in a common schoolyard fight) are not considered to be abusing each other.[362]

Sexual abuse

California law defines two types of child sexual abuse. "Sexual assault" includes incest, oral sex, anal sex (sodomy), sexual penetration, lewd and lascivious acts, child molestation, and *some forms of* statutory rape. Of these, oral and anal sex and object

---

[359] Though it isn't specifically tailored to California law, McCoy and Keen's *Child Abuse and Neglect* differentiates categories of abuse well.

[360] The U.S. Department of Health and Human Services' Child Welfare Information Gateway includes many resources on recognizing and responding to different kinds of abuse and neglect. Start with *Recognizing Child Abuse and Neglect: Signs and Symptoms*, which is a free factsheet.

[361] California Penal Code section 11165.4

[362] California Penal Code section 11165.6

penetration are fairly self-explanatory. Any penetration of the mouth or anal opening by the penis are considered oral or anal sex, even if they do not lead to orgasm.[363] Similarly, any penetration of the genitals or anal opening of another person using an object (including body parts) is considered to be abusive.

In addition to the kinds of behaviors that you would expect to be included in sexual assault (fondling, masturbating an another's presence, etc.) "lewd and lascivious acts" and "child molestation" broaden the scope of sexually abusive behavior to include such acts as videotaping children undressing, soliciting prostitution from a minor, flashing, and a variety of other behaviors.[364] Even when a child is willingly participating in these acts, they may still be reportable. (Lewd and lascivious acts are discussed in more detail below, under "Reporting consensual sexual activity.")

The other type of child sexual abuse is "sexual exploitation." It occurs when parents or other adults encourage a child to participate in sexually explicit acts, performances, or depictions. A caregiver is committing sexual exploitation if they allow such acts to take place, even if they do not play an active role in them.[365]

When adolescents of similar chronological and maturational age are engaging in heterosexual, vaginal intercourse, it may or may not qualify as sexual abuse under California's reporting laws. See "Reporting consensual sexual activity" on the next page.

Willful harm or endangerment

This category is not particularly defined in law. Any person causing a child **"unjustifiable physical pain or mental suffering,"** or any caregiver allowing it to happen, is committing this form of abuse.[366]

One way to think about this is that not all forms of pain and suffering involve the kinds of injuries that are captured in other categories of abuse. Adults who torture children with sleep deprivation, locking them in cages for long periods, and other similar

---

[363] California Penal Code section 11165.1(b)
[364] California Penal Code sections 288, 647.6, and 11165.1(a) and (b)
[365] California Penal Code section 11165.1(c)
[366] California Penal Code section 11165.3

tactics would arguably not be committing physical abuse, but their actions are certainly abusive – and reportable.

Neglect

A child is the victim of neglect if the person responsible for their welfare fails to provide adequate food, clothing, shelter, medical care, or supervision. Neglect is the only category of abuse that can occur by omission (the *failure* to do something). It is reportable even if it takes place by accident. It is also important to understand that a child need not have suffered actual harm before a report of neglect can be made.[367] So if a child is left locked in a car in the sun on a hot day, the simply fact that the child did not suffer ill effects would not prevent a report of neglect from being made.

The law allows parents to make "informed and appropriate" decisions regarding medical care on the child's behalf. These may include refusal of medical treatment or a choice to use spiritual treatment. These decisions on their own are not considered neglect.[368]

Abuse in out-of-home care

The law specifically lists abuse in out-of-home care (such as a day care) as its own category for reporting purposes. It is something of a catch-all category for **physical injury or death that occurs to minors in child-care or school settings.**[369]

Emotional abuse

If a child is suffering "serious emotional damage" or is at substantial risk of suffering such damage, a therapist is allowed to make a report of suspected child abuse. However, **the emotional abuse category is <u>not</u> a mandated report**. It is a *permissive* report,

---

[367] California Penal Code section 11165.2
[368] California Penal Code section 11165.2(b)
[369] California Penal Code section 11165.5

meaning that you can make a report, and are protected from lawsuits if you do. But there is no penalty for failing to report.[370]

The emotional abuse standard requires that there be some behavioral evidence of the emotional harm the child is suffering or at risk of suffering. This can include severe anxiety, depression, withdrawal, or aggression (including toward self).

Reporting consensual sexual activity

When specifically considering heterosexual, vaginal intercourse, it is important to bear in mind that behavior that is *illegal* is not necessarily *abusive*. When a 19-year-old engages in sexual intercourse with a 16-year-old, the 19-year-old is committing statutory rape.[371] However, this combination of ages does not qualify as child abuse under the law. The child abuse standards are specific in only including some categories of unlawful sexual intercourse as reportable:

Table 7.1: Is consensual sexual intercourse involving minors reportable?[372]

	Partner age			
Client age	Under 14	14-15	16-20	21 or over
Under 14	No*	**Yes - Report**	**Yes - Report**	**Yes - Report**
14-15	**Yes - Report**	No*	No*	**Yes - Report**
16-20	**Yes - Report**	No*	No*	No*
21 or over	**Yes - Report**	**Yes - Report**	No*	No*

* - In some instances, even when partners are of similar age their sexual activity can be considered coerced (and thus reportable). For example, if one partner was drunk, or if one partner was threatened or intimidated into the act, the sexual activity may be reportable even if the minor tells you they gave consent.

---

[370] California Penal Code section 11166.05
[371] California Penal Code section 261.5
[372] Adapted from *Understanding Confidentiality and Minor Consent in California*, which includes full legal referencing. Sources include California Penal Code sections 261, 261.5(d), and 11165.1

Other forms of sexual activity, including oral sex, anal sex, and object penetration for sexual purposes (including any part of the body other than a penis) are always considered child abuse under the law if a minor is involved.[373] However, this would appear to create different standards for reporting sexual activity of heterosexual adolescents as opposed to gay and lesbian adolescents. In April of 2013, the Department of Consumer Affairs (which oversees the BBS) issued a memo interpreting current law as allowing therapists to use their discretion in determining whether to report such acts if the acts were consensual and within acceptable age ranges as defined in the chart above.[374] Since this memo is simply one interpretation of the law, and the underlying statute is still in place, some attorneys are continuing to advise therapists that the safest route is to follow the statute.[375]

A different standard applies for "lewd and lascivious acts," which can involve flashing or other forms of activity geared toward sexual gratification that are not included in the categories above.[376] If a child is under age 14, lewd and lascivious acts are reportable regardless of the partner's age. If a child is 14 or 15, *and their partner is more than 10 years older than the child*, such acts are reportable. If a child is 16 or older, lewd and lascivious acts are not reportable as abuse.[377]

Sexting and other digital media

Under a 2015 change in state law, mandated reporters of child abuse must report any time they have reasonable suspicion that someone knowingly "downloads [...] streams, or otherwise accesses through any electronic or digital media" any images or videos that involve minors engaging in "an act of obscene sexual conduct."[378]

The aims of this bill were good. CANRA was written before the development of the Internet, and the legislature wanted to clarify that

---

[373] California Penal Code section 11165.1(b)
[374] Dobbs, D. R. (2013). Evaluation of CANRA reform proposal related to reporting of consensual sex between minors. Memo dated April 11, 2013.
[375] For example, Atkins, C. (2014 Jan/Feb). Reporting consensual sexual activity between minors: The confusion unraveled. *The Therapist, 26*(1), 79-82.
[376] California Penal Code section 288(a)
[377] California Penal Code section 11165.1(a)
[378] California Penal Code section 11165.1(c)(3)

digital distribution of child pornography qualifies as child abuse in the same way that print distribution of child pornography does. However, the bill's language has come to be seen by many as problematic. Minors who are voluntarily "sexting" each other pornographic images of themselves could be seen as committing child abuse based on this language. Even more troubling, those who *download* the images are considered to be abusers; in other words, both the sender and recipient of a sext can be considered to have committed a crime.

What if you're wrong?

The law is designed to encourage therapists to err on the side of reporting. From the perspective of protecting vulnerable children, it is better for the state to receive suspected child abuse reports that cannot be verified than it is for the state to *not* receive reports that *would* turn out to be verifiable.

A therapist is protected from any civil or criminal liability for making a good-faith report of suspected child abuse, even if investigators are unable to substantiate the report.[379]

Filing a report

Once you have developed reasonable suspicion that abuse has taken place, it must be reported to a local child welfare agency immediately. Such agencies include local police or sheriff's departments, the county welfare

> **Suspected child abuse must be reported by phone immediately.** This must be followed up with a written report within 36 hours.

department, or in some locations, the county's probation office. While your county will have specific procedures in regard to who ultimately investigates suspected child abuse, under the law you are allowed to make your report to any agency authorized to receive such reports.[380] They must take your report or immediately transfer your call to

---

[379] California Penal Code section 11172
[380] California Penal Code section 11165.9

someone who can, and it is then up to them to forward the report appropriately.

The phone report must be followed up with a written report within 36 hours. There are no exceptions to these timeframes for weekends or holidays. When making the initial phone report, be sure to ask where the written report is to be sent, and how they prefer to receive it (fax or mail). Most agencies will prefer to receive the report by fax, so that they will have it more immediately.

The written report form can be found online.[381] You should file the report even if you do not have all of the information it requests.[382]

Once you have filed the written report, if you keep a copy, it should be stored separately from the client record. Courts have determined that the report form can *only* be released to those specifically authorized by law to receive suspected child abuse reports, so releasing a copy to your client or a third party as part of the client's treatment record may actually violate the law.[383]

Penalties for failing to report

A therapist who fails to report known or reasonably suspected abuse can be sentenced to up to six months in jail, a $1,000 fine, or both.[384] The penalties are greater if the abuse results in death or severe injury.[385] Covering up a failure to report is considered a continuing offense until the time it is discovered, effectively meaning that a therapist can be punished for covering up a failure to report even if it is not discovered for many years.

Of greater concern than criminal penalties and lawsuits should be the human consequences of failing to report child abuse. Any time a mandated reporter knows of or reasonably suspects abuse and does nothing, that inaction enables the abuser to continue abusing children, while their victims go without protection or resources.

---

[381] http://oag.ca.gov/childabuse/forms (scroll to "Suspected Child Abuse Report Form")
[382] California Penal Code section 11167(a)
[383] Montgomery, A. (2015 May/June). Patient records under California law: The basics. *The Therapist, 27*(3), 47-51.
[384] California Penal Code section 11166(c)
[385] California Penal Code section 11166.01

Abuse that occurred out of state

Abuse that occurred out of state is still reportable. It should be reported to your *local* child welfare agency. It is then up to them to determine whether and how to forward the information to the place where the abuse happened.

Reporting when the abuser or victim has died

The law specifically requires reporting when the victim has died,[386] and does not make any exceptions to reporting for instances when the abuser has died. Even in these cases, there still is a compelling state interest in knowing about and investigating the abuse. There may be other victims in need of assistance, and there may have been others involved in committing the abuse.

Reporting when the abuser has moved away or no longer has access to children

These are two excuses I commonly hear therapists give for not reporting suspected child abuse. However, **the law does not make an exception for either of these**, and it makes sense that there would be no such exception. Abusers should not be able to escape responsibility for their actions simply by moving to a new place. Someone who does not have access to children now (for example, if they are incarcerated) may regain access to children in the future, and they still should be held responsible for any past abusive acts. In either instance, there may be additional victims of abuse who could benefit from resources being made available to them.

---

[386] California Penal Code section 11166.2

Reporting when the victim is now an adult

California law requires reporting when a therapist has knowledge of or witnesses *a child* who is the victim of suspected abuse. CAMFT has construed this to mean that therapists do not report when an adult client reveals they were abused as a child.[387] Of course, the victim can still be encouraged to report the abuse on their own to law enforcement.

---

[387] Tran-Lien, A. (2014 Jan/Feb). A look at the Child Abuse and Neglect Reporting Act. *The Therapist, 26*(1), 73-78.

▶ Reporting elder and dependent adult abuse

The reporting guidelines for elder and dependent adult abuse changed significantly in 2012. While the reportable categories of abuse stayed the same as they have been, the reporting process changed

> Recognized **types of abuse and rules for reporting differ** in important ways between child abuse and elder/dependent adult abuse.

significantly. Now, instead of a single rule for how quickly a report must be made and to whom it must be made, there are five different sets of standards, based on a number of factors surrounding the suspected abuse.

What is reportable

California law recognizes six types of elder or dependent adult abuse that, if reasonably suspected by a therapist, must be reported. As with children, it is also allowed, but not required, to report emotional abuse. Unlike the laws for children, mandated **reporters also have a permissive standard for reporting *any* other form of elder or dependent adult abuse not specified here**; they may make a report if they choose to, but they are not required to.[388]

Physical abuse

Physical abuse includes physical attacks (assault, battery, and the like), unreasonable physical restraint, and depriving a person of food or water. Various forms of sexual abuse are also included in the definition of physical abuse.[389]

One does not have to have been assaulted to have been physically abused, however. Physical restraints, chemical restraints,

---

[388] California Welfare and Institutions Code section 15630(c)(1)
[389] California Welfare and Institutions Code section 15610.63

and psychotropic drugs are all abusive if used for punishment or for any reason not authorized by a physician. This is one reason why you as a therapist do not need to see a physical injury in order to reasonably suspect abuse has taken place: Not all kinds of abuse, and even not all kinds of physical abuse, leave visible marks.

Abandonment

Caretakers for elder and dependent adults willingly take on responsibility for those adults' well-being. If a caretaker deserts their patient or gives up on their responsibilities when a reasonable person would not have done so, this is considered abandonment.[390]

Abduction

Under the abuse reporting statutes, for abduction to have occurred, the elder or dependent adult must have been *taken outside the state of California or prevented from returning* to the state, and they must not have the ability to consent to this.[391] If an elder or dependent adult is moved against their will within the state, this would not appear to qualify as abduction for the purposes of abuse reporting. However, it may fall within the definition of isolation.

Isolation

No elder or dependent adult should be needlessly kept from contact with their loved ones. Any attempts to prevent contact with outside individuals are considered isolation and are reportable as abuse. Examples in the law include preventing an elder or dependent adult from receiving their mail or telephone calls, telling callers or visitors that the person is not present or does not want to visit with them (when that isn't true), and physically restraining someone from seeing visitors.[392]

---

[390] California Welfare and Institutions Code section 15610.05
[391] California Welfare and Institutions Code section 15610.06
[392] California Welfare and Institutions Code section 15610.43

Financial abuse

Unlike minors, who rarely have significant financial resources of their own, elder and dependent adults are vulnerable to having their money or other resources taken. California law protects elders and dependent adults from such abuse. Note that financial abuse can occur even when the victim knowingly gave their money or property to another person, if that other person has an "unfair advantage" (that actually is language used in the law)[393] over the victim by virtue of their position of trust or authority or because of the victim's needs, distress, or weakness of mind.

As you can see, the law here is purposefully broad. Of course, elders and dependent adults still have control over their money and property, unless they have had their legal rights restricted for some reason. They can choose to give their money or possessions away. It is only financial abuse if the recipient took the gift "for wrongful use or with intent to defraud," or if they knew or should have known that taking the gift would be harmful to the elder or dependent adult.

Neglect

Neglect can be difficult to assess, particularly when the concern is that an elder is neglecting their own care. For this reason, the law defines neglect in some detail. There are four key areas: Hygiene, medical care, health and safety hazards, and malnutrition/dehydration.[394] Any person responsible for the care of an elder who is not ensuring that these four areas are being appropriately addressed can be reported for neglect.[395]

It is not only caregivers who may neglect an elder or dependent adult. Elder or dependent adults can be reported for neglecting themselves.[396] The intent of this law is not to punish those who are unable to adequately care for themselves, but rather to ensure that they are provided with a level of care appropriate to their needs.

---

[393] California Civil Code section 1575
[394] California Welfare and Institutions Code section 15610.57(b)
[395] California Welfare and Institutions Code section 15610.57(a)
[396] California Welfare and Institutions Code section 15610.57(a)(2)

Hearing directly from the victim

One key difference from the child abuse reporting standards occurs when an elder or dependent adult tells you directly that they are the victim of abuse. With a minor, you would use your professional judgment to determine whether you reasonably believe that report. With an elder or dependent adult, the law is specific that you *must* report any instance of abuse that an elder or dependent adult tells you about directly[397] – *even if you do not believe them* – unless *all three* of the following are true: (1) the client has been diagnosed with a mental illness or dementia (or is under a conservatorship for that reason), (2) you reasonably believe the abuse did not happen, and (3) you are aware of no evidence that would support the claim of abuse.[398]

Filing a report

Known or suspected instances of elder and dependent adult abuse *that occurred outside of a long-term care facility* must be reported by phone or Internet immediately, and in writing within two working days, to law enforcement or your local adult protective services agency.[399] If the initial report was filed by Internet, as is now possible in some counties, a separate written follow-up is not necessary.

For abuse that takes place *inside* a long-term care facility, how long you have to file the written report and who that report goes to will vary based on the circumstances of the case. In some cases, as many as three separate written reports must be filed within a specific timeframe. To see where these reports must go, and how long you have to file them, see "Decision tree for reporting elder and dependent adult abuse" on the next page.

As is the case with child abuse reports, any copy you keep of the written report should be stored separately from the client record. Courts have determined that the report form can *only* be released to those specifically authorized by law to receive suspected elder and dependent adult abuse reports, so releasing a copy to your client or a

---

[397] California Welfare and Institutions Code section 15630(b)(1)
[398] California Welfare and Institutions Code section 15630(b)(3)
[399] California Welfare and Institutions Code section 15630(b)(1)

third party as part of the client's treatment record may actually violate the law.[400]

Ombudspersons

If you are examining the reporting requirements for suspected abuse that occurs in long-term care, you may be wondering, *What exactly is an ombudsperson?* Each county has a long-term care ombudsperson, and there is a directory of them on the web site of the state's Department of Aging.[401]

Long-term care ombudspersons serve two purposes: (1) They receive and work to resolve complaints from individual long-term care residents, and (2) They work with the state Department of Aging and with other local and state officials to develop policies and practices that will best serve the larger long-term care population.[402] In both cases, ombudspersons exist to support and advocate for the interests of residents.

---

[400] Montgomery, A. (2015 May/June). Patient records under California law: The basics. *The Therapist, 27*(3), 47-51.

[401] www.aging.ca.gov/programs/LTCOP/Contacts/

[402] California Department of Aging: Long Term Care Ombudsman Program

Table 7.2: Decision tree for reporting suspected elder or dependent adult abuse

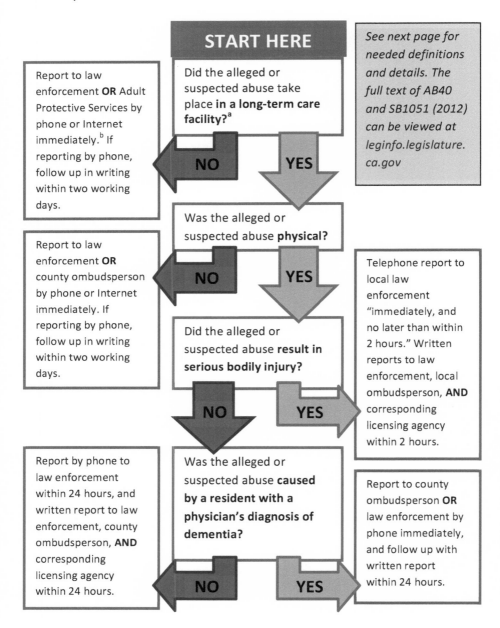

START HERE

See next page for needed definitions and details. The full text of AB40 and SB1051 (2012) can be viewed at leginfo.legislature.ca.gov

Did the alleged or suspected abuse take place **in a long-term care facility?**[a]

Report to law enforcement **OR** Adult Protective Services by phone or Internet immediately.[b] If reporting by phone, follow up in writing within two working days.

NO   **YES**

Was the alleged or suspected abuse **physical?**

Report to law enforcement **OR** county ombudsperson by phone or Internet immediately. If reporting by phone, follow up in writing within two working days.

NO   **YES**

Telephone report to local law enforcement "immediately, and no later than within 2 hours." Written reports to law enforcement, local ombudsperson, **AND** corresponding licensing agency within 2 hours.

Did the alleged or suspected abuse **result in serious bodily injury?**

NO   **YES**

Was the alleged or suspected abuse **caused by a resident with a physician's diagnosis of dementia?**

Report by phone to law enforcement within 24 hours, and written report to law enforcement, county ombudsperson, **AND** corresponding licensing agency within 24 hours.

Report to county ombudsperson **OR** law enforcement by phone immediately, and follow up with written report within 24 hours.

NO   **YES**

Definitions and clarifications

a – Other than a state mental hospital or state developmental center. If the suspected or alleged abuse occurred in a state mental hospital or a state developmental center, the report shall be made to designated investigators of the State Department of State Hospitals or the State Department of Developmental Services, or to the local law enforcement agency (Welfare & Institutions Code 15630(b)(1)(E)).

b – Unless otherwise specified, "immediately" means "immediately or as soon as practicably possible" (WIC 15630(b)(1) and (b)(1)(A)(iii)).

"Serious bodily injury" = "an injury involving extreme physical pain, substantial risk of death, or protracted loss or impairment of function of a bodily member, organ, or of mental faculty, or requiring medical intervention, including, but not limited to, hospitalization, surgery, or physical rehabilitation" (WIC 15610.67).

Elder abuse reporting form and instructions

www.dss.cahwnet.gov/Forms/English/SOC341.pdf

Find your local ombudsperson

www.aging.ca.gov/programs/LTCOP/Contacts/

Room for debate: Abuse and culture

by Emma Jaegle, MS

The United States is known for being a melting pot of cultures from all over the world. Different cultures have different standards for controlling the behavior of children. Some Latino matriarchs hit their children with sandals. Some Asian families force their children to study long hours, and verbally ridicule children when they do not perform up to standards. Many cultures follow a belief that children should be "seen and not heard," resulting in consequences for misbehavior such as being sent to bed early with no dinner. Are all children subjected to these parenting behaviors trauma victims? No. Many ultimately thank their parents for these efforts, and believe that children *should* be raised with some sense of fear in order to do well in life.

This illustrates the difficulty of even discussing culturally-bound parenting behaviors. If you support a culture's parenting, you see the later gratitude of children raised in that culture as illustrating that the parenting is not traumatic or otherwise problematic. But if you don't agree with a culture's parenting practice, you see the later gratitude of children raised in that culture as a symptom of the cycle of abuse, where the victim comes to believe that they "deserved it."

When a therapist hears of behaviors that qualify as abuse under state law, *even if those behaviors are culturally accepted parenting tactics*, the therapist needs to report those acts. When people from other cultures and countries make California their home, they are agreeing to follow California's laws. State law states that an act that willfully causes injury to a child is physical abuse. *It does not matter* whether that act is accepted within one's native culture. That may impact how a child protective service agency chooses to *respond* to an instance of abuse, but the client's cultural background should have *no impact whatsoever* on your decision to report or not report suspected abuse.

8

Business and Marketing

From an administrative perspective, a therapy business is just like any other business. It must operate in accordance with the law, and it needs to bring in enough money to survive.

Therapists often choose to begin work in private practice, or to take on leadership roles in clinics or group practices, without full understanding of what it means to run that kind of business. That's understandable! Our graduate degrees include very little business training. But there are risks when a therapist tries to run a business without a good sense of the rules. The mistakes therapists make in this area are often the result of simple naïvete, rather than a purposeful effort to disobey the law, but they still can have negative consequences.

This text is, of course, not a substitute for more meaningful business training. If you are considering forming your own business, I encourage you to consult with an attorney and an accountant. Here, I simply aim to give you a sense of some of your options and obligations.

Business structures

California law limits the contexts in which mental health services can be offered to the public. Most therapy practices will be organized in one of the following ways:[403]

Sole proprietorship

This is a common structure for individual private practices. It does not involve formal incorporation. The income from a sole proprietorship is typically taxed as personal income from self-employment. If you are planning to operate a sole proprietorship under your own name, you do not need to file documents with the state or county.

Partnership

Two or more therapists can get together to form a partnership. This also does not involve formal incorporation. While general partnerships are not required to register with the state, there is an optional process for filing a Statement of Partnership Authority. Partnerships typically use fictitious business names, which are discussed in more detail below. Partnerships do not appear to be especially common among therapists, perhaps because of how liability is organized; each partner can be held liable for damages caused by any other partner.

Corporation

A corporation is a legal entity separate from the people who own it. Corporations can raise capital and have shareholders. To form a corporation, you need to file articles of incorporation with the state,

---

[403] Much of the information here is drawn from the California Secretary of State's page on "Starting a Business: Entity Types." Visit the full page here: www.sos.ca.gov/business-programs/business-entities/starting-business/types/

and depending on the type and size of your business, you will need to follow up with regular corporate filings. While there are several different types of corporations, state law steers therapists toward what are called professional corporations.[404] Within that structure, the owners of a professional corporation can choose whether to designate it as an "S Corporation" for tax purposes. There are some advantages and limitations to that designation, making it again worthwhile to consult with an attorney and accountant.[405]

Nonprofit

Many agencies and clinics are set up as nonprofit organizations. A nonprofit is actually a type of corporation, and it must file articles of incorporation with the state. This structure is exempt from most taxes, but is also heavily regulated to ensure that those exemptions are not misused. The state and federal governments have their own *separate* processes of applying for tax exemption as a nonprofit organization.[406]

Other structures

Other, less common business structures are also sometimes used. Therapists are not restricted to *only* the types of businesses listed above, but there are some restrictions on the types of structures we can use. For example, a therapy business *cannot* be organized as a Limited Liability Corporation (LLC) or Limited Liability Partnership (LLP) in California.

---

[404] California Corporate Code section 13401(a)

[405] Tran, A. (2009 Mar/Apr). California professional corporations and the S Corporation. *The Therapist.*

[406] The California Franchise Tax Board has further information here: www.ftb.ca.gov/businesses/Exempt_organizations/California_Tax_Exempt_St atus_and_Federal_Exemption.shtml

Fictitious business names

Therapists can use fictitious business names to refer to their businesses. However, you cannot simply choose a name and start using it. You need to take steps to ensure that the name is not already in use. While the exact process varies by location, you typically need to apply for a fictitious business name with your county.[407] You may or may not also need to place an advertisement in a local newspaper announcing that you are planning to use the name, and providing information for anyone who wishes to challenge your use of the name.

Fictitious business names cannot be false or misleading. "Neighborhood Clinical Psychology Services" would be false if the therapists there were not Psychologists, and a therapist operating a solo practice should not use a business name that suggests a larger organization. Any client coming to a therapy practice that operates under a fictitious business name has to be informed of the owners' names and licensure status prior to the beginning of treatment.[408]

A business that wishes to obtain trademark protection for their name or logo can file an application with the United States Patent and Trademark Office.[409]

Additional licenses, permits, and documentation

Your professional license may not be the only paperwork you need to start a practice. Depending on where you are, your city or county may require you to obtain a **business permit**. (Nonprofit organizations may be exempted from permit requirements entirely, or may be exempted from fees but still required to get the permit.) Check the rules in the area where you are planning to set up shop.

---

[407] The process for Los Angeles County is described here: www.lacounty.gov/business/starting-a-business-in-the-county/filing-a-fictitious-business-name
[408] California Business and Professions Code section 4980.46
[409] www.uspto.gov

If you are planning to sell any physical products as part of your practice, such as guided visualization CDs, workbooks, or other goods, you need to obtain a **seller's permit** from the state. You also will need to collect sales tax on the physical goods you sell, and regularly report your sales (and pay the sales taxes you have collected) to the state.

If you are planning to work with insurance in any way, you will need to obtain a **National Provider Identifier** number. This is a quick and easy process that can be completed online.[410]

Employees

If your business is going to have employees, you need to obtain an **Employer Identification Number** from the federal government. This number helps the government keep track of tax payments and obligations. You can obtain an EIN online or over the phone in just a few minutes.[411]

You also need to file paperwork with the state of California for each new hire, and then regularly thereafter to report wages paid. State and federal labor laws can be complex, so you may want to use a payroll service provider to ensure you are correctly calculating wages, taxes, paid sick leave, and other obligations. For more information on labor and employment law, see Chapter 2.

---

[410] nppes.cms.hhs.gov/NPPES/Welcome.do
[411] www.irs.gov/businesses/small-businesses-self-employed/apply-for-an-employer-identification-number-ein-online

▸ Elements of marketing

Marketing a business involves all aspects of developing and promoting the products and services you sell. Choosing what services you want to offer, researching your local therapy market (to see where you should set up your office or how much others are charging), making choices such as whether to offer services online, and advertising are all components of marketing.

State and federal law offer guidance on some of these issues and not others. Fee setting is specifically addressed, as there are some ways of setting fees that would be legal violations. And advertising is covered in great detail, as discussed below.

▶ Fee setting

Recall from earlier discussion that clients need to be specifically informed of the therapist's fee and how the fee was computed before therapy begins. Ethically, you can set your fee at any amount that is not exploitive. As long as the process of setting fees is clear to clients (when you are using a sliding fee scale, for example), there is nothing illegal or unethical about charging two different clients different fees for the same service.

Therapists commonly set their fees by surveying the marketplace and evaluating their place in it. If other therapists who are similarly licensed and experienced, and work with similar clientele, charge an average of $120 an hour, a therapist new to the area might decide that the way to build their practice would be to come in a bit lower on price. On the other hand, a therapist who offers a specialization that isn't commonly found in the area, or evening and weekend appointments, may decide to charge more. There's no inherent problem with surveying other therapists' marketing materials, or even asking them directly, to get a sense of what your competitors charge.

Therapists sometimes get frustrated with low reimbursement rates from insurers, or with what they perceive as a flooded local market of therapists driving down how much they can charge. While this frustration can be understandable, one solution that they can't use is to band together for the purpose of setting fees.

Therapy practices are independent businesses. If therapists who are supposed to be competing with one another in the marketplace choose instead to all raise their fees to a certain level, this is no different from competing grocery stores all getting together and agreeing to sell milk for $100 a gallon. It's considered "anti-competitive behavior" (also known as "antitrust"), and can bring severe legal penalties.[412]

---

[412] Tran-Lien, A. (2012 Sept/Oct). Avoiding antitrust problems in practice. *The Therapist, 25*(5), 57-63. It's worth adding here that price-fixing isn't the only kind of anti-competitive behavior. Any time independent, competing businesses take collective action that artificially raises prices or keeps new competitors out of the market, they may be violating state or federal law.

If you want to charge more than other therapists who serve the same clients, find other ways to encourage clients to pay more to come see you. Highlight the unique aspects of your practice that clients may want to pay more to access. This way you are still competing in the marketplace – you're just winning the competition.

While we're on the topic of fee setting, one other note. Our discussion so far has focused on setting fees for clinical services, but these are not the only services you may be called upon to provide. You may be asked to check in by phone with clients between sessions; to consult with teachers, case managers, doctors, or others involved in client care; to testify in court; or to provide any number of additional non-clinical services on the client's behalf. You are allowed to charge for these services. Clarifying what non-clinical services you provide, and what you charge for those services, *at the beginning of treatment* makes it much easier to collect those fees when necessary. Some therapists also make a point of charging – with appropriate initial notice and consent, of course – extremely high fees for services that the therapist would prefer not to do.

▶ Advertising

The ability for therapists to advertise mental health services is good for everyone: It helps therapists build their preferred clientele (ultimately allowing them to make a living), helps prospective clients find the therapist who is the best fit for their needs, and helps raise broader public awareness about available mental health services. However, such advertising must protect and preserve the public trust placed in psychotherapists. This can be a challenging balance.

While California law can often be complex and highly specific, much of the law on advertising comes down to two simple ideas:

1. **Be truthful and honest in how you represent yourself to the public.**
2. **Include required disclosures, such as your licensure status, in all advertising.**

Much of this section focuses on the specific words and titles you are allowed or not allowed to use, and when their usage is appropriate. That's the letter of the law. California law is *also* written in such a way as to require adherence to its spirit. So you should not try to find ways to be *technically* compliant that would still violate either of the two principles above.

For example, if you are an Associate Clinical Social Worker, and you include this fact on your business cards in type so small that most people would need a magnifying glass to read it, you couldn't argue that you had followed the law when it comes to accurately disclosing your licensure status; your card could still be seen as misleading. The BBS defines any misrepresentation of *any* of the following to be unprofessional conduct:[413]

- The type of a license or registration held
- The status of a license or registration held
- Education
- Professional qualifications
- Professional affiliations

---

[413] California Business and Professions Code section 4982(f)

The term "misrepresentation" does not simply mean lying or making false statements. It would also apply to anything you produce that a reasonable person would find misleading.

The BBS gained what is commonly called cite-and-fine authority over advertising. While of course they could pursue an action against your license or registration if your advertising qualifies as false or misleading, that is a time-consuming and expensive process (see Chapter 3). It is much faster for the BBS to simply issue a cease-and-desist order and require you to pay a fine if they find your advertising to be problematic, and they can now do so.[414]

As you will see in this chapter, if your ads are truthful and honest, if they include your required disclosures in obvious places, and if you use good judgment in deciding what content to include in your ads, you should be in safe territory.

What qualifies as an advertisement

The definition of an advertisement in California law is very broad. Essentially, **any "public communication" about your services – in speech, in print, or in any other media, including the Internet – qualifies as an advertisement.** The only exceptions are signs posted in religious buildings and notices in bulletins mailed to religious congregations.[415]

The phrase "about your services" is important there. Just because you are a therapist does not mean that anything you say to anyone is an advertisement. However, it does mean that any time your professional role or professional services are mentioned in a venue that could lead someone to come to your practice, you are obligated to make sure the discussion of your services is truthful and accurate, and that you make the disclosures required in the law.

We will discuss several specific types of advertisements below. With all of them, the law does not specify how big the type has to be for your required disclosures, nor does it specify where those

---

[414] California Code of Regulations title 16 section 1811(e)
[415] California Business and Professions Code sections 4980.03(e), 4989.49, 4992.2, and 4999.12(j)

disclosures need to be (the front of a business card as opposed to the back, for example). However, the law specifically prohibits advertising that is misleading about one's licensure or registration status, and it stands to reason that **making your disclosures too small or too hard to find could be considered misleading**, even if you have included all of the required text.

Business cards

Business cards are among the most common tools therapists use to promote their practices, and to provide convenient contact information to colleagues and prospective clients alike. Because they are made to be widely distributed, business cards easily meet the definition of an advertisement if they include any mention of your professional role or services.

Flyers, postcards, and brochures

Printed materials like flyers, postcards, and brochures are commonly used to offer information about a therapist's practice, and all clearly fall within the definition of advertising. Even if you are simply planning to distribute a flyer for a new group to a limited audience of prospective group members, you are still likely to be considered to be advertising that group.

Therapist directories

Whether in print or online, therapist directories (such as those at GoodTherapy.org and PsychologyToday.com) qualify as advertisements. Some online directories may list you without any knowledge or action on your part, simply based on publicly available information. While it is not your job to police the Internet, if you do come across information about you that is inaccurate, you should attempt to correct it.

Email

Email occupies something of a gray area. A private message to individuals with whom you have a prior relationship seems unlikely to be considered "public communication." However, any email you send can be forwarded to people you do not know, so even private discussions of your practice should be approached with caution. Using email to promote your practice (through an e-newsletter, for example) would more clearly be public communication, and thus count as an ad.

Therapists who regularly include their title, or any mention of services offered, in their email signatures may be engaging in "public communication" under the definition in the law. It would seem safest to consider those signatures to be advertising and include all required disclosures.

CAMFT has noted a trend of prelicensed therapists using license titles or abbreviations in their email addresses.[416] This can be considered misleading and should be avoided. For example, if you are a registered associate MFT (or anything other than a licensed MFT), you should not use an email address that includes the initials MFT or LMFT. The same would apply to the abbreviations for counselors and social workers.

Web sites

If you advertise your practice through a web site, bear in mind that through search engines or even printouts of your site, someone may land on a specific page within your site without ever seeing your home page or a page with your biographical information. For this reason, therapists commonly **consider *each individual page* on a web site to be an advertisement.** They then include the required disclosures on each and every page of the site.

As is the case with choosing email addresses, you should choose your web domain name carefully to avoid misleading visitors. If you are not yet licensed, advertising your practice with a web domain like "JaneDoeMFT.com" or "JaneDoeClinicalCounselor.com" could be

---

[416] Tran-Lien, A. (2012 Mar/Apr). Ten advertising mistakes made by therapists. *The Therapist.*

considered misleading. Only include a professional title or abbreviation in your domain name if you are qualified to use that title or abbreviation.

Several requirements specific to counselors' use of web sites were added to the ACA Code of Ethics in 2014. These requirements include having links to relevant licensure and certification boards (in California, presumably that would mean including a link to the BBS web site at www.bbs.ca.gov), regularly ensuring that all the links on your site are working properly and are professionally appropriate, and providing accessibility to persons with disabilities. When feasible, counselors should also provide translation capacities for clients who speak a different language.[417] On the last point, web site translations can be fairly easily offered by including a service like Google Translate on your site; even the BBS itself does so. Of course, such translations are likely to be imperfect, a fact that you may want to ensure that your web site visitors know.

Blogs

Blog posts may or may not be considered advertising, depending on their content. A post that is informational in nature (for example, discussion of a recent scientific study that has been in the news) and makes no mention of your professional services seems unlikely to be considered an advertisement for those services. However, if you so much as suggest that you offer therapy services to the public – through your title, through mentioning that you see clients, or through any other means – you are advertising.

I struggled with this very issue in my own online writing. I maintain a blog on professional issues in psychotherapy at www.PsychotherapyNotes.com. Even though most posts do not mention my practice, I was reticent to take any chances. That's why each and every blog entry features my licensure information on the right-hand side of the page. That doesn't mean you have to do the same thing; it just means I chose to err on the side of caution.

---

[417] ACA Code of Ethics, subprinciples H.5.b through H.5.d

Social media

Social media cites certainly can qualify as advertising if you are publicly discussing your professional services on your page or profile. Posts on Facebook, LinkedIn, Instagram, Snapchat, and other social media sites and apps can function as ads, and if so, should include all of your legally required disclosures. This can be challenging to do in a manner that other users would be likely to see. As with other advertising, it is critical that anyone coming to you for services has been made aware of your licensure status and other required disclosures.

In addition to the new web site requirements noted above, a number of the additions to the ACA Code of Ethics in 2014 centered on counselors' use of social media. Even if you are not a counselor yourself, I would encourage you to review this portion of the ACA Code as a guide to best practices in this area, as it is particularly clear and well-written. Among other requirements, the ACA Code demands that counselors keep their personal and professional social media presences separated, that they explain their social media policies (including boundaries) in the informed consent process, that they respect the privacy of clients unless given specific consent to review clients' social media profiles, and that they not disclose any confidential information through social media.[418] These are surely good standards for any mental health professional to follow.

Tweets and Google ads

Twitter is a social media site that allows for "micro-blogging," or posting of messages that are 280 characters or less. Google ads (on their AdWords platform) run alongside search results, and are limited to a total of 95 characters plus a web address. As you can imagine, these limits often do not provide enough space to include both your legally-required disclosures and whatever meaningful content you had hoped to include.

You can advertise your practice on Twitter or through Google ads. You just need to use caution in doing so. The BBS

---

[418] ACA Code of Ethics, subprinciples H.6.a through H.6.d

reported in a board meeting that they had consulted with legal counsel on therapists' use of Twitter and their use of Google ads.

If the BBS were to receive a complaint about such advertising, they said they would consider the totality of the advertisement. In other words, if your tweet or Google ad *links* to your web site, they would consider the tweet and the site together.[419] As long as a potential client must have seen your legally mandated disclosures in at least one of those places, you should be safe. Another way to think of it is this: Do NOT include any direct contact information – like your phone number, email address, or office location – in a tweet, on your Twitter profile, or in a Google ad. If you do that, a potential client could come to you *just from the tweet or ad*, never having seen your required disclosures. Instead, make sure your Twitter profile, individual tweets, and Google ads ONLY include a link to a web site where you *do* meet all of California's advertising disclosure requirements.

---

[419] California Board of Behavioral Sciences: Minutes from the July 21, 2011 meeting of the Policy and Advocacy Committee (page 6)

▸ Who is allowed to advertise

Any licensed mental health professional can advertise their services. Associates are also specifically allowed to advertise,[420] though any advertisement of prelicensees' services must include additional disclosures (see "Advertisements for associates and trainees" later in this chapter).

Trainees cannot advertise on their own. However, it is common for the agencies and other workplaces where trainees work to advertise services provided by trainees. Such ads also require additional disclosures.

If you are working for an agency, group practice, or other organization, you should pay close attention to any ads that the organization produces that discuss you or your services. Even when you are not the person doing the advertising, you have a responsibility to ensure that any advertisements distributed on your behalf are not false or misleading. In other words, **you may be held responsible for any advertising that is *about* you, even if you yourself did not produce the ad.**

---

[420] California Code of Regulations title 16 section 1811(c)(d)(e)

▸ Professional titles

The law makes clear that mental health professionals must be up-front about their licensure status. **You must provide your licensure status in any advertising. Since April 1, 2013, this must be done by providing <u>all</u> of the following information:**

1. **Your specific license number** (for example, "LPC1234")
2. **Your full name, exactly as it is listed on your license**
3. **The fully spelled-out title of your license, or an acceptable abbreviation** (for example, "Licensed Professional Clinical Counselor" or "LPCC")[421]

References to your license should be specific to your profession. For example, you could not truthfully refer to yourself as a "licensed sex therapist," even if you were licensed as an LPCC and specializing in sex therapy, because there is not a sex therapist license in California. Similarly, there is no such thing as a "licensed associate" in California; associates are *registered*, not licensed.

Additional requirements for advertising the services of prelicensed persons are extremely specific (see "Advertisements for associates and trainees" later in this chapter).

Title protection

The mental health professions all enjoy what is commonly referred to as "title protection." Individuals cannot advertise themselves using the title of one of these professions unless they actually hold that license from the state of California. Even if an ad never uses the specific titles listed as protected here, it is illegal to use *any* titles, terms, or abbreviations that would lead a reasonable person to believe that an unlicensed person is actually licensed.[422]

---

[421] California Code of Regulations title 16 section 1811
[422] California Business and Professions Code sections 4980(b), 4999.82(c), and 4996(a)

Licensed Marriage and Family Therapists

The title "Marriage and Family Therapist" and the abbreviations "MFT" and "MFCC" are protected under state law. (MFTs were previously licensed as "marriage, family, and child counselors.") In addition, no one can advertise themselves as a "performing the services of a marriage, family, child, domestic, or marital consultant, or in any way use these or any similar titles" to imply that they perform marriage and family therapy without being licensed. Other licensed mental health professionals can say that they do marriage and family therapy, as long as such treatment is within their scope of practice.[423]

Licensed Professional Clinical Counselors

The titles "Licensed Professional Clinical Counselor," "Licensed Clinical Counselor," "Professional Clinical Counselor," and "LPCC" are all protected under the law.[424] The terms "counseling" and "counselor" by themselves are *not* specifically protected, and are sometimes used in other professions (including lawyers, career counselors, nutrition counselors, and so on). Other mental health professionals also sometimes refer to themselves as counselors, which is legal so long as they are not implying that they hold an LPCC license.

Licensed Clinical Social Workers

The title "Licensed Clinical Social Worker" is specifically protected under state law. As with the other professions, it is also illegal to use any other term or title that suggests you are an LCSW unless you hold that license.[425] Other mental health professions can do work of a psychosocial nature, but cannot present themselves with titles that include "psychosocial" or "Clinical Social Worker."[426]

---

[423] California Business and Professions Code section 4980(b)
[424] California Business and Professions Code section 4999.82(b)
[425] California Business and Professions Code section 4996(a)
[426] California Business and Professions Code section 4996.13

Abbreviations

State regulations currently require the use of both the license number and a license title or acceptable abbreviation in advertising. Below are the acronyms that are acceptable to distinguish different licensure types:[427]

LMFT or MFT: Licensed Marriage and Family Therapist.
LPCC: Licensed Professional Clinical Counselor.
LCSW: Licensed Clinical Social Worker.

Prelicensed therapists have additional requirements when they use acronyms in place of their full registration titles. For more on this, see "Advertisements for associates and trainees" later in this chapter.

It is also worth noting here that **neither law nor common practice allows for any abbreviation of the term "trainee" in any of the mental health professions.** I have occasionally seen (with great concern) MFT trainees using the abbreviation "MFTT" to denote their title. This would almost certainly be seen as an attempt to mislead regarding one's trainee status. If you are a trainee, always spell out the word when giving your title.

"Psychotherapy" and "psychotherapist"

Professionals licensed by the BBS can use the terms "psychotherapy" and "psychotherapist" in their advertisements provided that they have included all of the required information listed above (license number, full name as it is listed on your license, and your license title or an acceptable abbreviation).[428]

The regulations on this issue specifically apply to licensees, leaving the matter unclear for associates. However, MFT, PCC, and CSW associates are all defined as psychotherapists in other places in

---

[427] California Code of Regulations title 16 section 1811
[428] California Code of Regulations title 16 section 1811

the law.[429] So, some associates simply follow the same guidelines, also including all of the other legally required disclosures for their ads (see "Advertisements for associates and trainees" later in this chapter). However, you may wish to consult with your supervisor and an attorney before doing so.

You should avoid terms like "licensed psychotherapist," "licensed behavioral therapist," "licensed couple therapist," and so on. These terms could be considered false because there are no such licenses in California.

---

[429] As two examples, California Business and Professions Code section 728(c)(1) and California Evidence Code section 1010 both include associates in their definitions of the term "psychotherapist." However, these definitions are clear in specifying that they only apply to their sections of law, so it may be inappropriate to interpret them as having any meaning relevant to advertising rules.

▶ Professional qualifications

In addition to the required information about licensure status, therapists often include additional information in their ads to show prospective clients that they are well qualified to provide particular types of treatment. **None of this information is required to be in an advertisement,** but the law and some professional ethical codes encourage informing clients as fully as possible about your education, training, and experience. Prospective clients often find it helpful in making informed choices about whom to call. When information about professional qualifications is included in ads, the law does include requirements that the information be truthful and relevant.

Degrees

Legally, **you can advertise any earned degree from an accredited or approved university so long as it is relevant to the discipline in which you are working**. If you have a master's degree in counseling and a PhD in physics, you could not advertise your counseling services using "PhD" after your name.

The law does not specify where it is or is not acceptable to include the word "doctor" or the abbreviation "Dr." It should go without saying that any such usage that creates a mistaken belief that you are trained or licensed as a medical doctor would be illegal. If you have a doctorate degree relevant to your practice, however, the rules are less clear. While I am not an attorney, it would seem far safer to advertise the specific degree type (by putting "Ph.D." after your name, for example) than to use "doctor" in any context where it might be misunderstood.

Some therapists in doctoral degree programs use the initials "ABD" to indicate that they have completed coursework requirements for the doctorate degree. ("ABD" stands for "All But Dissertation.") Since this is not a formal license or degree status, it is better not to include this in any advertising. Similarly, some therapists will use the term "candidate" to note that they are progressing toward a particular degree. Many universities do have formal processes for advancing a student to candidacy. However, a consumer may not understand this designation, so it too presents some risk.

Specializations

State law does not specifically mention the advertising of specializations. However, professional codes of ethics prohibit a therapist from working in or advertising an area of specialization unless the therapist has appropriate training, education, experience, or combination thereof, to ensure competency in the specialization.[430] It could be considered misleading to advertise a specialization in an area where you have an interest but no additional training or experience to speak of.

When advertising a specialization, you also should bear in mind that such an advertisement may obligate you to a higher standard of care while working in that area; clients could reasonably expect that your skills and services within that specialization would be comparable to other therapists *who share that specialization*, and not simply other therapists in general.[431]

Certifications

Many private organizations offer certifications in specific areas of training. These certifications are not regulated by the state, and no outside certification is necessary to practice in any area that is within your legal scope of practice. However, as with other qualifications you hold, you cannot advertise yourself as certified in a particular area of practice unless you actually hold that certification.

It is also important to bear in mind that being "certified" to perform a particular type of treatment is not the same as having a continuing education (CE) *certificate* from a particular training. In other words, going to a two-hour training on motivational interviewing, and receiving a certificate for the CE hours, does not mean you can list yourself as "certified" in the motivational interviewing approach. (You can, of course, truthfully say you have attended the training.)

---

[430] AAMFT Code of Ethics subprinciple 9.7; ACA Code of Ethics subprinciple C.2.b; NASW Code of Ethics subprinciple 1.04(b)
[431] Pelchat, Z. (2001 May/June). The standard of care: Definitions and examples. *The Therapist*.

Association membership

If it is true, it is legal to include in an advertisement that you are a member of your professional association. Be warned, however, that some associations specifically require in their ethics codes that any advertising mentioning your membership also clearly indicate what type of member you are (student member, associate member, or clinical member, for example).[432] In addition, presenting the initials of your association after your name as if it were an academic degree or a license (for example, "John Doe, LPCC, *ACA*") could be considered misleading.

---

[432] ACA Code of Ethics subrinciple C.4.f; CAMFT Code of Ethics subprinciple 10.9

▸ Advertising content

The state laws that apply to all business advertising also apply to therapists. You cannot produce ads that are fraudulent, that make false claims about you or your competitors, and so on. There are some additional laws that apply more specifically to ads by or for health care professionals, including psychotherapists.

Claims of effectiveness

As a general rule, you should avoid making any claims in advertising psychotherapy that could be construed as a guarantee (for example, "feeling depressed? Therapy will help!"). Even the best therapies do not *always* work. Even if you are not intending to lie or mislead, the law prohibits any claim that "is likely to create false or unjustified expectations of favorable results."[433] This is why it is common for therapists' ads to use language noting that their therapy "can be" or "could be" an effective way to resolve a particular problem, not that it "will be."

If you make specific claims of effectiveness for a method or technique you use (for example, if you say that your method has been shown to work in 4 out of 5 cases), you must be able to back up those claims with published, peer-reviewed studies of the method or technique.[434]

Fees

Informed consent requires that clients must be informed of the fee and how it was computed prior to the beginning of services.[435] While ads do not need to include fee information, many therapists choose to include this information in their advertising. This must be done with caution, however, especially if you operate on a sliding fee scale. **The law requires that advertisements including prices be**

---

[433] California Business and Professions Code section 651(b)(3)(A)
[434] California Business and Professions Code section 651(b)(7)
[435] California Code of Regulations title 16 section 1881(j)

exact. The law does not allow ads to include terms like "as low as," "and up," "lowest prices," or anything similar.[436] Therapists or agencies working on sliding fee scales should be cautious to avoid misleading all prospective clients into believing they will get the lowest fee.

Testimonials

California law prohibits advertisements from including any testimonials that are likely to create false expectations in the eyes of consumers.[437] Professional codes of ethics go farther than this, specifically declaring it unethical for mental health professionals to solicit testimonials of any kind from their clients.[438] While a professional code of ethics does not carry the same weight as state law, it is a reference point that the BBS uses when seeking to determine whether a therapist has engaged in unprofessional conduct.

Questions surrounding testimonials have grown more complex in the age of Yelp, Angie's List, Health Grades, and similar web sites where clients may openly post about their experiences with particular therapists. While other types of businesspeople will sometimes respond to negative reviews on these sites, therapists rarely do so, out of concern for the client's confidentiality. Of course, in posting a review, a client may be telling the world that they have been in therapy with you – but that does not give the therapist permission to go online and discuss anything about the client's therapy.

---

[436] California Business and Professions Code section 651(c)
[437] California Business and Professions Code section 651(b)(8)
[438] ACA Code of Ethics subprinciple C.3.b; CAMFT Code of Ethics subprinciple 10.6; NASW Code of Ethics subprinciple 4.07(b)

▶ Advertisements for associates and trainees

As previously mentioned, associates are allowed to advertise their services if they include additional specific disclosures.[439] Trainees cannot advertise themselves, but their employers can place advertisements on the trainees' behalf.

Before we address the additional disclosure requirements for ads for the services of trainees and registrants, a common question:

Who pays for ads for associates?

For associates, the question often arises of who is expected to pay for advertising of their services. While the law disallows MFT and CSW associates from renting their own office space, buying their own furniture, buying equipment, or paying for any other "obligations of their employers," the law does not name advertising as an employer's expense.[440] As such, it seems that associates can pay for their own advertising. However, because the law is not specific, it is helpful to have a clear advance agreement with your supervisor that specifies who will be paying for what when it comes to marketing costs.

Associate advertising disclosures

Registered associates are specifically allowed to advertise under the law. Associates' ads must not be false, fraudulent, misleading, or otherwise deceptive.[441]

Any advertising by or on behalf of an associate must include all of the following:

---

[439] California Code of Regulations title 16 section 1811
[440] California Business and Professions Code sections 4980.43(i) and 4996.23(l)(3). There is no similar language for PCC associates, who are simply restricted from having a proprietary interest in the employer's business (section 4999.47(f)).
[441] California Business and Professions Code section 4992.3(q)

1. The associate's formal title or an acceptable abbreviation
2. The associate's registration number
3. The name of the associate's employer (or the agency where they volunteer)

Ads for PCC associates must specify that the associate is unlicensed and under supervision.[442] Similarly, ads for MFT associates must indicate that they are supervised by a licensed person.[443] In a private practice setting, the employer and the supervisor would be the same person, so providing their name and license number would meet the requirement to name the employer *and* the MFT and PCC requirement to indicate that they are under supervision. It would make sense to say something like "Employed and Supervised by" followed by the supervisor's name and license number. In an agency setting, the same associate may have multiple supervisors or there may be frequent supervisor turnover, so it is sufficient to provide the name of the employing agency (#3) and a simple statement that the associate is under licensed supervision.

Titles and abbreviations

The following are acceptable titles for associates to use: [444]

- **MFT:** "Registered Associate Marriage and Family Therapist" or "Registered Associate MFT"
- **PCC:** "Registered Associate Professional Clinical Counselor" or "Registered Associate PCC"
- **CSW:** "Registered Associate Clinical Social Worker" or "Registered Associate CSW"

Each of the professions also has an abbreviation that associates can use, but it comes with an important condition: To use the

---

[442] California Business and Professions Code section 4996.18(h)
[443] California Business and Professions Code section 4980.44(d)
[444] California Code of Regulations title 16 section 1811. As we noted back in chapter 1, technically these titles were in *pending* regulation at press time for the book. We expect them to be fully in force in March 2018.

abbreviation in an ad, that same ad also must include the *fully spelled out* version of the title without any shortening of *any* of the words. For example, associate MFTs can use the abbreviation "AMFT," but the abbreviation can never be used on its own. It can *only* appear in an advertisement that *also* includes the fully spelled-out title "Registered Associate Marriage and Family Therapist." The abbreviated title "Registered Associate MFT" does *not* meet the requirement here – if you want to call yourself an AMFT in an ad, you must also call yourself a "Registered Associate Marriage and Family Therapist."

PCC associates can *only* use "APCC" in an ad that *also* uses the full and exact title "Registered Associate Professional Clinical Counselor."

CSW associates can *only* use "ASW" (note that *isn't* "ACSW," out of concern that would create confusion with the Academy of Certified Social Workers) if they *also* use the fully spelled out title "Registered Associate Clinical Social Worker" in the same ad.

Ads for trainees

The laws surrounding advertising for the services of trainees are a bit less specific, for a couple of reasons. Trainees typically cannot advertise on their own; their services might be advertised by their employers, but the employers are more likely to be advertising specific *programs* than specific *therapists* who are completing trainee hours there. Note, however, that MFT trainees do have detailed guidelines, even when others are advertising on their behalf.

Any advertising by or on behalf of an MFT trainee must include all of the following:

1. The trainee's name
2. That the person is a Marriage and Family Therapist trainee
3. The name of the trainee's employer
4. That the trainee is supervised by a licensed person
5. The supervisor's license type or abbreviation, and license number[445]

---

[445] California Business and Professions Code section 4980.48(b) and (c)

Providing the name and license number of the supervisor would seem to meet the requirements of #4 as well as #5. The most important change from prior law is the inclusion of the employer's name, which was not required before 2012.

Clinical counselor trainees are required to inform clients prior to the beginning of treatment that they are unlicensed and under supervision.[446] Ads on behalf of clinical counselor trainees regularly include this information. As with the other professions, clinical counselor trainees cannot advertise on their own.

There are not advertising laws specific to clinical social work trainees, who cannot advertise their own services. Agencies and organizations advertising trainees' services typically do so cautiously.

---

[446] California Business and Professions Code section 4999.36(d)

▶ Networking groups

Some clinicians choose to participate in networking groups to help spread the word about their services. These groups typically aim to bring together businesspeople representing a wide variety of goods and services in a specific local area, for the purpose of exchanging referral information on potential customers.

The aims of these groups are very positive. If you know someone who needs a plumber, a dentist, a computer expert, or any other service, wouldn't you rather send them to someone you know than simply have them pick a name out of the phone book or a Google search? Networking groups often serve to build trust and community among those who work in the same area, and can do so very effectively.

These groups can also represent dangerous territory for therapists, however. Such groups may require that when you make or receive a referral within the group, information on the prospective customer be recorded by a group administrator who tracks referrals, raising confidentiality concerns. More worrisome are those groups that reward referrals or penalize group members who don't make a certain number of referrals to other group members each year. Recall from chapter 3 that state law specifically prohibits paying, accepting, or soliciting a fee for referrals.[447] Even if the reward for referrals within the group is simply avoidance of what would otherwise be a financial penalty, it could still be argued that you are, in essence, receiving a fee for referrals by not having to pay.

It may be helpful here to consider why the rules against fees for referrals exist. The idea is to make sure that clients can be fully confident our referrals are based solely on *what is best for them*, and not in any way on what is best for *us*. When we receive a direct personal benefit from referring a client out to another professional, it raises at least the *appearance* of a conflict of interests. That undermines the credibility not just of the individual therapist or that specific referral, but of *every* referral made by that therapist – and arguably, any referral made by *any* therapist.

---

[447] California Business and Professions Code sections 4982(o), 4992.3(p), and 4999.90(o)

Networking groups can be very useful if they allow you to get to know other local businesspeople, to make presentations about your services, and to exchange business cards and other marketing information about your practice. But if membership in such a group requires making a certain number of referrals each year, if you would receive payment (or avoid financial penalties) for making referrals to others within the group, or if referral information has to go through a group administrator, participating in such a group may not be worth the risk.

Room for debate: Testimonials

It can be difficult for prospective clients to find a therapist they trust. While therapists often go to great lengths to advertise their services, clients can still struggle to find meaningful information they can use to compare therapists, other than on obvious issues like fees and office locations. Because our work is confidential, a therapist who is ineffective may be able to make up for client dropout (as clients find the therapist to be ineffective and move on to another) with good marketing (to recruit replacements).

It is hard to blame clients for wanting to hear about others' personal experiences with the therapist they are considering. Such first-person reviews have become vital in the hotel and restaurant industries, and for a variety of other service and health care professions. Sites like Yelp, Health Grades, Angie's List, and more seek to provide clients with the experiences and recommendations of others who have used therapists in the past. It's word of mouth advertising, just online. And right now, it's prohibited by the codes of ethics of each major mental health professional association. Therapists are not allowed to solicit testimonials from clients.

Despite the bans, online reviews are growing. Therapists cannot respond to these reviews, even when they contain false or misleading information, without violating confidentiality. It presents a major problem for therapists who have suffered negative reviews online, especially when those reviews were posted by people who were never clients.

Should the bans on soliciting testimonials be reconsidered? And if so, should therapists be able to respond to online reviews without risking complaints for violations of confidentiality?

Protect clients from harms they can't foresee

by Emma Jaegle, MS

Of course therapists have to be accountable for their work. But clients posting reviews online may cause more harm than good for therapists and clients alike.

Any reviews posted by clients would be under the condition of volunteering, even if the ban on soliciting testimonials were to be lifted. There is the concept of *volunteer bias*, which means that people who volunteer data or contribute to studies have different personality characteristics, privileges, and lifestyles from those who do not (Dollinger & Leong, 1993). Another concern, already experienced by other industries more open to online reviews, is *negativity bias*. People tend to hold onto negative emotions longer than they do positive ones (Wu, 2013). Together, these issues mean that the reviews of a therapist are not likely to be representative of the therapist's work. Negative comments can seriously tarnish a therapist's reputation.

In addition, a client disclosing on the Internet that they have been in therapy can potentially harm them in the future. Potential employers or legal investigations can run searches and see that this person had a mental health issue at one point. Especially if the client's comment is negative, it could show that the person's mental health issue was unresolved.

Online reviews are great for rating consumer goods and services, where it is easy to objectively define good performance and value. But one client's experience may be completely irrelevant to how a therapist's theory of choice works with another person. Complicating things further, therapists who work with particularly challenging clients may be placing themselves at greater risk for negative online reviews. Clients diagnosed with personality disorders, mood regulation disorders, and other diagnoses may act out via these forums. A prospective client reading the reviews would not know the whole story or diagnosis.

We should be steering clients *away* from selecting a therapist through such questionable data, not toward it.

Lift the ban on soliciting testimonials

by Benjamin E. Caldwell, PsyD

Accountability is a major problem in the mental health professions. Many therapists never bother to truly measure the effectiveness of their work, leaving them overconfident in their skills and unaware of their deficits. It is little wonder that prospective clients don't trust us to be the sole sources of information about how great we are. They want to hear from others we have worked with.

I am in agreement with Emma that volunteer bias and negativity bias make online reviews of therapists inherently untrustworthy... as they are now. There is a solution to this problem, though, and it's allowing therapists to ask *more* clients to share their experiences online.

We've all had an experience at a hotel, restaurant, or store where employees were pushy in asking for reviews. If therapists started similarly begging, we would come off as tacky salespeople, and it would alter the power dynamic between therapist and client. But lifting the ban on solicitation of testimonials would not be likely to have this effect, for one key reason: The existing rules against abusing therapist power *would remain in place*. So *asking* for an online review could become acceptable, while *pressuring* for it or *demanding* it would still be prohibited.

Existing clients can (as they already do) make informed choices about when to value their confidentiality and when to value sharing their experience. Prospective clients clearly hunger for a broader range of information about therapists than just what we use to try to sell ourselves. Our policies should allow them access to the better, broader range of information that client testimonials could provide.

On those rare occasions when clients post reviews that include false or misleading information, therapists should be legally allowed to respond *minimally*, solely for the purpose of addressing the false or misleading information, without risking professional discipline. This too ensures that the information prospective clients see online is accurate and diverse.

9

Technology

If you utilize the telephone, Internet, or videoconferencing in the delivery of mental health services, you are engaging in what the state calls "telehealth." (Many practitioners are more familiar with the older term "telemedicine.") Telehealth involves the delivery of health care services through interactive audio, video, or data connections.[448] The term "delivery of services" is important – simply using the phone or email for routine administrative contacts, such as appointment scheduling, is not considered to be within the definition of telehealth.[449]

Telehealth offers a number of potential advantages to both consumers and therapists, particularly regarding access to care. Clients in rural areas or with specific language needs can access qualified providers via telehealth without having to drive for hours for each therapy session. Providers can expand their practices beyond their local communities, which is especially helpful if you serve a highly specific clientele or specialize in working with less-common problems.

However, telehealth also brings with it a number of potential problems. The therapist needs to be skilled in utilizing the technology,

---

[448] California Business and Professions Code section 2290.5
[449] Atkins, C. (2011 Nov/Dec). A 2011 recap of the 1996 Telemedicine Development Act. *The Therapist.*

and also must be prepared to address emergency situations for clients who may not be located in areas the therapist is familiar with. There are also concerns about privacy and confidentiality of client data.

In spite of these concerns, telehealth is increasingly practiced among mental health providers. In a 2015 survey, about half of CAMFT members said they provided at least some of their services via telehealth.[450] As we saw in Chapter 1 (Licensing), all three of the professions covered in this text are able to gather a portion of their hours of experience for licensure by providing services by phone or Internet.

While our focus in this text is California law, it is helpful to understand the federal laws and ethical rules governing telehealth to ensure that you are providing telehealth services in an appropriate manner if you are going to offer these services at all. In this chapter, we focus on California's rules, but also briefly review the requirements found in professional ethical codes and some of the rules found in federal law. As is the case with the rest of this book, the coverage here is not meant to be all-inclusive. You also should keep in mind that both technology and the rules surrounding its use can change quickly.

If you are interested in providing services via telehealth, you may want to become familiar with some of the businesses and professional organizations that specifically work in this area.[451] The American Telemedicine Association regularly publishes best-practice guidelines for telehealth practitioners in a variety of areas; their 2013 guidelines for video-based mental health care offer useful and highly specific guidance on security protocols, bandwidth, and much more.[452] The Online Therapy Institute trains exclusively in this area, and offers a number of certifications for online practitioners.[453] MyTherapyNet is an example of a platform that aims to provide secure and legally-

---

[450] Babayan, M. (2015 Sept/Oct). CAMFT's 2015 demographic survey: A snapshot of the "typical" California MFT. *The Therapist, 28*(5), 56-63.

[451] As is the case with all references to outside groups in this book, please do not take this paragraph as an endorsement of these organizations or as an indication that they endorse this book. These are just intended to give you a sense of the kinds of resources available if you want to learn more about telehealth. Of course, this is by no means an exhaustive list.

[452] www.americantelemed.org

[453] onlinetherapyinstitute.com

compliant videoconferencing connections between therapists and the clients they serve.[454] And SimplePractice is one of several companies specializing in handling therapists' scheduling, billing, and documentation in a secure manner.[455]

Ultimately, if you are interested in providing services via telehealth, there is no shortage of individuals and groups eager to train you for such practice, provide the platform for connecting, and assist you with the administrative elements. Just remember that the ultimate responsibility is on you to ensure that your practice stays current with all legal and ethical requirements.

---

[454] mytherapynet.com
[455] www.simplepractice.com

▶ Licensure stops at the state line

Your license or registration is issued by the state of California, and only allows you to practice with clients located within the state of California. **Providing services by phone or Internet to a client who is physically located in another state at the time of the service could be considered practicing in that other state without a license.** While prosecutions for interstate practice are rare, California has prosecuted a Colorado psychiatrist who prescribed medication to a California teenager through an online pharmacy, arguing successfully that the psychiatrist was practicing in California without a license.[456]

This is reinforced in ethical code language. CAMFT includes this in their Code of Ethics:

> 3.11 Electronic services. Marriage and family therapists provide services by Internet or other electronic media to patients located only in jurisdictions where the therapist may lawfully provide such services.[457]

The key word there is "located." As in, *the physical place where the client's body is at the time of service.* You could not argue that doing therapy across state lines is acceptable because the client is a California *resident* who is on vacation or away for work; if the client is outside of the state of California, you are subject to the licensing rules of the state they are physically in at the time of service.

The ethical code of the American Mental Health Counselors Association is similarly strict:

> 6 [...] a) Counselors only engage in distance counseling when they are licensed in the state of the client. In the case of an emergency, counselors should first attempt to attain permission from the client's state licensing entity and only proceed when failure to do so could result in harm to the client.[458]

---

[456] Local television news coverage: www.youtube.com/watch?v=aftPEFSHExQ
[457] CAMFT Code of Ethics, subprinciple 3.11
[458] AMHCA Code of Ethics, standard 6a

While the other professional codes of ethics are arguably less clear on this issue, it ultimately is a legal concern as well as an ethical one. Again, your scope of practice is set by state law, and only applies in the state where you are licensed.

Exceptions and carve-outs

Recognizing the growing mobility of Americans and the growing capacity of technology to serve as a vehicle for the delivery of health care services, a number of states have crafted laws and regulations about distance counseling. Most of these states have specifically noted that when the client is physically located in their state at the time of service, the therapy is considered to have occurred in that state, regardless of where the therapist is located. This simply reinforces that your licensure stops at the state line.

A handful of states have considered or taken different stances. Arizona, Colorado, Florida, and Wyoming provide short windows of time for online practice by out-of-state licensees, usually under specific conditions (like informing the client about the therapist's licensure). Kansas and New Jersey have such windows but require filings with the state first. Utah allows temporary practice by out-of-state licensees only when clients are actually moving to Utah.[459]

Most licensing boards do not allow practitioners to practice in their state, even for brief periods, if they don't have a license from that state. (California takes that stance.) State laws exist to protect those inside the state, and licensing boards are proceeding with caution given the likelihood that a therapist seeing a client in a different state will not be familiar with that state's rules for child abuse reporting, crisis intervention, and other important issues. In any case, the onus is on the therapist to determine whether practicing by phone or Internet with a client in another state is allowed there.

This calculus becomes more complicated when a client is outside of the country. Since many other countries do not have formal licensure for mental health professions (and among those that do, many only license Psychologists), you could argue that you *do* have the

---

[459] Tran-Lien, A. (2016 September/October). The practice of marriage and family therapy across state lines. *The Therapist, 28*(5), 65-76.

required qualifications to practice in a country where there are no required qualifications for your profession.

Clients in transition

In spite of the risks involved, some therapists do continue to meet with their clients via phone or other technology while the client is out of state. The argument these therapists often make is one of *continuity of care* – they worry that leaving a client without familiar and accessible mental health resources while they are travelling out of state could be seen as client abandonment. So therapists sometimes choose to keep seeing such clients, at least on a limited-term basis.

How much risk is involved in doing this depends in part on the nature of the services the therapist is providing. If a therapist is merely checking in on the progress of a client who has moved, and ensuring the client is getting connected with a therapist licensed in the client's new home state, that seems likely to be a low-risk proposition. Similarly, a therapist who checks in on a client vacationing out of state in order to make sure the client is maintaining medication compliance and not experiencing any worsening of symptoms is probably not taking a significant risk by doing so. When a therapist is *providing therapy* to out-of-state clients, the risk to the therapist is higher. This risk seems particularly high if the client has moved permanently and the therapist is making no effort to transition the client to resources closer to their new home.

We are an increasingly mobile society, and as the use of technology in the delivery of psychotherapy services becomes more common, the demand for licensure to operate on a national level (rather than state by state) is likely to continue to grow. Until a truly portable license can be achieved, though, the safest course of action appears to be to only see clients physically located in those places where you are authorized to provide services.

▶ Legal requirements when providing services by telehealth

Both state and federal law establish requirements surrounding therapists' use of technology. The California Telemedicine Act, the later California Telemedicine Advancement Act, and 2016 changes to California regulation have the most direct rules for working with patients, while other state laws address the use of technology in supervision. Federal laws (including the Health Insurance Portability and Accountability Act, or HIPAA, and the Health Information Technology for Economic and Clinical Health Act, or HITECH) also govern telehealth services provided by mental health clinicians. This text focuses on state law, so the discussion of HIPAA and HITECH here is only a very brief overview.

The California Telemedicine Act

As mentioned above, there are two primary pieces of state legislation that govern telemedicine in California: The California Telemedicine Act of 1996 and the California Telemedicine Advancement Act of 2011.[460]

The California Telemedicine Act and most related laws are not specific to psychotherapy, covering instead a wide scope of health care services. A 2003 law clarified that the state's telemedicine rules do apply to mental health practitioners.[461] While these laws focus largely on billing and payment, and are not the only telehealth rules in California law, the consent process is particularly important for therapists to know and follow when working in telehealth:

- Prior to any service delivery by telehealth, the client must be informed that telehealth services will be used
- The client must give verbal consent for telehealth services

---

[460] Senate Bill 1665 (1996) and Assembly Bill 415 (2011)
[461] Assembly Bill 116 (2003)

- The client's verbal consent must be written in the client's record[462]

Note that these requirements are above and beyond the standard requirements for informed consent for therapy, which were discussed in Chapter 5.

California telehealth regulations

In an effort to clarify the board's expectations for providers who offer services via telehealth, the BBS created regulations on telehealth services that took effect in 2016.[463] These regulations specify that anyone engaging in the practice of marriage and family therapy, professional clinical counseling, or clinical social work with a client physically located in California at the time of service needs to be licensed or registered with the BBS. (Trainees can provide telehealth services as well, this is just established separately in law.) This is important because it represents the state's effort to ensure that therapists in other states don't treat California-based clients without proper authorization *from the state of California.* This applies even if the therapist's licensing board in their home state says that the location of the therapist determines where therapy is seen as having taken place.

The new regulations further require that therapists do the following *in advance* of providing therapy via technology:

- Obtain informed consent for the use of telehealth (this is consistent with existing requirements as noted above)
- Inform the client of potential risks and limitations of telehealth treatment
- Provide the client with the therapist's license type and number
- Document efforts made to gather contact information for relevant resources (particularly crisis or emergency resources) local to the client

---

[462] California Business and Professions Code section 2290.5(b)
[463] The specific language of the new regulations can be reviewed here: www.bbs.ca.gov/pdf/regulation/2016/1815_00a.pdf

In addition, therapists under BBS jurisdiction must do the following *at the beginning of each session* using telehealth:

- Obtain and document the full name and current location of the client (i.e., the specific address)
- Assess whether the client is appropriate for telehealth services
- Use industry best practices to ensure client confidentiality and the security of the communication platform

On the last point, while it can be confusing for state law to refer to "industry best practices" that are not further defined, the important takeaway is that there is no exception built into the security requirement based on client consent. Even if a client is willing to use a less-secure platform for telehealth, their desire for convenience does not waive a therapist's responsibility to provide a secure connection.

HIPAA

HIPAA places a number of requirements on therapists who are governed by it. It is important to note, however, that not all therapists are required to follow the HIPAA rules. You are considered to be a "covered entity" if you transmit sensitive health information electronically for the purposes of billing, referrals, eligibility inquiries, or a number of other covered transactions.[464] If you are a part of a clinic or organization that is covered by HIPAA, you are obligated to follow the law, even if you personally do not transmit information electronically.

The rules put in place by HIPAA are quite complex, reflecting the law's effort to balance protecting the privacy of individuals with allowing the free flow of information needed for effective care and for analysis of providers. Thankfully, there are a number of excellent reference guides on the rules of HIPAA available to you. I particularly recommend the Heath Information Privacy section on the Department of Health and Human Services' web site.[465] I also found Lorna Hecker's

---

[464] Office of Civil Rights, U.S. Department of Health and Human Services: Summary of the HIPAA Privacy Rule
[465] http://www.hhs.gov/ocr/privacy/

book, *HIPAA Demystified: HIPAA Compliance for Mental Health Professionals* to be both highly informative and easily digestible.[466]

HHS breaks down HIPAA into three key rules for practitioners, and I've added a fourth to emphasize an important new component (numbers and emphasis added):

1. "The **HIPAA Privacy Rule**, which protects the privacy of individually identifiable health information;
2. The **HIPAA Security Rule**, which sets national standards for the security of electronic protected health information; and
3. The **confidentiality provisions of the Patient Safety Rule**, which protect identifiable information being used to analyze patient safety events and improve patient safety."[467]
4. The **Breach Notification Rule**, which requires providers to inform HHS of data security breaches and to inform those patients whose data has been breached.

The HIPAA Privacy Rule

The HIPAA Privacy Rule protects all identifiable information about a client, including common identifiers (like name and birthdate), information about the client's health care treatment, and information about their payment for services. Health information that has been de-identified – that is, all personally identifiable information has been removed – is not protected under the HIPAA Privacy Rule.[468] This allows for health care providers to give data sets to researchers for research purposes. Several recent studies comparing mental health professions' effectiveness in treating various problems have relied on large, de-identified data sets from health care organizations.

If you are part of a covered entity, you must protect your clients' information in accordance with HIPAA. Among your requirements are:

---

[466] Hecker, L. (2016). HIPAA Demystified: HIPAA Compliance for Mental Health Professionals. Crown Point, IN: Loger Press.

[467] Office of Civil Rights, U.S. Department of Health and Human Services: Health Information Privacy

[468] Office of Civil Rights, U.S. Department of Health and Human Services: Summary of the HIPAA Privacy Rule

- Developing and implementing privacy policies and procedures
- Designate a privacy official responsible for maintaining adherence to the policy and handling complaints
- Training all staff members on your privacy policy and procedures
- Formally disciplining staff members who violate the privacy policy
- Repairing any harmful effects of violations of the privacy policy
- Maintaining specific reasonable safeguards to protect against the release of private information
- Having procedures for clients to make formal complaints about violations of privacy
- Maintaining records of the privacy policy, all complaints, and related information for at least six years

These requirements apply even if you are an individual working in a private practice. You would still need to develop formal written policies for the protection of private information, and for clients to make complaints, along with all of the requirements listed earlier in this chapter and others spelled out in the law. While this may at first appear to be a significant burden, a therapist in private practice who is thoughtful in maintaining privacy is unlikely to need to handle complaints very often.

As of September 2013, therapists who are covered by HIPAA must ensure that any third party they use to store or transmit protected health information *also* follows the HIPAA requirements to which the therapist is bound. The safest companies for a HIPAA-covered therapist to work with are those who are willing to sign a HIPAA Business Associate Agreement, a document attesting that they meet (and, importantly, commit to continue to meet) legal requirements for data privacy and security. The Department of Health and Human Services has a great deal of information online about when these agreements are necessary and what responsibilities a therapist has relative to their business associates.[469]

---

[469] www.hhs.gov/ocr/privacy/hipaa/faq/smaller_providers_and_businesses offers a lengthy and helpful list of common questions and their answers, though note that it is relevant to smaller providers like a private practice or a

The HIPAA Security Rule

The Privacy Rule described above applies to client information in all forms, including in writing. In contrast, the HIPAA Security Rule applies specifically to client information that is created, received, transmitted, or maintained in *electronic* formats.[470]

The therapist or organization covered by HIPAA must respond to the Security Rule by:

- Ensuring the confidentiality, integrity, and availability (to appropriate persons) of all electronic health information
- Protecting against anticipated threats to the security of any electronic health information
- Protecting against anticipated improper uses or disclosures of electronic health information
- Ensuring compliance with this rule by all staff[471]

In another contrast with the Privacy Rule, the Security Rule acknowledges that there are meaningful differences between the protections that will need to be put in place by a large organization (like a hospital) and those that will need to be put in place by a single individual (like a therapist in private practice). In either case, given the rapid changes in technology, the provider must regularly review and update their practices to best protect the security of electronic health information.[472]

---

small clinic. Larger clinics, hospitals, and other larger practices are held to more stringent guidelines, since they are responsible for protecting more health information.

[470] Office of Civil Rights, U.S. Department of Health and Human Services: Summary of the HIPAA Security Rule

[471] Office of Civil Rights, U.S. Department of Health and Human Services: Summary of the HIPAA Security Rule

[472] Office of Civil Rights, U.S. Department of Health and Human Services: Summary of the HIPAA Security Rule

The Patient Safety Rule

While the rules generally move toward the protection of protected health information (PHI), the government also recognizes the importance of understanding the safety records of various health care facilities. For example, there is great value in knowing whether your risk of death from infection is higher at one hospital than another. In order to make that kind of a determination, patient records must be made available for research and analysis.

The Patient Safety Rule, added to HIPAA in 2009, establishes a voluntary system for the reporting and analysis of safety events. Most mental health providers will not be impacted by this rule. However, if you work for a large organization such as a hospital or large clinic, your organization may participate in the voluntary reporting system. Under the confidentiality provisions of the Patient Safety Rule, information used in the reporting and analysis of safety events is considered both confidential and privileged under federal law.[473]

The Breach Notification Rule

Under new rules taking effect in September 2013, all HIPAA-covered entities must monitor their systems for breaches of unsecured health information, and report such breaches to HHS as well as to the clients whose information was potentially impacted. Breaches do not have to be intentional; if your computer or cell phone contains unencrypted client information and is stolen, that may be a reportable breach, even if you have no way of knowing whether the protected data was actually accessed. Data breaches involving fewer than 500 clients are reported on an annual basis. Larger breaches have more immediate and complicated reporting requirements.[474]

---

[473] Office of Civil Rights, U.S. Department of Health and Human Services: Understanding Patient Safety Confidentiality
[474] American Psychological Association (2014). *Are you aware of HIPAA breach notification standards?* Available online at www.apapracticecentral.org/update/2014/10-23/hipaa-breach.aspx

HITECH

While HIPAA works largely to protect patients by *restricting* how health information can be shared electronically, HITECH is a law largely designed to *facilitate* the sharing of electronic health records. At least in theory, if more health care practitioners are using electronic medical records with consistent standards, it should be easier for practitioners to obtain necessary medical information about a patient's history. This is especially important in an emergency.

One way the HITECH act encourages the use of electronic health records is with financial rewards and punishments for physicians and other providers who accept federal funding through Medicare and Medicaid. For eligible providers, there were rewards for adopting electronic health records early, and punishments for those who were meaningfully using electronic health records as of 2015 (with increasing penalties in future years). **These provisions do *not* apply to mental health professionals, though the American Psychological Association has argued that they should.**[475]

One part of HITECH strengthens the enforcement provisions of HIPAA, increasing the criminal and civil penalties that can be applied when a health care provider or organization fails to appropriately protect electronic records. HITECH also strengthened the government's ability to enforce HIPAA requirements on the companies that create and store electronic health records.

---

[475] American Psychological Association (2012). *The HITECH Act and eligible professionals: FAQ for psychologists.* Available online at www.apapracticecentral.org/update/2012/07-30/hitech-act.aspx

▶ Ethical requirements when providing services by telehealth

While this book focuses on state law in California, it is worth noting here that the legal guidelines above are not the only standards to follow when providing services via electronic technology. The professional ethics codes of all three major mental health professions covered in this text have moved toward specific additional requirements for therapists providing services through such technology. The American Counseling Association's code is the most specific, though many of its requirements are effectively duplicated in the codes of the other associations.

The chart below outlines how each of the associations has tackled issues surrounding therapist use of technology. Bear in mind that the fact that something is not discussed specifically does not mean the therapist is free from that obligation. For example, the ACA Code of Ethics does not directly provide specific added guidelines for the electronic storage of client records, beyond that the therapist should follow the law and also should inform clients about the security and length of electronic record storage.[476] However, other parts of the ACA Code would suggest that a therapist would take precautions with electronic records that they may not take with paper records. Subprinciple B.6.b requires counselors to "ensure that records and documentation kept in any medium are kept in a secure location and that only authorized persons have access to them."[477] Ensuring security and limited access would logically seem to logically require more precautions for electronic records than paper records.

Note that the references to specific subprinciples in Table 9.1 are only the most *directly* applicable to that issue; other subprinciples within that association's Code of Ethics may apply, regardless of whether the task is listed by name in the code. All of the listed tasks are certainly good practices for all mental health professionals using technology.

---

[476] ACA Code of Ethics subprinciple H.5.a
[477] ACA Code of Ethics subprinciple B.6.b

Table 9.1: Ethical requirements linked to technology*

Therapist is required to...	Included in Association's Code of Ethics?[478]			
	AAMFT	CAMFT	ACA	NASW
...inform client of benefits and limitations of using technology	Yes 6.1(b)	Yes 1.4.2	Yes H.4.a	Yes 1.03g
...determine that technology-based services are appropriate to client needs and abilities	Yes 6.1(a)		Yes H.4.c	Yes 1.03g
...consider face-to-face services if technology-based services are ineffective			Yes H.4.d	
...provide reasonable access to computer applications			Yes H.4.e	
...ensure that all use of technology is in keeping with applicable law	Yes 6.1	Yes 3.11	Yes H.1.b	Yes 1.04e
...ensure that electronic communications with the client are appropriately secured	Yes 6.1(c)		Yes H.2.d	Yes 1.07m
...be appropriately trained in the use of the specific technology used to provide service	Yes 6.1(d), 6.6		Yes H.1.a	Yes 1.04d
...provide specific additional informed consent and disclosure (information needed varies by association)	Yes 6.2, 6.3	Yes 1.4.2	Yes H.2.a	Yes 1.03f
...provide an emergency process to follow if the therapist is not available		Yes 1.5.3	Yes H.2.a	
...adhere to additional standards for web sites and social media			Yes H.5, H.6	Yes 1.07f, g, h
...reasonably protect confidentiality of information transmitted electronically	Yes 2.7	Yes 2.3	Yes H.2.b	Yes 1.07m
...reasonably protect the security of records stored electronically	Yes 6.4		Yes H.5.a	Yes 1.07l

Notes: (1) Specific wording of the required tasks varies by association. (2) The absence of a "yes" in any particular box should NOT be interpreted to mean that the therapist does not need to do the listed task. Rather, it only means that the task is not specifically mandated in that ethics code. The task may be reasonably required by subprinciples in the code that do not mention the task by name. Additional standards apply in each code.

---

[478] See Appendix for links to each organization's full Codes of Ethics.

▸ Telehealth platforms

The scope of the legal and ethical requirements outlined above are enough to scare many mental health professionals away from providing services through telehealth. That's unfortunate. As technology continues to improve, more prospective clients will have ready access to the hardware and software they would need in order to work with you.

It's also true that hardware and software providers are rightly seeing commercial opportunities here. There are dozens of videoconference platforms that advertise themselves as being suitable for psychotherapy, some of which cost nothing to use. And most will provide you the Business Associate Agreement necessary for you to maintain HIPAA compliance when using such a platform.

Of course, clients often prefer the convenience and familiarity of using software they already own. This presents problems for therapists who seek to protect client privacy, even when the client isn't especially concerned about doing so. **Unlike confidentiality, the therapist's responsibility to protect the security and privacy of electronic communications is *not* one that a client can simply waive with a signature.** So while your client might be more than happy to use a non-secure video platform, that does not mean it would necessarily be a good idea for you to agree to it.

FaceTime

With so many therapists and clients owning iPhones, some therapists have started experimenting with doing sessions via Apple's FaceTime videoconferencing.[479] While Apple does not provide a Business Associate Agreement for use of FaceTime, there is an interesting legal argument that suggests it may still be safe for therapists to use.[480]

---

[479] The Apple, iPhone, and FaceTime product names are all registered trademarks of Apple.
[480] Taylor, J. (2015). Is FaceTime HIPAA compliant? Available at https://www.linkedin.com/pulse/facetime-hipaa-compliant-jon-taylor/

HIPAA contains a small exception, called the Conduit Exception, that was intended to protect companies like your cell phone provider and your internet service provider. In a technical sense, these companies *do* transmit protected health information on your behalf, which would bring them under HIPAA's authority.

However, these companies do not *store or maintain* any protected health information on your behalf. They merely carry it from one point to another. For this reason, they can be considered conduits, and not business associates, under HIPAA's definitions.

Since FaceTime provides end-to-end encryption, and creates a peer-to-peer connection (don't worry if you don't know the technical definitions of these terms), there is no way for Apple to decrypt the data going from one end of a FaceTime connection to the other. Even if they *wanted* to gather and store the content of your FaceTime calls, they couldn't. In this way, Apple appears to be a simple data conduit – and thus you would not need to get a BAA to use FaceTime for client sessions.

Bear in mind here that no particular *platform*, in and of itself, is HIPAA compliant. It is only *providers* like you and me who can be compliant or non-compliant. So a platform like FaceTime, which seems as though it could be used in a HIPAA-compliant manner, could still also be used in a *non*-compliant manner, depending on how you used it. The fact that it's a secure platform would not matter much if you were conducing sessions from a Starbucks, where other customers could see and hear the conversation.

▶ Communicating with clients

As discussed above, a phone call with a client for administrative purposes like scheduling the next session would not qualify as telehealth since you are not actually providing therapy services on that call. However, electronic data transmission and storage -- including storage of protected health information -- is now so common that it often happens without our taking conscious action to make it happen. This is important to consider when you weigh the best ways to keep in touch with your clients.

Email

Under HIPAA requirements that took effect in late 2013, therapists covered by HIPAA must inform their clients and get specific consent for communicating with clients via unsecured email. (As a general rule, your email is unsecured; a few secured-email providers have sprung up in recent years, but very few people use them, and you generally have to pay to use such a service.) This rule caused therapists some alarm, though it generally just means you need to acknowledge to your clients that there's risk inherent in sending messages this way.[481]

In my experience, clients tend to welcome a brief discussion of email security. They appreciate that I am thinking of their privacy, and it can be a helpful reminder to them to use privacy options like two-factor authentication. Clients also tend to appreciate when I include a notice of confidentiality at the bottom of my email signature and on fax cover sheets to further clarify the risks. Whether you are a HIPAA-covered entity or not, it is worth giving careful consideration to what kinds of information you will discuss over email, and making sure clients are aware of your email-related policies.

Consider what happens to email once it is sent. Depending on the software and service providers being used on both ends, there can

---

[481] This article offers a common-sense approach: www.personcenteredtech.com/2013/10/clients-have-the-right-to-receive-unencrypted-emails-under-hipaa/

easily be *six* copies of that email instantly created: one each on your computer, cell phone, and email provider's server, and one each on the recipient's computer, cell phone, and email provider's server. The more devices you or the recipient use to send and receive email, the more copies will be created. In addition, many of us (myself included) now use email providers that basically never require deleting old messages -- meaning that, if you discuss clinical information via email, there is the potential for protected health information to remain in your account forever, always susceptible to prying eyes of outsiders if your email account is hacked.

Texting

Texting can provide added convenience for therapists and clients alike. It can bring clients peace of mind to know that they can text you to let you know that they are running 10 minutes late for their session. Again, though, it is worth giving careful thought to what kind of information will ultimately be stored on your phone (and on the cloud, if you regularly back up your phone using a cloud-based service). Text messages are typically unsecured, which arguably goes against new ethical standards from AAMFT and ACA requiring reasonable security protections for all forms of electronic communication (see Table 9.1).

Perhaps more concerning, if a phone you have used to text with clients is lost or stolen, whoever is lucky enough to find it may be able to access a great deal of information about those you work with. Simple password protection does not qualify as encryption of this kind of data, meaning that even a password-protected phone may need to be reported as a data breach if it contains client information.

The intention here is not to scare you into thinking we should all go back to the time of telegrams or carrier pigeons. *No* form of communication is entirely secure. It is precisely because electronic communication is so easy to *not* think about that we have an added duty to think about it, to act as careful stewards of health information on our clients' behalf.

As is the case with email, if you plan to communicate with clients via text, it can be helpful to make sure clients are very clear on your policies for such communication and how you protect their information. Some have speculated that texting will be the focus of the next wave of HIPAA enforcement standards. Perhaps better, HHS could aid in the development of a secure standard for text messaging of health information.[482]

---

[482] Department of Health and Human Services (HHS) Text4Health Task Force (n.d.). *Health text messaging recommendations to the secretary.* Available online at www.hhs.gov/open/initiatives/mhealth/recommendations.html

Room for debate: Interstate practice

Having the states in charge of professional licensing *theoretically* allows each state to enact licensure requirements tailored to the needs of that state. In practice, though, differences between state licensure requirements are typically small. At the same time, therapists and clients have become more mobile, regularly moving or travelling to new states. And online practice continues to grow.

The time is surely coming when we will be able to practice across state lines. The question is simply how we will get there. At least three possibilities exist.

Interstate compacts are agreements between states to honor each other's laws or regulations. In counseling, four states have signed on to an interstate compact allowing counselors licensed in one of the states an easy pathway to licensure in each of the others.[483] The other professions could do the same.

National licensure is a possibility over the longer term. The Association of State and Provincial Psychology Boards has been working on PSYPACT, a multi-state agreement to facilitate psychology practice across state lines.[484] Psychologists would need to be licensed at the state level first, then could apply for a credential that would allow them to engage in interstate practice.

A court case leading to federal regulation. This actually strikes me as a meaningful possibility. If a therapist is prosecuted – as therapists inevitably will be – for practicing without a license because they engaged in online practice with a client in another state, the therapist could push back in court. They could argue that when a therapist is in one state and their client is in another, that is plainly *interstate commerce*, the regulation of which is expressly given to the federal government in the Constitution. State licensure would not go away, but a federal license would need to be created for interstate practice.

---

[483] www.psychotherapynotes.com/the-first-interstate-compact-for-counselor-license-reciprocity/
[484] www.asppb.net/?page=PSYPACT

10

Advocacy

Licensed mental health professionals are recognized and respected as being the community's experts on human functioning. While doctors are looked to for physical health and lawyers are looked to for knowledge of the rules of society, mental health professionals are rightly seen as uniquely educated and experienced in resolving interpersonal problems and reducing human suffering.

So why don't we have more impact on the law?

In short, **not enough of us are working to have that impact.** Policymakers are eager to hear from us and want to do what is best for the health of their constituents.

I realize that may arouse skepticism in some readers. When I started doing advocacy work, I certainly had that skepticism. But having now done advocacy work in some form or another for about 10 years, I can say with pleasant surprise that this has absolutely been my experience. In most cases, I only know state legislators' party affiliations from what I have read about them elsewhere; I have experienced every policymaker and staffer I have met as trying to do what is right for the people of their districts, regardless of party affiliation. They have a real and genuine hunger for facts and expertise, and often wish they had more of it from mental health professionals. Multiple surveys of legislators from various parts of the country back this up: Policymakers want to hear from us.

The failing is on our end.

Karen Bogenschneider has written a tremendous amount in the family studies field about how good research can be used to influence policy decisions, and why that doesn't happen nearly enough. She surveyed researchers who had been involved in carefully planned events with legislators and staff, where their research findings were heard and considered important. Most of the researchers, unfortunately, failed to follow up on these events, leaving the legislators and their staff hungry for a relationship that didn't exist and for additional facts they couldn't obtain.[485] Mental health professionals can have a greater impact on public policy by not just getting involved once, but actively maintaining relationships with policymakers. I'll review her findings more in the next section.

There are many good reasons to be involved in changing policies that don't work well for you, for your profession, or for the clients you serve. While it does happen, most mental health professionals do not get involved in advocacy purely out of self-interest. Instead, we generally respond to our ethical calling to service.

Ethical obligations

The mental health professions have long recognized that with our positions and our expertise comes a responsibility to act not just on behalf of our clients, but also on the larger communities we serve. This means maintaining awareness of the laws and policies that impact our clients, and working to change those policies that are not in the community's best interest as we see it. While our professional organizations may phrase this obligation differently, most of them include it. Organizations' requirements and encouragements for professional advocacy are quoted in Table 10.1 below. Simply put, you are expected to use your specialized knowledge and training to benefit the larger community. It is part of holding the title of a mental health professional.

---

[485] Friese, B., & Bogenschneider, K. (2009). The voice of experience: How social scientists communicate family research to policymakers. *Family Relations, 58*(2), 229-243.

Table 10.1: Professional associations' ethical standards supporting advocacy

Association	Code of Ethics Language[486]
AAMFT	**Preamble.** Marriage and family therapists are concerned with developing laws and regulations pertaining to marriage and family therapy that serve the public interest, and with altering such laws and regulations that are not in the public interest.
ACA	**A.7.a. Advocacy.** When appropriate, counselors advocate at individual, group, institutional, and societal levels to address potential barriers and obstacles that inhibit access and/or the growth and development of clients.
AMHCA	**F2. Advocate.** Mental health counselors may serve as advocates at the individual, institutional, and/or societal level in an effort to foster sociopolitical change that meets the needs of the client or the community.
CAMFT	**7.6 Developing Public Policy:** Marriage and family therapists are concerned with developing laws and regulations pertaining to marriage and family therapists that serve the public interest, and with altering such laws and regulations that are not in the public interest.
NASW	**6.04 Social and Political Action.** (a) Social workers should engage in social and political action that seeks to ensure that all people have equal access to the resources, employment, services, and opportunities they require to meet their basic human needs and to develop fully. Social workers should be aware of the impact of the political arena on practice and should advocate for changes in policy and legislation to improve social conditions to meet basic human needs and promote social justice.

---

[486] See Appendix for links to each organization's full Codes of Ethics.

Solving real problems

Though their underlying philosophies differ (see "Differences between professions" in Chapter 1), each of the mental health professions seeks to understand the rules that govern human behavior and relationships, and ultimately to have an impact on not just individuals but communities and cultures. It is this notion that tends to draw the therapists most passionate about advocacy work.

Consider, as an example, the statements of various professional organizations on same-sex marriage. While some therapists are understandably reluctant to wade into such a politically controversial area with their professional hat on, mental health researchers have produced a great deal of well-grounded scientific literature on the functioning of families with same-sex couples. We see in our therapy offices the real impacts of discrimination, in the stresses and symptoms of our clients. Who is better equipped than the mental health community to share with legislators the impact of societal oppression on same-sex couples and families, or to inform legislators of what we can safely say we know about the long-term impact of growing up with same-sex parents? If mental health professionals do not fill this information need with good, objective research findings, others will happily fill the information vacuum with pseudoscience or scare tactics. **When mental health professionals inform a debate, it does make a real difference:** When the Iowa Supreme Court ruled that a ban on same-sex marriage was unconstitutional,[487] they heavily cited the policies and findings noted in a brief filed by the American Psychological Association, detailing a number of studies that suggested same-sex couples and their children suffer needlessly from being unable to marry.[488]

This is, of course, simply an example. Your personal politics of course do not need to agree with those of your professional association, and many practitioners oppose same-sex marriage for

---

[487] The case was formally *Varnum v Brien*. The full ruling of the Iowa Supreme Court can be read here:
hosted.ap.org/specials/interactives/_documents/iowa040309.pdf
[488] The APA brief can be read here:
www.apa.org/about/offices/ogc/amicus/varnum.pdf

religious or other reasons. My point here is not to argue with such a viewpoint, but rather to stress the importance of therapists being involved in policy discussions. Even when that means therapists will be representing both sides of a debate, the policymakers involved will be making more fully-informed decisions than they might without the involvement of therapists.

► Why therapists struggle to influence policy

It seems most therapists are unaware of just how much the BBS and the state Legislature hunger for our opinions.

Most meetings of the California Board of Behavioral Sciences (our licensing board) and its committees are open to the public. These meetings are the breeding and testing ground for law and regulation ideas that can dramatically impact the mental health professions. The current legislation that (if adopted) will significantly change the requirements for supervisors, for example, was developed in a series of open board meetings around the state where representatives from universities, the profession, and community agencies all were able to speak about their needs and desires for changes in supervision standards.

For as important as these meetings are, and as welcoming as they are to the public, most professionals never go to a BBS meeting. They wait to be told what happened there by professional associations, whose representatives are quite often the *only* attendees in the room.

It is ironic, then, that professionals often lament that their research findings and clinical experience are ignored by policymakers. Since both policymakers and mental health professionals want the voice of professionals to be included in policymaking, why doesn't it happen?

In writing about the difficulty experienced by researchers in the field of family studies, Bogenschneider developed several recommendations to promote "a more active, reciprocal engagement" between policymakers and professionals.[489] Her findings are highly relevant to the work of mental health clinicians and researchers. She offers a total of 10 recommendations, paraphrased here:

---

[489] Friese, B., & Bogenschneider, K. (2009). The voice of experience: How social scientists communicate family research to policymakers. *Family Relations, 58*(2), 229-243.

1. Think of policy work as developing relationships, not just providing facts
2. Be willing to reach out to policymakers
3. Learn about the policymakers you are working with
4. Communicate information in ways policymakers will understand
5. When discussing vulnerable populations, use clear, specific language
6. Be familiar with the legislative process
7. Provide rapid responses to questions that arise in policy debates
8. Approach policy work as an information provider, not an advocate
9. Respect the wisdom and experience of policymakers
10. Exercise patience and flexibility

A brief comment on her eighth recommendation is important. Bogenschneider was primarily addressing researchers who would be interested in *informing* a policy debate, and not necessarily *taking a position* in that debate. In contrast, this chapter is quite purposefully about taking positions in policy arenas and moving ideas for change forward. However, these are not mutually exclusive. If you are approaching the advocacy process skillfully, you will arrive at policy debates well informed, and your primary investment should be that the problem you have identified gets solved – not a specific *way* that it gets solved. Policymakers and other stakeholders can and will argue about the best methods of solving a problem, and you can provide them with information to move that debate forward. Approach those discussions knowing that everyone involved is doing their best to serve their constituents, and you will be able to engage in a healthy, respectful debate. Even if your efforts are unsuccessful, you will have earned the respect of those on the other side of the issue, which will be helpful when working in the future on the same issue or on any other.

In fact, researchers in Bogenschneider's study pointed to three key rewards of being involved in policy work (paraphrased here), none of which involve being on the winning side of a policy argument:

1. They were able to have a meaningful impact on the community
2. They were able to see their research applied to real-world problems
3. They felt respected for the wisdom and expertise they brought to policy discussions

You can and should experience these same rewards. The policymaking community truly does want to hear from you.

▶ What it takes to be a successful advocate

In a moment, I will discuss the actual process of changing a law, regulation, or policy that you feel is not working as it should. First, a review of what makes for a successful advocate.

Information

Your expertise will be well respected in the policymaking community, especially when you can make specific recommendations backed up by clearly documented facts. The more you know about the issue at hand, the clearer your arguments will be, and the easier it will be to get stakeholders[490] and policymakers on your side.

Motivation

Passion for change is not a liability in policy work. It is an asset – as long as your passion is harnessed as motivation to inform and to act, rather than to attack. Depending on the issue, it may take months or years to see a change (more on that momentarily), but persistence and a good argument will often win out.

Allies

When you can identify a clear and real problem in policy, you may be surprised at how many existing groups and organizations will take an active interest. The BBS and professional associations are just two examples of groups that have the infrastructure in place to write new rules and lobby legislators; there are also mental health consumer

---

[490] I realize this is the first time I've used this term. In case you aren't familiar with it, in policy circles it tends to be broadly used to categorize all those individuals and organizations who have a "stake" in the outcome of a policy discussion.

groups, family member groups, labor organizations, and special interest groups that, like you, want to get involved when they see that they can have a positive impact.[491] Use what they have to offer! Your passion and information combined with their connections can make for a powerful and effective team.

Patience

Simply put, meaningful change takes time. The fields of family therapy and counseling have been lobbying for Medicare inclusion for almost 10 years now, and continue knocking on the door.[492] The BBS works on a cycle of quarterly meetings, and issues must be put on the agenda, heard in committee, and forwarded to the full Board before they even vote on it – a process that can easily take six months.

Similarly, the state Legislature operates on an annual cycle. Introducing an issue to a legislator in May might mean that even under the best of circumstances, where the legislator throws their full support behind your proposed solution and is willing to author a bill that would change the law as you recommended, that bill may not be formally proposed until early the next year. It could be as late as September of the next year before you knew whether your bill made it into law, and that's if your bill wasn't pushed back by a year.

The time lag can certainly be demotivating at first, but it has a couple of indirect benefits. One is that it allows for careful consideration of the specific language of a proposal, to ensure that it doesn't have unintended consequences. Another is that if you remain heavily involved in pushing your proposal forward, the long process of moving through committee hearings and the rest of the legislative process means that you typically don't need to take huge chunks of time out of your job or your private practice to move your idea

---

[491] For a list of common stakeholder groups in mental health law, see the Appendix at the end of this book.

[492] Each profession has gotten a bill through at least one house of Congress, but has not managed to get a Medicare inclusion bill through both houses of Congress at the same time. They are actively working together in Washington on this issue. If you are an MFT or PCC, your national association could use your help!

forward. In theory, that should make it easier for more of us to act on our ideas.

Courage

Therapists are notoriously conflict-averse. Indeed, many of us got into mental health work precisely because we experience interpersonal conflict as being especially burdensome, and want to help others to experience less of it. So it is understandable that therapists would shy away from situations where we are likely to be directly confronted on the weaknesses of our arguments, and actively opposed by people and groups who have a vested interest in the status quo. Advocacy requires that we not only not avoid conflict, but in some cases, *actively seek it out* in order to clarify opposition arguments and see whether there is any opportunity to work together with those who disagree with us.[493]

To be courageous, you first have to recognize that the situation requires that courage. In other words, there is something to fear in the conflict we are about to face. It is admittedly much easier to face that fear when you approach it from a position of greater power and privilege. When you stake out a public position on an issue that is controversial, people involved on the other side may not like you. They may seek to undermine your credibility. Advocacy work can be polarizing even to your friends and colleagues; some will admire and respect your work, while others may pull away from you. This is a risk that comes with advocacy. While my own experience suggests that younger therapists *overestimate* these risks (for example, people sometimes worry about losing their jobs for simply stating their position on a professional advocacy issue, and that rarely if ever actually happens), it would not be accurate to say there's *no* risk of it.

Even so, experienced advocates are good at making their best arguments, sometimes winning and sometimes not, and still getting along well afterward. Courageous advocates respect other courageous advocates, even when on different sides of a specific issue.

---

[493] Goodman, J. M., Morgan, A. A., Hodgson, J. L., & Caldwell, B. E. (2018). From private practice to academia: Integrating social and political advocacy into every MFT identity. *Journal of Marital and Family Therapy, 44*(1), 32-45.

▶ The advocacy process

Now that you know why you should be an advocate, and the qualities you need to have to move a policy idea forward, how do you do it? The process can be broken down into specific stages, each of which I will discuss in some detail:

1. Recognize a problem or concern
2. Identify the specific policy issue
3. Gather information
4. Strategize
5. Take action
6. Adapt and (sometimes) accept compromise
7. Repeat as needed

As you will see, these same steps apply regardless of whether the specific policy concern is institutional (like a concern about a policy at your university), professional (such as a problem with the wording of one of your ethical requirements), legal (something that requires a new law in order to fix), or regulatory (something that requires licensing board action to change a regulation, but does not need the involvement of the legislature).

1. Recognize a problem or concern

Many of us first get into policy work because we can see something that is not working. Maybe a law is having unintended consequences, or the field has changed such that a new policy is needed. When a problem directly impacts you, that can be a powerful motivator to fix the problem – not just for you, but for anyone who may follow you and run into the same problem.

It is helpful at this very early stage to give serious thought to whether your problem is specific to your own immediate situation, or whether it is actually an issue that is likely to impact many others. If the problem only impacts you, you may want to first see whether an exception can be made for your situation before embarking on a much larger process of policy change. For example, if your university has a policy that is negatively impacting you because of unique personal circumstances, you may have the best success by reaching out to your faculty or dean to see what options exist for granting policy exceptions.

2. Identify the specific policy issue

The next step is to very specifically locate the problem. You may know that there is a policy issue, but what is the particular rule that is causing or worsening the problem you see? The BBS publishes an updated booklet each year of the laws and regulations for LMFTs, LPCCs, and LCSWs,[494] which is a good place to start if your problem is in law or regulation. You should find, at this stage, the specific section of law, ethics code, or institutional policy that you want to change.

Naturally, laws and regulations are written in legal language, so you may want or need some help deciphering them. If you are experiencing a problem you believe might be a policy issue, you can work with colleagues, supervisors, or your professional association to find the exact language that is of concern. They also can let you know whether your issue is impacting more of their members.

You may already have a potential solution in mind at this point, but it will be important to not be too locked into that solution at this time. As you will see in the next stages, there may be other solutions available.

3. Gather information

Has anyone else run into the same problem you are now facing? Internet searches, conversations with colleagues, and discussions with your professional association can help answer that question. If others have run into the same issue, how have they gone about trying to resolve it? What solutions were attempted, even if they failed? What were the impacts of those efforts? All of this information will be helpful to you in figuring out how to move forward.

---

[494] Board of Behavioral Sciences (2018). *Statutes and Regulations Relating to the Practice of Professional Clinical Counseling, Marriage and Family Therapy, Educational Psychology, and Clinical Social Work.* Sacramento, CA: BBS.

Gathering information also means contacting those groups you believe will be stakeholders in the issue, including (perhaps *especially*) those who you believe are likely to disagree with you on the problem or proposed solution. You will not be giving anything away by letting them know you are acting on the issue; they will have plenty of time to hear your concerns and proposed solution no matter what, and coming to them early in the process may lead them to try working with you on a compromise rather than battling against you later.

With all stakeholder groups, you should ask them about their knowledge and experience of the problem, their investment in fixing it (including any previous efforts they may have made), and whether they are interested in working with you in the advocacy process. A good information-gathering process will result in a team of allies, all sharing information, and committed to working together to solve the problem you helped bring to their attention.

4. Strategize

At this stage, if you have stakeholders working with you, you will transition from being an individual with a problem to being part of a team pushing for a specific solution. An adage often repeated by the Dean at a university where I taught was "Don't bring me problems, bring me solutions." This is a common desire among policymakers. With your team, you will likely discuss and debate several possible avenues for solving the problem, settling on the one that the team believes is most likely to be adopted. You then will work on how to push that idea forward – who needs to talk to whom, when the contacts should be made, and what they hope to get from each stage of the process.

There are two important things to keep in mind at this stage. One is to be a team player. Working as part of a group means accepting the group's wisdom and influence. Stakeholders may have knowledge of the policymaking process that you lack. There is a good balance to be struck between maintaining your personal voice in the process and working with the group to get the problem solved.

The second important thing to keep in mind at this stage is that you are likely to encounter opposition as you push your cause forward. Part of strategizing is anticipating the arguments of those who disagree with you, and being prepared with more convincing responses. With a plan in hand, you can walk into any debate about the issue confident that you have the right plan.

5. Take action

You and your allies have a plan. Now you need to carry it out. Depending on the issue, this can involve meeting with policymakers, letter-writing, phone calls, organizing others with the same concern, involving the media, or any number of additional actions. If the strategy you developed in the previous stage is solid, you simply need to see it through.

If you are part of a group, and the group agreed on a strategy at the previous stage, follow that plan. Make sure you have the understanding and agreement of the group before making any changes to the plan. Venturing away from the agreed-upon plan, even if your intentions are good, risks undermining the group's efforts and ultimately making success less likely. More than once, a coalition with a good plan to change a policy has come unraveled when one member of the group decided to go their own way.

As you are acting toward the change you desired, you will likely find yourself faced with stakeholders who disagree with you. While you may be able to make more convincing arguments and get policymakers to take your side, a better path is to work with those opposing stakeholders and see whether you can come to a point of agreement. If you can address their concerns, you may actually be able to get those stakeholders who initially opposed you to instead help you move the idea forward.

6. Adapt and accept compromise

Even with a good plan, there may be roadblocks along the way that were not anticipated. Action plans need to be able to adapt to changing circumstances; arguments need to be formulated on the fly when others disagree with you for reasons you had not expected. Adapting your plan and your arguments is a normal part of the process. Particularly in longer change processes such as the process required to get a bill through the legislature, your proposal is likely to be amended along the way.

As the old saying goes, you should not let the perfect be the enemy of the good. A policy change that is a step in the right direction, even if not as big of a step as you were hoping for, is still a success. As mentioned in the previous stage, if your proposal encounters opposition from other stakeholders along the way, see whether your proposal can be changed to address the opposition's concerns. Often policy opposition does not come from disagreement about the nature of the problem, but instead differences in preferred solutions. Legislators are conflict-averse; they like to see stakeholder groups come together to eliminate opposition to bills. As you might expect, it is much easier for them to vote for a bill when they know that their vote will not be angering groups of their constituents.

Accepting compromise works to everyone's benefit. Your idea moves forward, opponents become friends, and policymakers become much more comfortable with accepting whatever it is you have proposed. While compromise is not always possible, it is worth going to great lengths to pursue.

7. Repeat as needed

If you have moved successfully through the previous stages and seen your idea through to the end of the advocacy process, congratulations! You have very likely made a change that will impact significant numbers of professionals or the clients we serve.

Success in policy work is addictive. It brings you new contacts who are like-minded, colleagues or clients who are grateful for your work, and most importantly, a very real, concrete impact on the community around you. Once you have had that success, you may decide that your policy work is done. But that's unlikely. More likely, you will have encountered other policy problems along the way, or been left less-than-fully-satisfied by whatever compromises were made on the journey toward the policy change you initially proposed.

Whatever your specific outcome, I hope you choose to remain active in policy work. Even if it means we will disagree, you are my colleague, you should have a place at the table in policy discussions, and we can make changes that will improve the quality of life for the clients we serve and the professionals who will follow us.

▸ How new rules are made

The most important thing to know about making or changing the rules for a profession is that the rules are meant to be adaptive. They are set forth in living documents, and while the process for changing them should be cautious and deliberative, rules should be able to adapt to changes in the profession and in the larger social environment.

This section outlines in general terms how the rules governing our profession are changed. The process will often vary depending on the kind of problem being solved and just how major or controversial the proposed change is.

Institutional policymaking

Any non-governmental agency – a hospital, a university, a mental health clinic, even a small private practice – has a set of policies and practices it follows. Generally speaking, the larger the institution, the more of its policies will be in writing to ensure that everyone who works there acts in a responsible manner consistent with those policies.

Of course, every specific institution is different. **However, there are some common processes used by larger institutions in changing their policies**. Most will field a suggestion about a new policy or a change in existing policy within some form of committee, tasked with discussing the potential impact of such a change. Often, the person who suggested the change will be invited to speak at a committee meeting, answer questions from committee members, and offer additional detail about the need for the proposed change. Typically, the committee would then make a recommendation to the individual or group who actually has the power to change the policy. Depending on the organization, there may be a second hearing where that person or group again considers the issue.

Professional rulemaking

When discussing the rules that exist on the professional level, we typically are talking about professional Codes of Ethics. Each major mental health association has its own code (links to which are offered in the Appendix).

Ethics codes are updated every few years, though they may be changed more often if the larger professional context demands it. The NASW Code of Ethics was last updated in 2018, making it the newest current code among the professions discussed here. The AAMFT updated its Code in 2015, ACA updated theirs in 2014, and CAMFT updated theirs in 2011. In each instance, meaningful updates were made that reflected changing standards within each profession.

Proposed changes to a code of ethics are typically first raised to the association's staff or Board of Directors, who collect such suggestions when there is not an active revision process underway. Once that process has started, a committee of professionals is assigned to review the code and the suggestions collected from members, and consider those in the context of the current professional environment. Typically, the committee then recommends specific language to the association's board. Because a code of ethics is binding upon all members of the association, it is sometimes put before all of the association's members for additional feedback, a broad vote, or both before taking effect. The specific process varies a bit by association.

The California legislative process

The state of California uses a similar process to the one described in "Institutional policymaking," though it is much more structured.[495] The California legislature consists of two houses, or groups of lawmakers: the Assembly and the Senate. If you are a California resident, you are represented by both a state Assembly member and a state Senator. It is helpful to know who your

---

[495] This is a summary and leaves out some key pieces. The Legislature offers its own more detailed explanation of the California legislative process at www.leginfo.ca.gov/bil2lawx.html

representatives are, as they are especially receptive to input from the specific people they represent.

Whoever has an idea for a new or amended law must find an *author* – that is, a legislator (from either house) willing to write the bill and formally propose it. Associations and licensing boards typically will have a much easier time convincing legislators to author bills because they have relationships with the legislators; this is part of why it is a good idea to get stakeholder groups on board with your idea before moving forward.

Once a legislator has proposed a bill, it gets assigned to a policy committee for consideration. These committees consider, in detail, the likely effects of the bill; they also accept public input. When outside organizations say they have taken a position on a bill, that typically means they have informed the author and the legislature of their position, and they may also testify about the bill during committee meetings. Most outside groups take positions on bills while they are still in the policy committee stage, to have the most input on the bill.

Next, the policy committee votes on the bill. If they move it forward, it may go to another committee or to the full house (that is, a bill proposed in the Assembly would go to the full Assembly) for a vote. If it passes there, it follows the same process in the other house, starting with the other house's policy committee.

Bills can be amended at any step of the legislative process, up to the final vote of the second house of the legislature. If the bill was amended while going through the second house, there will be a final vote on the amended version of the bill in both houses. Once the final bill has passed both houses, it cannot be further amended. It moves to the Governor for consideration. The Governor must then sign the bill into law, or veto it. If the Governor takes no action, the bill automatically becomes law. A veto can be overridden with a 2/3 vote of both houses. Most bills signed into law take effect January 1 of the next year.

The California regulatory process

Many of the rules that govern California professions come from regulation, and not legislation. The difference is that regulations are put into place by licensing boards and other governmental agencies and do not need the approval of the Legislature or the Governor. They largely serve to make legislation clearer and more specific, so that agencies like licensing boards can apply the rules equally to all of their licensees. Any time there is a conflict between legislation and regulation, the regulation is ignored and the standard set in legislation applies.

When the BBS wants to change regulation, they first determine through staff input, Board and committee meetings what changes need to be made. These meetings are open to the public, and indeed many of the changes to regulation pursued by the BBS come from suggestions made by ordinary licensees or their professional associations.

Once the BBS has decided on specific language, they vote to send the proposal forward to the Department of Consumer Affairs and the state's Office of Administrative Law.[496] If those groups have no suggested changes, the proposed regulations are posted online for a period of public comment. The BBS is required to respond to *every single comment* made during this time, from any individual or organization. They do not need to agree with the comment, but they must offer a justification for why they are refusing that comment or suggestion. They typically get few such comments.

As one recent example, the BBS has been working to change the process of how it handles complaints against its licensees. This process is set in regulation, not legislation, so it must be changed through regulation.

---

[496] The Office of Administrative Law offers a more detailed explanation of the regulatory process here:
http://www.oal.ca.gov/Regular_Rulemaking_Process.htm

▶ Examples of the advocacy process

So far, I have talked in general terms about the process of advocacy. It can be helpful, of course, to see specific examples – including examples of efforts that *didn't* work, so that you will see that sometimes even good efforts fall short.

Below are three examples of the advocacy process at work: the birth of the LPCC license in the state, the change of title for prelicensed MFTs and PCCs from "interns" to "associates," and California's first-in-the-nation ban on so-called "reparative therapy" for minors.

The LPCC license

For an example of a much more significant change in the law being successful, one need look no further than the very existence of the Licensed Professional Clinical Counselor license in California.

In the early 2000s, LPCs continued earning licensure across the country, and had achieved licensure in most states – but not California. The problem was clear (step 1): Without licensure, those with LPC training could only work in license-exempt settings. Their other option was to try to qualify for an existing form of licensure (such as LMFT), but this would often mean taking significant additional coursework and training. Furthermore, as was the case for LMFTs at the time, having states without licensure laws hindered LPCs' efforts at inclusion in federal programs like Medicare.[497]

To achieve licensure, counselors would need to add a new profession to state law (this was their specific problem, step 2). They developed a coalition of counselors of various types, who banded together and raised funds for their effort under the name "California Coalition for Counselor Licensure." As they gathered information and

---

[497] You'll notice I'm using the abbreviation LPC here, rather than LPCC. The LPCC in California denotes that it is a *clinical* counseling license; that is, it is specific to mental health work. Other states use a variety of titles for the profession, but the LPC designation is the most broad for including licensed professionals in counseling across the country.

began work on their proposal (step 3), they quickly found stakeholders to be unwilling to offer what they had hoped for: A broad-based LPC license in California. The BBS was only willing to support a license specific to mental health. Psychologists, social workers, and family therapists wanted specific restrictions on the counseling scope of practice. Making the counselors' journey even more complicated, these stakeholders sometimes had demands that conflicted with those of other stakeholders. Compromising with one stakeholder group would mean alienating another. The issue of grandparenting was particularly problematic: For those licensed in California as LMFTs, how easy or difficult should it be for them to qualify for a counseling license?

The CCCL's first strategy (step 4) was to go through the legislature's "sunrise" process. This is where a new profession seeks to demonstrate the need for licensure in the state. When they pursued this path in 2006 (step 5), their effort ended without a positive recommendation from the sunrise committee.[498] Wisely, the CCCL adapted (step 6), and sought to push forward in negotiations with stakeholders in spite of the failure of the sunrise process. They worked with CAMFT, a key stakeholder, on compromise language on grandparenting that led CAMFT to remove its opposition to counselor licensure. They worked with the BBS on language that would make their license an "LPCC" license specific to mental health. They worked with the California Psychological Association on compromise language around counselors' ability to use psychological tests. They worked with AAMFT-CA on language limiting LPCCs' ability to assess or treat couples or families without first having training to do so. And they worked with all stakeholder groups on the language of the LPCC scope of practice. While these negotiations took time to reach points of agreement, in 2009 the last key stakeholders removed their opposition. The LPCC licensing bill passed through the legislature and was signed by then-Governor Schwarzenegger. The first LPCC licenses in California were issued through grandparenting in 2011, and through the regular licensure process in 2012. Since the 2009 licensure bill, there have been several other pieces of legislation that have clarified the LPCC profession and its place in the law (step 7). These clarifying bills have largely moved forward with minimal opposition.

---

[498] The Assembly Appropriations Committee's January 18, 2006 analysis of AB894 (2005) describes the outcome of the sunrise process on its final page.

Changing "interns" to "associates"

What does it mean to be an intern? Socially, the term is usually understood to mean someone who is still in school, and is gaining work experience in their chosen field. It's also often understood to mean someone who gets coffee and runs errands for the professionals doing the real work.

The intern title was, at best, a questionable fit for therapists who had completed master's degrees. While MFT and PCC interns *were* gaining supervised experience on the pathway to becoming licensed, they also were out of their educational programs and were doing much of the same work as those who are licensed.

The title created problems in the career pipeline (step 1), as working without pay after graduation makes the process of becoming licensed much more expensive. Many employers (and interns themselves) made the mistaken assumption that because they were called interns, it was legal to have interns in unpaid volunteer roles – or even that their roles *must* be unpaid. Under the law, quite the opposite was true. Most for-profit organizations would fail the government's six-point test for determining whether an unpaid "internship" program was legal. And even many non-profit organizations would be considered "commercial enterprises" under the law, which means that they *also* would be required to pay their employees at least minimum wage.

Unpaid "internships" in psychotherapy have persisted for a number of reasons. One is the simple misunderstanding of the term, as described above. Another is that therapists are sometimes reluctant to "rock the boat" by pushing employers to pay them, even when their position is required by law to be a paid one. They worry about getting fired, not being able to get credit for their hours, or even about their work setting deciding to no longer work with prelicensed therapists.

A change in title would not resolve all of these issues. But it *would* go a long way toward clarifying for therapists and employers alike that prelicensed therapists are doing real, professional work, and that they should be classified and paid accordingly.

That the intern title was problematic was not news. I had initially raised the issue with the BBS several years ago. At that time, they refused to take action on it because they were dealing with a number of more urgent problems, such as a months-long delay in processing licensure applications. Part of effective advocacy is timing, and the timing was not ideal then for concerns about the title to be addressed.

I more formally proposed the title change in August of 2015.[499] My presentation to the BBS included data on the problem and a specific proposed solution (step 2). After that presentation and some more discussion in committee (step 3), counselors were added to it. This way the proposal would provide parallel titles for all three master's level psychotherapy professions. (Post-degree, pre-license clinical social workers in California already carried the title "Associate.") CAMFT and AAMFT-CA added their support as well (step 4).

With the professions in agreement and no known opposition, the BBS sponsored the change themselves (step 5).[500] The title change law took effect in 2017, but it included a one-year delay in implementation (to January 1, 2018) to help therapists and their employers prepare new marketing materials reflecting the new title (step 6). The professional associations will continue attending to issues within the career pipeline to determine whether the change improves pay and employment conditions (step 7), and in the meantime, a number of new resources have been developed for prelicensed therapists who are specifically seeking paid employment. Prelicensed.com is an example.

Banning reparative therapy for minors

In 2012, California passed a law that made it unprofessional conduct for any therapist to provide so-called "reparative therapy" to minors. This law, the first of its kind in the country, did not originate from the mental health professions themselves. It came from a state legislator, who used the advocacy process effectively to earn the support of most professional associations and many outside groups.

---

[499] If you're interested, you can see me present to the BBS about it here: youtu.be/iAnmyJLqAus?t=3h7m16s

[500] Senate Bill 1478 (Business, Professions, and Economic Development Committee), 2016. The title changes are described under item 7 in the Legislative Counsel's Digest of the bill.

The bill that became law in California has since been used as a model in a number of other states.

State Senator Ted Lieu learned about reparative therapy in the months preceding the 2012 legislative session, and was horrified at what he learned (step 1). Reparative therapy – also sometimes known as conversion therapy, or ex-gay therapy – aims to change a client's sexual orientation, based on the assumption that homosexuality is a pathological condition.[501] There is no objective scientific evidence that the therapy is generally effective at changing the sexual orientation of clients, though there are some anecdotal accounts of it working. Unfortunately, there are also many anecdotal accounts of the therapy doing long-term harm to those who have gone through it.[502] The absence of scientific support coupled with the apparent risk of harm from this form of therapy have led all of the major mental health associations to caution against its use. However, none of these organizations have directly banned the practice.[503]

He brought representatives of all of California's mental health professions together in his office early in the year to see why the professional groups had not explicitly banned the practice of reparative therapy, and whether they would object to his moving a bill forward that would have that effect (step 2). He wanted to know what the relevant dynamics were among mental health professionals (step 3).

Working with the associations and with other interested groups (step 4), Senator Lieu initially put forward a bill (step 5) that would have allowed therapists to provide reparative therapy for adults if the therapist engaged in a very specific informed consent process

---

[501] Nicolosi, J. (2009). Shame and attachment loss: The practical work of reparative therapy. Downers Grove, IL: InterVarsity Press.

[502] APA Task Force on Appropriate Therapeutic Responses to Sexual Orientation (2009). *Report of the task force on appropriate therapeutic responses to sexual orientation.* Washington, DC: American Psychological Association.

[503] For an explanation of why they have not banned reparative therapy by name, watch this video: www.youtube.com/watch?v=Ki-TQvVhpi4 (this specific issue comes up at the 4:11 mark)

with the client, acknowledging that there was little evidence of success and the possibility of significant risk with this form of treatment.[504]

The professional associations all objected to this approach. Advocacy work sometimes means looking out for how rules might be misused and misinterpreted, and this was a great example of such a time. The associations feared that this informed-consent process would actually be creating a "safe haven" for the practice of reparative therapy, putting into law that California found the practice to be within legal requirements (the fact that it included specific conditions for informed consent did not resolve this issue).[505] Far better, the associations felt, to leave the law gray than to have a specific statement in the law that reparative therapy was allowed, even with restrictions.

So Senator Lieu and his staff wisely regrouped, and worked with the associations on a better approach (step 6). When he changed his bill to make it a simple ban on reparative therapy for minors, he quickly earned the support of NASW-CA and AAMFT-CA, and most other professional associations ultimately joined this support.

The bill was signed by the Governor in September 2012, and immediately challenged in court. Supporters of the bill remained engaged in the process, submitting dozens of amicus briefs (these are papers used to inform courts about the underlying scientific or legal issues in a case, filed by individuals or groups who are not directly involved; "amicus" here means "friend of the court") arguing that the law should be allowed to take effect.[506] The fight went all the way to the US Supreme Court; when they refused to hear the case, the law finally did take effect.[507]

---

[504] Senate Bill 1172 (Lieu), 2012. Use the pull-down menu in the upper right corner to select the April 9, 2012 version.

[505] Caldwell, B. E., & Kahn, A. C. (2012). California prohibits therapists from working to change a minor's sexual orientation. *Family Therapy Magazine,* *11*(6), 8-11. Available online at newsmanager.commpartners.com/aamft/downloads/CaldwellArticle.pdf

[506] All amicus briefs filed in this case at the US Ninth Circuit Court of Appeals can be found here: www.ca9.uscourts.gov/content/view.php?pk_id=0000000635

[507] McGreevy, P. (2014 June 30). Supreme Court rejects challenge to law banning gay-conversion therapy. *Los Angeles Times.* Available online at www.latimes.com/local/political/la-me-pc-california-supreme-court-gay-conversion-therapy-20140630-story.html

This is an example of a very time-consuming, but ultimately effective, advocacy effort. It demonstrated the importance of all of those factors listed earlier in this chapter: Information, motivation, allies, and patience. The change it made in state law was significant, protecting untold numbers of children from the potentially damaging effects of reparative therapy. Had the bill not been signed by the Governor, or had it been defeated in court, its proponents surely would have tried again, using knowledge gained from that failure (step 7). However, in this instance, they didn't need to.

Instead, the California law has been a model for those debated in at least eight other states, including laws passed in Illinois, New Jersey, Oregon, Vermont, and the District of Columbia. Now that California's law has survived its court challenge, it seems likely that other states will feel safer in following suit. The initial efforts of just a few advocates in California will thus continue to have impact all around the country.

▸ Be the change

In closing, let me offer perhaps an overly-brief summary of this text: You've learned many of the specific rules governing master's-level mental health professionals in California, and just as importantly, you've learned how to change those rules that aren't working very well.

I hope you will join me and your professional associations in that task of change. As you will see many times through your career as a therapist, sometimes actions taken with the best of intentions have negative consequences. And, as you will also see many times through your career as a therapist, simple insight into these failures is not enough. **We do neither our clients nor our professions any favors if all we ever do about the rules that govern our lives is talk.** When something in life – whether it be the life of a client, or the life of a profession – isn't working, our calling should be develop understanding *and then to act,* thoughtfully and collaboratively, to fix the problem.

One of my greatest joys as a teacher has been seeing my students take up this charge, becoming advocates for their clients and their professions in the truest sense of the word. I hope and trust that you will do the same.

I look forward to working with you.

Room for debate: Slacktivism

New technologies have made it easier to get involved in activism at a variety of levels. You can now sign a petition or email your government representatives in just a few clicks. You can join social media groups connected with a specific cause. Raising awareness of an issue within your network may simply be a matter of sharing links or videos.

Precisely *because* activism is now so convenient, some of its modern forms are seen skeptically by policymakers and advocates alike. There's even a derisive term for advocacy conducted via email, online petition, and related efforts: *Slacktivism*. In other words, advocacy for slackers.

This chapter has described activism as a *process*, rather than a single event, and it could be argued that one problem with slacktivism is that it presents advocacy as a single act. It also could be argued that by making activism so accessible, we bring more people into advocacy work.

Effective activism for the digital age

by Emma Jaegle, MS

  While online activism has a number of limitations, there is no evidence that it negatively impacts participation offline. It can be argued that overall, online activism represents an important social good. While online petitions and form emails may do little to actually influence policymakers, they can do a great deal to inform the public. In doing so, they bring new voices in to the advocacy process, and may inspire some people to get more involved in issues they may not have been aware of before.

  An example of this is the movement in 2013 of having the Human Rights Campaign logo as Facebook profile pictures. It drew awareness of the marginalized LGBT group and demonstrated a trendy call to action for people to create a supportive environment. The tremendous amount of participation caught the attention of multiple news platforms, creating awareness offline and inspiring more action to be made.[508]

  A meta-analysis of studies of the impact of Internet use on civic engagement found evidence that the impact is increasing over time.[509] In addition, it can help mobilize the younger generation into offline forms of activism. An example of this is the Ice Bucket Challenge that went viral in 2014. The challenge was to pour a bucket of ice water on your head and/or donate to Amyotrophic Lateral Sclerosis (ALS) Foundation. Participants posted their challenge onto their social media pages and nominated others to complete the challenge. People were so influenced by the stories shared that over $115 million was raised. The ALS Association later announced that the money helped to develop a disease model, identify biomarkers, conduct clinical trials, develop new drugs, and identify a new gene linking to the

---

[508] Vie, S. (2014, April 7). In defense of "slacktivism": The Human Rights Campaign Facebook logo as digital activism. Retrieved October 10, 2016, from http://journals.uic.edu/ojs/index.php/fm/article/view/4961/3868
[509] Boulianne, S. (2009). Does internet use affect engagement? a meta-analysis of research. *Political Communication, 26*(2), 193-211.

disease.[510] The attention of younger people was attracted through the means of the Internet and helped contribute further to the cause.

Though these examples are outliers in a number of attempts for activism online, they still prove the potential of what slacktivism can achieve. The concern should not be whether slacktivism is effective. Instead, the focus should be on how government agencies and other activists can use their creativity and marketing resources to turn the Internet into a tool for slacktivists to make more of an impact.

---

[510] Wolff-Mann, E. (2015, August 21). What Happened to the Money Raised From the Ice Bucket Challenge. Retrieved October 10, 2016, from http://time.com/money/4000583/ice-bucket-challenge-money-donations/

The illusion of impact

by Benjamin E. Caldwell, PsyD

Policymakers have ways of telling how much you care about an issue. As the saying goes, people vote with their feet – meaning that your true investment in an issue can be measured not by what you *say* about that issue, but by how much you are willing to *do* about it.

I've often heard from elected officials that they presume every phone call or letter they receive (excluding form letters) on an issue is worth a certain number of votes. The people willing to take the time to call or write on an issue, and provide their thoughts in their own words, care about that issue enough to act meaningfully on it, and will probably remember how the official responded when that person is next up for election.

Form emails, form letters, and petitions – the kinds of activism that can now be done in seconds – are presumed to be worth *zero* votes. These tasks are so easy that they will likely be forgotten by the next week, and certainly by the next election. So they are given very little weight. And they have little to no impact.

Unfortunately, one problem with slacktivism is that it can present the *illusion* of impact. If you sign an online petition at around the same time that others are taking more meaningful action on an issue, you might understandably think that you helped make the change happen. You may think that signatures on an online petition, in and of themselves, are influential. You may then be in for a rude awakening when future online efforts don't produce the changes you want.

Effective advocacy takes work, and it is a process. Slacktivism isn't *bad*, it just isn't much of anything. Simple clicks and likes, no matter how well-intentioned, don't actually do much. It is possible – and important, and often surprisingly easy – to have a meaningful impact on whatever policy areas you wish to impact, no matter what career stage you're in. Part of the reason it can be so easy is that relatively few therapists are willing to truly invest – to take *meaningful* action – in creating change.

Caring about an issue is great. Acting on it is better.

Appendix

▸ Old supervised experience requirements

New, streamlined options for supervised experience toward LMFT and LPCC licensure took effect in 2016. Anyone who submits their hours of experience for licensure before the end of 2020 can come in under either the old structure or the new one, whichever they prefer. The experience requirements outlined in Chapter 1 reflect the new, streamlined requirements. For those using this book in a graduate-level law and ethics course, it is possible but unlikely that you would finish your hours in time to qualify under the old rules. However, we include them here for those at other career stages, including current associates and supervisors.

Old requirements for LPCC licensure

Category	Minimum/maximum[511]	
Individual or group counseling	**Minimum 1,750 hours,** including a **maximum of 500 hours** of group counseling and a **minimum of 150 hours** in a hospital or community mental health setting.	
Counseling via telehealth	**Maximum 375 hours.** Note that you generally may not counsel clients outside of California (see Chapter 1, Scope of Practice).	
Supervision	Part of combined maximum →	**Maximum 1,250 hours** in these four categories combined.
Client-centered advocacy	Part of combined maximum →	
Workshops and trainings	**Maximum 250 hours.**	
Testing, writing clinical reports, and writing notes	**Maximum 250 hours.**	

---

[511] California Business and Professions Code section 4999.46(b)

Old requirements for LMFT licensure

Category	Minimum/maximum[512]
Individual psychotherapy	**No minimum or maximum.**
Couple, family, and child psychotherapy	**Minimum 500 hours.** Up to 150 hours of couple and family (that is, *not* individual child) psychotherapy are double-counted toward the 3,000 total hours required for licensure.
Group therapy	**Maximum 500 hours.**
Telephone and Internet counseling	**Maximum 375 hours.** Note that you generally may not counsel clients outside of California (see Chapter 1, Scope of Practice).
Client-centered advocacy	**Combined maximum 500 hours** for these two categories. "Client-centered advocacy" involves efforts to link clients with resources outside of a therapy session.
Writing clinical reports, administering tests, and writing notes	

Category	Minimum/maximum[512]	
Supervision	Part of a combined maximum. →	
Workshops, trainings, and seminars	**Maximum 250 hours.** For agency in-service and similar trainings, it is at the discretion of the supervisor what will qualify within this category.	**Combined maximum 1,000 hours** for these three categories.
Personal psychotherapy (when the applicant is the client)	**Maximum 100 hours.** These hours are triple-counted, for a total of up to 300 hours of credit toward the 3,000 total supervised hours required for licensure.	

---

[512] California Business and Professions Code section 4980.43(b) and California Code of Regulations title 16 section 1833

▶ List of Tables

▶ Topic Index

A

AAMFT, 18, 82, 105, 163, 270, 274, 279, 294, 320, 322
AAMFT Approved Supervisor, 98
AAMFT-CA, 53, 298, 300, 302, 321
Abbreviations, 232, 237-239
   see also Acronyms
ACA, 89, 105, 159, 161-164, 234, 269, 270, 274, 279, 294, 320, 322
Acronyms, 21, 239
   see also Abbreviations
Advertising, 229-250
   false or misleading, 113
AMFTRB, 62
AMHCA, 258, 279, 322
Angie's List, 151, 245
Antitrust, 227
Arizona, 259
Assent agreements, 166
Associates
   advertising, 236, 246-248
   definition, 21, 41
   experience requirements, 52-60
   title change, 56, 299-300
Association membership, 126-127, 243
Audiotaping, 164

B

Background checks, 44, 107
Bellah v. Greenson, 134, 136

B (cont.)

Billing, 145, 154, 162, 257
Blogs, 233
Brochures, 231
Business cards, 229, 231
Business permit, 224

C

CACREP, 49
California
   legislative process, 294-295
   regulatory process, 295-296
California Telemedicine Act, 115, 261-262
CALPCC, 53, 321
CAMFT, 77, 164, 256, 258, 270, 279, 294, 298, 300, 321
Caregiver's Authorization Affidavit, 164, 192
Cancellation policy, 159
CCCMHA, 320
Certifications, 242
Child abuse
   definition, 203-208
   exception to confidentiality, 143
   failure to report, 116, 210
   reasonable suspicion, 201
   reporting, 209-212
Child custody
   see Custody

F

Facebook, 161, 234, 306
FaceTime, 271-272
Fees
    advertising, 113
    disclosure, 113, 155-156
    for licensure, 44
    for referrals, 105
    setting, 227-228
    splitting, 89-90
Fictitious business names, 224
5150 holds, 137, 141
Firearms
    see Guns
Florida, 259
Flyers, 231
Fraud, 102, 108
Freedom of speech, 99

G

General misconduct, 116-117
Google ads, 234-235
Gross negligence, 116-117
Guns, 140-142
    gun violence restraining
    orders, 141-142

H

Health Grades, 151, 245, 252
HIPAA, 143, 158, 261, 263-267,
    268, 271-275
    Conduit exception, 272
Homicide
    see Danger to Others
Hospitalization, 137-138, 141

I

Impairment, 106
Impersonation, 108
Independent contractor, 87
Informed consent, 115, 154-166
    with minors, 164-166, 193
    technology-based services, 115,
    261-263
Internet advertising
    see Advertising
Internet therapy
    see Technology
Interns
    see Associates ☺
Interstate practice, 258-260
Investigations, 120-121

K

Kansas, 259

L

Licensing
    exams, 61-63, 109-111
    exemptions, 45-46
    renewals, 44-45
    requirements, 43-63
    statuses, 41-42
Life coaches
    see Coaching

M

Misconduct
    see Unprofessional conduct

N

NAMI California, 320
NASW, 18, 22, 82, 90, 105, 162-164, 270, 279, 294, 320, 322
NASW-CA, 302, 321
NCMHCE, 63
Negligence, 116-117
Networking groups, 250-251
New Jersey, 259
No harm contracts, 136
Notice of Privacy Practices, 158

O

Ombudspersons, 217, 219
Online therapy
  see Technology

P

Paid sick leave
  see Sick leave
Policymaking, 282-284, 288-296
Privilege, 131, 146-148, 197
Practicum, 47, 50, 54-56, 57-58, 60, 70, 73
Probation
  see Disciplinary actions
Professional Therapy Never Includes Sex, 105
Professional titles
  see Titles
Progress notes, 167-168
Professional liability insurance, 20, 106, 118, 121, 127
Psychological testing, 33, 37
Psychologists, 27
Psychology Today, 231

Psychotherapy notes, 168
"Psychotherapy" and "psychotherapist" in advertising, 239-240

R

Recklessness, 116-117
Records
  access, 171-174
  disposal, 169-170
  failure to maintain, 114
  maintaining, 114, 169-170
  requests, 143-144, 171-174
  storage, 169-170
  types, 165-168
  see also Progress notes
Registrant, 21
Regulations, 295-296
  telehealth, 262-263
Release of information, 143-144
Revocations
  see Disciplinary actions
Rulemaking, 294

S

Safety plans, 135-136, 139
Salary
  see Wages
Scope of competence, 30, 42, 115
Scope of practice, 30-39, 115
Sexual misconduct, 104-106
Sick leave, 93
Specializations, 242
Stakeholder groups, 290-292, 295, 298, 319-321
Standard of care, 18-19, 112, 120, 134, 153, 155, 167, 197, 242

▶ Directory of key stakeholder groups

The following groups can be useful allies on issues where state policy would benefit from a change. They are organized here into three categories: Government; Consumer, Family, and Provider Organizations; and Professional Organizations. If you have suggestions for organizations to add to this list for future editions, please feel free to send them! See "About the Author" at the end of this Appendix.

Government

Board of Behavioral Sciences
1625 North Market Blvd., Suite S-200
Sacramento, CA 95834
www.bbs.ca.gov

Board of Psychology
1625 North Market Blvd., Suite N-215
Sacramento, CA 95834
www.psychboard.ca.gov

Department of Consumer Affairs
Consumer Information Division
1625 North Market Blvd., Suite N-112
Sacramento, CA 95834
www.dca.ca.gov

Department of Health Care Services
(mailing address varies by program)
www.dhcs.ca.gov

National Professional Associations

American Association for Marriage and Family Therapy
www.aamft.org

American Counseling Association
www.counseling.org

American Mental Health Counselors Association
www.amhca.org

National Association of Social Workers
www.socialworkers.org

Consumer, Family, and Provider Organizations

California Council of Community Mental Health Agencies
1127 11th St., Suite 925
Sacramento, CA 95814
www.cccmha.org

National Alliance on Mental Illness, California
1851 Heritage Ln., Suite 150
Sacramento, CA 95815
www.namicalifornia.org

State Professional Organizations

American Association for Marriage and Family Therapy, California Division
PO Box 6907
Santa Barbara, CA 93160
www.aamftca.org

California Association for Licensed Professional Clinical Counselors
1240 India Street, Unit 1302
San Diego, CA 92101
www.calpcc.org

California Association of Marriage and Family Therapists
7901 Raytheon Rd.
San Diego, CA 92111
www.camft.org
CAMFT Code of Ethics (last revision 2011):
www.camft.org/ias/images/PDFs/CodeOfEthics.pdf

National Association of Social Workers, California Chapter
1016 23rd St.
Sacramento, CA 95816
www.naswca.org

▶ Additional resources

Licensing

California Board of Behavioral Sciences
www.bbs.ca.gov

California Law

Full text of the California Business and Professions Code
leginfo.legislature.ca.gov/faces/codes.xhtml (choose BPC)

Statutes and Regulations for BBS-governed Mental Health Professionals
www.bbs.ca.gov/pdf/publications/lawsregs.pdf

Codes of Ethics

American Association for Marriage and Family Therapy
AAMFT Code of Ethics (last revision 2015):
www.aamft.org/imis15/content/legal_ethics/
code_of_ethics.aspx

American Counseling Association
ACA Code of Ethics (last revision 2014):
www.counseling.org/Resources/aca-code-of-ethics.pdf

American Mental Health Counselors Association
AMHCA Code of Ethics (last revision 2015):
www.amhca.org/?page=codeofethics

National Association of Social Workers
NASW Code of Ethics (last revision 2018):
https://www.socialworkers.org/LinkClick.aspx?fileticket=ms_A
rtLqzeI%3d&portalid=0

▸ About the author

Benjamin E. Caldwell, PsyD, is a practicing Marriage and Family Therapist (California license number MFC42723) who teaches Law and Ethics for California State University Northridge in Los Angeles and The Wright Institute in Berkeley. He has served as chair of the Legislative and Advocacy Committee for the California Division of the American Association for Marriage and Family Therapy, and was honored for his service in 2013 with the AAMFT Division Contribution Award. His research has been published in the *Journal of Marriage and Family Therapy, American Journal of Family Therapy, Journal of Couple and Relationship Therapy,* and in *Family Therapy* and *Self* magazines. He maintains a private practice specializing in the treatment of distressed couples. He lives in Los Angeles, CA.

Photo by Tracy Teague / Trace Images, courtesy Casey Caldwell.

Other books by Ben Caldwell

Practice Tests for the California MFT Law & Ethics Exam
Preparing for the California MFT Law & Ethics Exam
Preparing for the California Clinical Counseling Law & Ethics Exam
Preparing for the California Clinical Social Work Law & Ethics Exam
Saving Psychotherapy

Find me online

Web: www.BenCaldwellLabs.com
Facebook/Twitter/Instagram: bencaldwelllabs
Blog: www.PsychotherapyNotes.com